Second Edition

THE PRACTICE
OF FAMILY THERAPY

Key Elements Across Models

Second Edition

THE PRACTICE
OF FAMILY THERAPY

Key Elements Across Models

Suzanne Midori Hanna

Joseph H. Brown

University of Louisville

Brooks/Cole • Wadsworth
I(T)P®An International Thomson Publishing Company

Belmont • Albany • Boston • Cincinnati • Detroit • Johannesburg • London
Madrid • Melbourne • Mexico City • New York • Pacific Grove • Paris
Singapore • Tokyo • Toronto • Washington

Sponsoring Editor: *Eileen Murphy*
Editorial Assistant: *Julie Martinez*
Marketing Team: *Steve Catalano, Jean Thompson, Aaron Eden, and Jay Honeck*
Permissions Editor: *Elaine Jones*
Cover and Interior Designer: *John Edeen*
Cover Art: *T. Shiozu/Photonica*

Production Editor: *Mary Anne Shahidi*
Copy Editor: *Frank Hubert*
Art Editor and Illustrator: *Lisa Torri*
Compositor: *Joan Mueller Cochrane*
Interior Printer: *R. R. Donnelley–Crawfordsville*
Cover Printer: *Phoenix Color Corporation*

For more information, contact Wadsworth Publishing Company, 10 Davis Drive, Belmont, CA 94002, or electronically at http://www.wadsworth.com

International Thomson Publishing Europe
Berkshire House
168–173 High Holborn
London, WC1V 7AA, United Kingdom

International Thomson Editores
Seneca, 53
Colonia Polanco
11560 México D.F. México

Nelson ITP, Australia
102 Dodds Street
South Melbourne
Victoria 3205 Australia

International Thomson Publishing Asia
60 Albert Street
#15-01 Albert Complex
Singapore 189969

Nelson Canada
1120 Birchmount Road
Scarborough, Ontario
Canada M1K 5G4

International Thomson Publishing Japan
Hirakawa-cho Kyowa Building, 3F
2-2-1 Hirakawa-cho, Chiyoda-ku
Tokyo 102, Japan

International Thomson Publishing Southern Africa
Building 18, Constantia Square
138 Sixteenth Road, P.O. Box 2459
Halfway House, 1685 South Africa

Printed in the United States of America
2   3   4   5   6   7   8   9   10

Library of Congress Cataloging-in-Publication Data

Hanna, Suzanne Midori [date]
    The practice of family therapy : key elements across models /
Suzanne Midori Hanna, Joseph H. Brown. -- 2nd ed.
      p.   cm.
    Includes bibliographical references and index.
    ISBN 0-534-35768-7 (hbk.)
    1. Family psychotherapy. I. Brown, Joseph H. II. Title.
RC488.5.H337 1999
616.89'156--dc21
                          98-37385
                           CIP

To Phillip, for bringing out the best in me.

—SMH

To Carolyn, whose love and
support makes everything possible.

—JHB

CONTENTS

Part Two
STRUCTURAL AND EXPERIENTIAL SKILLS   **123**

Chapter Six
THE INITIAL INTERVIEW: PROVIDING STRUCTURE   139

Chapter Seven
THE ASSESSMENT: EXPLORING CLIENT EXPERIENCE   167

Part Three
RELATIONAL AND DIRECTIONAL SKILLS   203

PREFACE

Since the first edition of this book, we have continued to explore the question, "What is marriage and family therapy?" We know we are not alone. At this time, 41 states have regulatory statutes that address the question from a legal perspective. This is evidence of the exponential growth and institutionalization of our field during the past decade. In addition, the Commission on Accreditation for Marriage and Family Therapy Education describes marriage and family therapy as based on a "systems/relational" curriculum. This defining feature comes from that part of the field that must document marriage and family therapy as a separate discipline with a distinct body of knowledge.

We approach the definition of marriage and family therapy with an additional question. "What should be the focus of beginning clinicians as they learn entry-level skills in the field?" As new approaches continue to flourish—some as long-term trends and some as passing fads—we think it is especially important to emphasize the conceptual roots and the innovative traditions of the field. We think that theories about family process and theories about change should be applied to problems of individuals, couples, families, and other diverse systems.

We think that beginning practitioners need to know how to work from a systemic and relational perspective regardless of the type of client, problem, or setting. When they can develop multiple views of a problem and integrate common skills using diverse approaches, we have seen them adapt their systemic practice to traditional and nontraditional practice settings. Thus, we have presented the material with this end in mind. Organized into three sections, content follows the logical order of therapeutic process.

❋ PART ONE: FROM THEORY TO PRACTICE

Chapter One begins with a brief review of the diversity within the field, on the basis of a specific case example. Differences in content and process between models are emphasized to provide the beginning student with a conceptual background from which to appreciate the challenge of integration. We have added more information on narrative and cognitive-behavioral approaches. As we move further away from privileging any one approach to family therapy, we see even more unifying trends in the field. In this edition, we have clarified the contributions of constructivism and social construction. In Chapter One, we have also provided evidence that family therapists have been integrationists from the very beginning.

Chapter Two examines areas of family process most pertinent to a given situation. Each section provides a list of questions that the family therapist can use to maintain a sense of direction while conducting an assessment. Suggestions are made regarding the circumstances in which each area might be most useful. Proceeding from macro factors such as gender and race to micro factors such as individual phenomenology, the chapter also helps the student of family therapy to see the value of exploring content on a multidimensional continuum.

Chapter Three reviews common elements that can be found across models in terms of the therapist's role, interventions, and assumptions about change. This chapter continues the process of integration by identifying areas of overlap among the various schools that can serve as a starting point. We have maintained a strengths perspective and have provided more encouragement for collaboration with our clients. There is also new information about the value of therapeutic relationships and the importance of understanding theories of change. In this chapter, we underscore our definition of marriage and family therapy as the application of theories about relationships integrated with theories about change.

In Chapter Four, we review sequences and interactions that are common elements of process, from referral through evaluation. These are discussed as part of a general progression through the therapeutic process that all models contain either implicitly or explicitly. We recommend that the therapist discuss these stages explicitly with clients, as a way of encouraging collaboration in the therapeutic process. This chapter becomes an operational guide as therapeutic process evolves. A new section outlines our approach to the basic elements of in-session process. These elements are structure, client experience, relational change, and a shared direction. Emphasizing what we consider to be the defining features of marriage and family therapy, we use these four elements as a template on which all remaining aspects of the book rest.

❄ PART TWO: STRUCTURE AND EXPERIENCE

Chapters Five and Six review intake and initial interviews in practical ways that direct the student to provide leadership and structure in the therapy process. We emphasize exploration, negotiation, and collaboration as important aspects. Joining is considered an ongoing process that underlies all other transactions. Defining the problem in interactional terms underscores the relational aspects of this work. The agreement between therapist and client is given particular attention as the foundation for further cooperation. This information constitutes a way of organizing the beginning stage of treatment; administrative and relational processes that promote clarity in the early stages of the therapeutic process are itemized. The major points in these chapters are summarized in a series of boxes, which serve as a guide to help entry-level clinicians stay on task. Chapter Six concludes with answers to common questions about difficult situations such as suspected substance abuse, suicide risks, violence, and family secrets.

Chapter Seven helps students with pragmatic skills that explore client experience and gather multidimensional information. While some might associate genograms and circular questions with a specific family approach, this chapter clarifies how these techniques can be used to accommodate multiple views of the problem. In the same manner, tracking interactional sequences is described in a way that generalizes across models, and tracking longitudinal sequences introduces a way of integrating historical information into narratives that are both systemic and interactional. We have added more figures and case material to illustrate how information is organized graphically when diagramming during a session.

❄ PART THREE: RELATIONSHIPS AND DIRECTIONS

Chapter Eight describes skills necessary to facilitate relational and systemic change. This chapter breaks down complex skills into behaviors that can be easily learned. The chapter can also be used as a supervisory resource by matching the therapist's therapeutic intent with several skills designed to accomplish that intent. Some skills relate to facilitating cognitive change and others to facilitating behavioral change. Taken together, these sections provide a foundation for integrating the most common interventions in the field.

We have added information on solutions, exceptions, and paradox, tailored to the beginning student.

In Chapter Nine, the practitioner will gain a sense of direction in therapy by focusing on how to develop concrete goals, how to enlist the involvement of family members, and how to structure collaboration with large systems involved with the family, such as school representatives. Lists of guidelines help the reader remember key principles.

Chapter Ten is aimed at helping family therapists understand how an evaluative process can be an integral part of treatment. We provide material on the evaluation of family therapy from multiple perspectives, in terms of both process and outcomes. A section on evaluations for termination or follow-up offers practical guidelines by which the clinician can help clients continue the process of change and mobilize their resources. In the final section, we discuss the possibility of integrating clinical practice with clinical research by seeing the two as examples of systematic inquiry. Evaluation provides a context for learning from client feedback, which is essential if the beginning clinician is to advance to intermediate-level practice.

Chapter Eleven integrates all elements of the book through the use of case examples. Partial transcripts, case summaries, and supervisory commentary provide a view of the case from "behind the mirror" as it progresses from session to session. Summary tables help students review the basic elements of marriage and family therapy and how they can implement each element.

❄ INSTRUCTOR'S MANUAL

The Instructor's Manual contains a conceptual overview of each chapter, points of interest to guide the learning process, learning objectives for each chapter, discussion and examination questions for personal growth and evaluation, and quizzes to assess recognition and comprehension of information. The Instructor's Manual is available in traditional print format and on disk in ASCII files.

❄ ACKNOWLEDGMENTS

We are truly indebted to our editors and their staff for talented guidance during the production of this edition—Eileen Murphy for her diplomatic urging and insightful vision to get the ball rolling and Mary Anne Shahidi for her skillful management as all the pieces fell into place. We thank the following reviewers for their helpful suggestions: Lennis Echterling, James Madison

University; Arnell Etherington, College of Notre Dame; Clarence Hibbs, Pepperdine University; Arthur Horne, University of Georgia at Athens; Billie Slater, El Paso Community College; Susan Stern, Boston University; and David Westhuis, University of Southern Indiana.

We also thank important others who have been invaluable and generous with their time and talents. Our program assistant, Christina Pickard, made this project possible. She keeps going and never gives up, even when we want to. Dr. Sally St. George at Lindsay Wilson College was an important voice for change and provided a thoughtful critique of the first edition with many excellent insights. Our colleagues in the Raymond A. Kent School of Social Work at the University of Louisville have been patient and dedicated role models as we have forged our interdisciplinary collaboration. The influence of that collaboration has made its way into this book.

We are also gratified by our long-standing relationship with Family and Children's Counseling Centers and their commitment to us as our joint efforts at marriage and family therapy education have continued. Their staying power has helped us focus on the real world beyond the ivory tower. Our students in the Family Therapy Program are our most valuable gift as they allow us to view the learning process through their eyes and challenge us to help them more effectively. We are energized by their enthusiasm and inspired by their commitment to helping the disadvantaged.

Finally, we pay tribute to the experts, those resilient survivors of life who come to us for help but who, in reality, allow us to join them on a journey where we discover more of ourselves along with the miracle of human potential.

Suzanne Midori Hanna
Joseph H. Brown

Part One

FROM THEORY
TO PRACTICE

Chapter One

FAMILY THERAPY: A FIELD OF DIVERSITY AND INTEGRATION

SAMPLE CASE: THE NELSONS

EARLY MODELS
Structural Family Therapy
Strategic Family Therapy
Intergenerational Therapy
Experiential Family Therapy

INTEGRATIVE MODELS
The Milan Systemic Approach
Narrative Approaches
Collaborative Approaches
Cognitive-Behavioral Family Therapy

SUMMARY

The history of marital and family therapy has always been one of professional diversity. The early interests of clergy, physicians, and social workers led researchers across the United States to study communication and behavior related to schizophrenia and the family. The collaboration between these groups led to an exchange of publications and joint presentations at major national conferences. As it evolved, the practice of these groups produced a paradigmatic shift in thinking: Rather than view problems within the individual, therapists began to see problems within the relationship.

From these developments, the field of family therapy emerged in the mid-20th century. With the organized efforts of those early pioneers came a variety of family therapy practices and backgrounds. From anthropology and communications to psychiatry and hypnosis, the ancestors of present-day family therapy extrapolated the knowledge of their original discipline and integrated it with other knowledge bases. Their synthesis occurred as these multidisciplinary networks dialogued and debated across the country. Gradually, experimentation gave way to models of intervention that developed around the practices of various charismatic innovators.

Today, the field of family therapy is characterized by numerous approaches, all claiming this common heritage. Nichols and Schwartz (1991) note that:

> *Theoretical positions tend to be stated in doctrinaire terms that maximize their distinctions. While this makes interesting reading, it is somewhat misleading. The truth is that the different systems of family therapy are more alike in practice than their theories suggest. Moreover, each new approach tends to become more eclectic over time. Practitioners start out as relative purists, but eventually discover the validity of theoretical concepts from other approaches and the usefulness of other people's techniques. The result is that, with increasing experience, most family therapists gradually become more eclectic. (pp. 512–513)*

These writers use the word "eclectic," which suggests choosing from an array of options, but we prefer "integrative" because it relates to making connections between parts. Thus, the field of marriage and family therapy started—and continues—as a field of diversity with many approaches. However, a history of integration between approaches also exists within this field.

In addition to this integration between approaches, the field's focus is shifting to include important relationships outside of formal family ties. For some, relationships between family and school may be targeted for intervention (Amatea & Sherrard, 1989). For others, non-blood kin may be more influential than their biological family (Boyd-Franklin, 1989). The Commission on Accreditation for Marriage and Family Education (1997) has stated that curricula should be based on a "systems/relational" point of view. Therefore, any system or any set of relationships may be identified as the primary context of the problem. As a relational network becomes the focus of treatment, the family therapist develops an approach that fits with the nature of these relationships as they emerge through families, friendships, or various community ties.

The intent of this book is to find a common ground from which to begin practicing family therapy in a broad range of situations. While the remaining chapters address the overlap between models, this chapter introduces distinctions between the major categories of family therapy practice. It does not contain every model practiced at present, and discussion is limited to concepts and interventions that are considered unique to a given approach. The models chosen for review are samples of early models and recent integrative models that provide the reader with examples of diversity and integration in the field. Thus, this survey illustrates the many avenues of creativity open to contemporary family therapists. Table 1.1 summarizes the concepts and interventions generally associated with some of the leading figures in the field, and Chapter Two covers many of these concepts in greater depth.

By reviewing these general models and identifying their unique contributions, beginning family therapists are introduced to concepts and skills that they may ultimately integrate into their practice. To illustrate the primary differences between the various approaches, the same case material is examined through different perspectives to illustrate how a family therapist from each approach might address the issues in practice.

❄ SAMPLE CASE: THE NELSONS

Paul Nelson, 14, was admitted to a residential group home for adolescent males when his truancy and behavior problems became such that his parents could no longer keep him at home. He had been held back in seventh grade because of absences and was in the eighth grade at the time of his placement. A caseworker was assigned through juvenile court, and Paul was in a local facility where parents were involved in parent education and family therapy. The adolescents had a structured school experience and could earn weekend visits home through good behavior.

Paul's parents, Roy, 45, and Lilly, 42, were a white, working-class couple who had three children, Ed, Janet, and Paul. Ed, 18, had dropped out of high school 2 years earlier and was working at a local gas station. His girlfriend, Roxanne, 17, was pregnant. Ed was living at home, trying to save enough

Table 1.1

Model	Leading Figures	Concepts Emphasized
Structural	Minuchin	Hierarchy Boundary Subsystem Alignment Coalition
Strategic	Haley	Symptoms as messages
	Mental Research Institute (MRI)	Solutions as problems Utopian thinking
Intergenerational	Bowen	Differentiation Family projection process Family losses
	Boszormenyi-Nagy	Relational ethics Family ledger
Experiential	Satir	Self-concept Communication Family rules
	Whitaker	Growth as an interpersonal process Therapy as an encounter
Systemic	Milan team	Hypothesizing Circularity Neutrality Information that makes a difference
Narrative	White	Oppression Liberation Narratives Unique outcomes
Collaborative	H. Anderson Goolishan Hoffman	Problem-defining and problem-dissolving system Dialogues Multiple interpretations
Cognitive-Behavioral	Jacobson Christensen Baucom	Cognitions (thoughts, expectations, attitudes) that trigger and maintain behavior Spouses' subjective nature of relationship

Goals	Unique Interventions
Strengthen parental subsystem Realign coalitions	Joining Enactments Unbalancing
Interrupt problematic sequences	Directives
Second-order change of unsuccessful "solutions"	Reframing Paradox
Decrease emotional reactivity Address losses	Genogram
Restore trust and fairness	Multidirected partiality
Relieve family pain	Sculpting Acceptance Communication skills
Interpersonal competence Intimacy	Use of self Modeling Confrontation Cotherapy
Relief of symptom	Circular questions Positive connotation
Rewrite problem-saturated story	Questions of influence Questions of invitation Externalization
Establish egalitarian relationships Promote respectful dialogue	Conversational questions Questions exploring the implications of diverse views

Restructure family interaction through
   cognitive and behavior change
	Analysis of behavioral sequences
	Exploration of acceptance related to
	   relationship themes

money to support this forthcoming child. At the time of treatment, Ed was uncertain whether he would marry Roxanne, although they were currently seeing each other on a regular basis. Janet, 17, was a senior in high school. She was an A student and enjoyed such school activities as cheerleading and chorus. She hoped to finish high school and go on to college.

❄ EARLY MODELS

The early pioneers of marriage and family therapy represent a wide range of professional training in a variety of mental health settings. For example, structural family therapy was developed by Salvador Minuchin, a psychiatrist who worked extensively with poor inner-city youth and their families at the Wiltwick School in New York. Murray Bowen, Ivan Boszormenyi-Nagy, and Carl Whitaker were also psychiatrists, but they worked more with middle-class clients in traditional psychiatric settings. Jay Haley, with his master's degree in communication, associated himself first with the Mental Research Institute in Palo Alto, California, and then with the Philadelphia Child Guidance Clinic, a nonprofit social service agency. Virginia Satir began her professional life as a teacher and then was drawn to the profession of social work through her keen interest and concern for the disenfranchised.

These leading figures brought to the developing profession of family therapy the courage to critique the prevailing practices of their day and a willingness to experiment with new methods. With respect to the early models these leaders proposed, each has elements that are unique to the person as well as to the setting within which they practiced. In applying each approach to the Nelson family, we invite the reader to imagine the various contexts and populations that stimulated this new thinking about relationships and interactions.

Structural Family Therapy

In this approach, family therapists focus on the interactions and activities of family members to determine the organization or structure of the family. Symptoms are regarded as consequences of organizational difficulties. This theory is closely identified with Salvador Minuchin, MD, who emphasized how, when, and to whom family members currently relate as a way of understanding the problem.

In the case of the Nelsons, structural family therapists would be interested in determining who interacts with whom, for what purpose, and how often.

For example, when Paul was truant from school, who would find out first? What would be his or her reaction? Who would be told next? What would be his or her reaction? What would Paul do in response to their reactions? How would other family members get involved? While gathering this information, structural family therapists also observe whether the family relationships appear close, distant, chaotic, or rigid. Who sits by whom during the initial session? Could their placement in the session be symbolic of how relationships are conducted at home? In this case, Paul's parents accompany him to the first session, and he sits next to his mother. During the session, the therapist notices that Lilly often leans toward Paul and away from her husband.

The therapist asks the Nelson family to describe their interactional process related to Paul's truancy and discovers that, when Mrs. Nelson is called by the school, she responds by leaving work and confronting Paul. When Paul refuses to interact with her and withdraws to his room, she complains to Mr. Nelson about the situation. Mr. Nelson usually responds by confronting Paul about his behavior and threatening him with punishment if his behavior does not improve. When Janet becomes aware of the problem, she usually spends time with Paul, encouraging him to behave better. She has also become Lilly's sounding board, providing a listening ear as her mother worries out loud. The therapist asks Paul about his relationship with each family member. Of his parents, Paul spends the most time with Lilly and is uncomfortable with Roy. Of his siblings, he is closest to Janet and feels some disgust that Ed has gotten himself into trouble. Roy and Lilly are asked about the time they spend together. Because they work different shifts, they have very little time together until the weekend. Recently, Roy has been asked to work overtime at the meat-packing plant as a result of employee cutbacks.

The structural family therapist might hypothesize from this information that the marital subsystem has become distant as a result of the family's economic situation. In addition, Lilly seems to be overinvolved with Janet and Paul in contrasting ways. By confiding in Janet, she has elevated Janet from the status of child to that of peer. By engaging in repetitive interactions with Paul, she is equally enmeshed with him, but in a way that produces opposition rather than peer status. Because Paul has persistently misbehaved, he has rendered the parental subsystem ineffective at this time, obtaining an inappropriate level of power.

Structural goals are based on hypotheses formulated from interactional sequences in the family (Aponte & Van Deusen, 1981). These goals are often specified in the form of altered transactional patterns or sequences of behavior related to the problem. Goals for the Nelsons include strengthening the marital subsystem to unite the family around parental functions. For example, instead of a pattern in which each makes ineffective threats to Paul, their sequence might be changed so that they first interact with each other to decide on a position or plan of action. Additional goals would be to help Roy become closer to his children and to help Lilly develop some distance in her responses. Since they have developed complementary roles with their children (i.e., one close, one distant), another goal is to develop more flexible personal boundaries, becoming more balanced in their roles and less rigid and extreme.

Therapeutic Process   In structural family therapy, the therapist's goal at the beginning of the session is to join with the family and become a part of the family system. Joining requires the therapist to build rapport by being personable and responsive to family members. Colapinto (1991) suggests that the role of the structural family therapist is that of producer, stage director, protagonist, and narrator. Further, he suggests:

> The structural model requires from the therapist a respectful curiosity about diverse forms of family experience and strengths, a commitment to help families change, a preference for concrete behavioral changes over talk about changed feelings, a disposition to construct hypotheses on the basis of scanty data and to have them corrected through a close encounter with clients, the ability to set clear goals and to express them frankly, a willingness to direct, a directedness of expression, a tolerance for intensity in human transactions, and the courage to raise intensity when necessary. (p. 436)

In the session with the Nelsons, the structural therapist joins the family by discussing Roy's work and Lilly's hobbies. Paul is asked about his hobbies and what musical groups he prefers. The therapist looks for strengths in the system as well as patterns of interaction. As patterns become evident and hypotheses are formulated, the therapist becomes directive, asking the family to participate in specifically designed enactments. For example, Paul and Roy are asked to sit together and discuss a family activity. The therapist nudges them to be direct and honest with each other. Lilly is asked to explore her own reaction to the suggestion that Roy become more involved in addressing Paul's behavior. When she tries to interrupt the discussion between Roy and Paul, the therapist stops her and directs Roy and Paul to continue. Suggestions are made regarding ways that Roy and Lilly can alter their roles. The therapist shares personal stories that demonstrate an empathy with the family's struggle. As Roy's isolation becomes more evident, the therapist works to strengthen the therapeutic bond with him, pointing out his strengths and acknowledging his good intentions. As the session concludes, the family is asked to bring Janet and Ed the next time. Eventually, the therapist discovers that Roy's mother is also very involved with Paul and persuades the family to include her in sessions as well.

The structural therapist relies heavily on in-session interventions to produce initial behavioral changes. These changes are thought to stimulate cognitive and perceptual changes as well. By involving many family members, the structural therapist attempts to help the family reorganize itself so that the parental subsystem is strengthened with appropriate hierarchical boundaries.

Strategic Family Therapy

Strategic models of family therapy emphasize a particular approach or strategy for each presenting problem. The principal contributors to this type of practice are communication theorists at the Mental Research Institute (MRI) in Palo Alto, California, including Don Jackson, Paul Watzlawick, Gregory Bateson, and Jay Haley. Jackson's early collaborations with Bateson led to many significant contributions such as the double-bind theory of schizophrenia (Bateson, Jackson, Haley, & Weakland, 1956). Their ideas about symptoms as a form of communication provided a theoretical model for strategic therapy. Concurrently, Milton Erickson was pioneering hypnotic and paradoxical techniques that emphasize the uniqueness of the symptom and the importance of behavioral directives. Haley incorporated these ideas into the model he called strategic family therapy.

Symptoms in the family are interpreted as metaphors that also describe some aspect of the family system. The idea of metaphor is used in the symbolic rather than the literary sense. Because metaphors often communicate meaning on more than one level, the symptom can contain an explicit message (e.g., "I have a stomachache") as well as an implicit message (e.g., "I want more affection"). Since these therapists view all behavior as communication, a symptom is a communicative act between two or more family members that symbolizes some problem within the interpersonal network (Watzlawick, Weakland, & Fisch, 1974).

Symptoms often occur when a family is stuck in a particular stage of life; that is, while Paul Nelson's behavior may be a metaphor for conflictual interactions between his parents, it may also be a statement about a transition in the family. In this way, the symptom is often an attempted solution for some other problem that goes unacknowledged or unnoticed by others in the system.

Such metaphoric messages help the therapist conceptualize the relationship between symptoms and interactional patterns within the family.

The strategic family therapist assumes that Paul Nelson's behavior is a metaphor or nonverbal message about something else going on in the family. It might be related to problems in the marriage, challenges of a new transition in the family, or some other aspect of the family's well-being that has not yet come to light. As strategic therapists explore opinions and interactions within the family, they search for possible clues to clarify the message of the symptom.

In developing a treatment strategy, therapists at MRI emphasized an analysis of the client's attempted solutions as a way of assessing which interactions were unsuccessful (Watzlawick, Weakland, et al., 1974). Their work ushered in a type of strategic family therapy known as *brief family therapy*. After defining the problem, brief family therapists explore what solutions have been tried to resolve it (Weakland, Fisch, Watzlawick, & Bodin, 1974). Often, the family's attempt to solve the problem actually has worsened the original situation. In exploring the Nelsons' attempts at solving Paul's behavior problem, the therapist discovers that their primary solutions have been verbal (nagging, criticizing, and threatening), as have the responses (Paul's refusal to answer); furthermore, none of these attempted solutions has been successful. These would be considered first-order attempts at change rather than second-order solutions that do change the nature of the interaction. A second-order solution would require Lilly and Roy to identify options they could implement to be more action-oriented and less verbal and negative. To withhold privileges or other pleasures is generally considered a more action-oriented option, provided the parents can accomplish it with a minimum of argument or discussion. In addition, since Paul may be aligned with Lilly, a second-order plan might also incorporate a shift in the relationship by having Lilly administer the consequences while Roy rewards Paul's good behavior.

Therapeutic Process   The strategic family therapist serves as a stage director who hypothesizes about the problem and provides a directive to the family in an attempt to solve it. In the process of discussing the problem, the Nelson family is asked what changes they would like to see in the family. The therapist asks, "What do we need to work on?" or "What needs to happen for you to be successful here?" Lilly begins to explain something about Paul's recent behavior, focusing primarily on her own frustration and helplessness. As family members describe the problem, the therapist is careful not to confirm the family's perception that (a) the identified patient is the problem and (b) the identified patient or symptom is unchangeable (Stanton, 1981). By accepting the family's definition of the problem, the therapist participates in its perpetuation (Madanes, 1981). Instead, it is critical to redefine the presenting problem from an individual condition (e.g., Paul's stubbornness) to a behavioral or interactional difficulty (e.g., not going to school or disobeying parents) that can be alleviated.

The therapist begins to look for sequential patterns of behavior. When one family member speaks, does another family member interrupt or reject what is being said? When this happens, what happens next? The therapist is thinking about the sequence of interactions surrounding the presenting problem. Lilly is the first to speak. Roy remains silent. Both Roy and Paul wait to be spoken to by the therapist. When the therapist asks Roy to describe what happens when Paul is stubborn, Roy outlines the usual sequence of interactions: his arrival from work, Lilly's complaints about Paul's truancy, Roy's questions to Paul about why he is behaving this way, and Paul's silence. At that point, in exasperation, Roy tells Paul that, if he continues this behavior, he will never amount to much of anything. With this, Paul finally retreats to his room and listens to his collection of heavy metal music.

The therapist now directs Roy and Lilly to discuss the problem to see if they can talk about it in the presence of Paul. When Paul interferes, the therapist identifies a problem area and directs Lilly to ignore Paul's comment and continue the discussion with Roy. The therapist is careful not to be central to this interaction. As Roy and Lilly interact, family structure and hierarchy begin to emerge. As noted in the structural family therapy section, Lilly is overinvolved with Paul, whereas Roy is underinvolved. When the therapist asks Roy and Paul to talk without interference from Lilly, the directive has both diagnostic and therapeutic value. The therapist works on the premise that small initial changes lead to greater changes in the Nelsons as time goes on (Weakland et al., 1974).

As the therapist helps the family interact differently in the session, it is important to attribute positive motives to clients (Stanton, 1981). Problem behaviors are relabeled to have more positive meaning. For example, a positive label for Lilly's interference is "caring," and Paul's anger is relabeled "desired attention." The new labels provide family members with a new way of thinking about the problem so that it can be resolved. Further interaction with the therapist might generate a list of attempted solutions other than the caring that Roy and Lilly have employed so that they can begin to see what has worked to their benefit and what has not.

As the session concludes, the strategic therapist must decide what type of task to assign for the week. Sometimes, strategic therapists use straightforward tasks on the assumption that clients will comply with the suggestions. Other times, strategic therapists use paradoxical directives on the assumption that clients are ambivalent about change, even though they are distressed by the problem. Families with a schizophrenic member or an addict and those in which one or more members are characterized by personality disorder generally have difficulty completing straightforward tasks (Stanton, 1981). These families are very effective in getting the therapist to work hard for improvement, but they resist his or her efforts (Haley, 1976).

Since the therapist is new to the Nelson family, a straightforward task is assigned. This serves the purpose of assessing the family's ability to comply with direct suggestion and provides direction for changes in their interactional sequences. Since Paul is currently in residential treatment, some of the family's typical interactions are already disrupted. Therefore, the therapist assigns Roy to be in charge of the weekly telephone call to Paul and suggests that he ask Paul about his future ambitions. What would he like to be when he grows up? Whom does he consider to be his heroes? If he had $1 million, how would he spend it? The therapist suggests that Roy keep his opinions and advice to himself so that he can focus entirely on understanding and recording what Paul says. Once Roy returns and reports on his efforts with the task, the therapist can decide whether more straightforward tasks are in order or whether to shift focus toward more indirect and paradoxical tasks.

Strategic models assume that change takes place through client response to in-session directives and out-of-session tasks. The interruption of current behavior patterns is thought to be the most important starting point for change. This entry point allows family members to experience the new and the unfamiliar with the help of the therapist. With that experience comes the increased likelihood that the family will view new possibilities for themselves and extend their experimental behaviors outside of the session. Positive labels and an analysis of solutions strengthen this momentum by stimulating changes in thinking.

Intergenerational Family Therapy

Intergenerational family therapy includes the work of several pioneers who share an attention to family dynamics across several generations and a history in psychodynamic theory. These practitioners conceptualize families and their problems in terms of psychological dynamics passed from generation to generation. They see the past as operating in the present and have evolved theories that help them chart a therapeutic course across time.

The practitioners sampled for this category are Murray Bowen, MD, who pioneered family treatment and research of schizophrenia in the 1960s, and Ivan Boszormenyi-Nagy, MD (the last syllable is pronounced *Nahzsh*), who developed contextual family therapy, which is based on the concepts of loyalty and trust in family relationships. Although they each developed various ideas that are unique to their separate approaches, together they represent the primary roots of most intergenerational therapy practiced today.

Intergenerational therapists assume that the parenting and marital patterns of the Nelsons have been influenced by experiences in each parent's family of origin. Unlike structural and strategic therapists, the practitioners of this model consider information about past relationships to be a meaningful springboard from which to design interventions in the present. Bowenians would assert that both Roy and Lilly respond out of emotion rather than rationality when addressing Paul's behavior. This imbalance of emotionality over rationality is referred to as a *lack of differentiation*. The fact that they engage in repetitive interactions that bring about the same unsatisfactory results indicates the intense anxiety that motivates their behavior. This model suggests that, if the Nelsons can begin to discern the difference between the anxiety of their current behavior and the logic of alternative solutions, they can develop healthier relationships in the future.

Additionally, Bowenians assume that patterns of differentiation are transmitted from parents to children. They would reason that Paul and his siblings are mirrors of a transmitted family process (family projection process) rooted in the historical evolution of previous generations. As parents pass on their level of differentiation to children, relationships are often fused (too close and too emotionally reactive). This model of family therapy assumes that each member of the family acts impulsively out of emotion or tradition and is unaware of how the power of reason could generate improved relational patterns. Thus, Paul's behavior is thought of as coming from some gut-level instinct that manifests the same level of differentiation as his parents'.

In exploring the historical development of the Nelsons, a family map called a *genogram* is constructed. This diagram identifies each member of their three-generation extended family, noting dates of births, deaths, marriages, and divorces. The intergenerational family therapist discovers that Roy's mother lives in their neighborhood and has been widowed for 5 years. As family members begin discussing the loss of Grandpa, Paul becomes animated and talkative for the first time. He relates his memories of Grandpa, giving particular emphasis to the sadness that he still vividly remembers feeling on the day of the funeral. Other family members describe the vacations that Grandpa organized and the great void his death left in the family. Since his death, there have been no family vacations. The year after his death, when Paul was 10, Lilly went to work outside the home for the first time.

Intergenerational family therapists often inquire about deaths and losses experienced in the family. Such events are often linked with the subsequent development of symptoms in the family (Petker, 1982). When viewing the problem as part of a sequence of family events, some families are seen as going through emotional shock waves from which they may not have recovered fully (Bowen, 1978). The Nelsons can be seen as having not recovered fully from Grandpa's death. The void in the family was not filled by anyone else taking on the planning of family vacations. For Paul, the void may have widened when Lilly went to work and Janet graduated from elementary school, leaving him to attend school alone for the first time. The historical development of the Nelsons illustrates how a lack of differentiation can be passed down through the generations and also how it can be exacerbated through traumatic life events.

Other intergenerational therapists might utilize contextual family therapy in helping the Nelsons. Boszormenyi-Nagy (1987) might assume that individuals in the family are motivated, in part, by a subjective sense of fairness that can only be understood from their unique development (relational ethics). Paul's motivation for skipping school could come from an unspoken sense of entitlement based on some contribution that he perceives himself to be making to the family. For example, having seen his brother drop out of school at age 16 (a perceived privilege), Paul may think he is entitled to the same privilege in return for the loyalty he manifests to his mother against his father. Understandably, Roy and Lilly may also be motivated by a sense of justice that comes from their experience in their own families (e.g., "We were expected to obey our parents unconditionally, and we are entitled to the same obedience from our children"). This ledger system provides a framework by which the family therapist discovers each person's subjective justification for his or her current behavior (Boszormenyi-Nagy & Krasner, 1986).

From an intergenerational perspective, the goals for this family could include teaching Roy and Lilly how to differentiate, helping the entire family recover more fully from Grandpa's death, and rebalancing the family ledger system to improve their sense of trust and fairness.

Therapeutic Process   In an intergenerational session, the therapist remains central to the process. Bowen usually worked with individuals or couples, gathering family information and coaching them into new behaviors.

Boszormenyi-Nagy usually works with the entire family, learning about their sense of loyalty and fairness within the family. The first session with the Nelsons includes all members of the household. For this model of practice, no purpose is served by asking family members to interact with each other. Instead, family therapists ask questions about the history of the symptom and pay specific attention to significant life events in the chronology of the family. This is how the therapist discovers the nodal event of Grandpa's death. However, the therapist begins by asking about the parents' courtship and marriage and then traces significant family transitions from that time to the present. It emerges that Paul's behavior did not become problematic until the sixth grade, approximately 1 year after Grandpa's death. This was also the year that Lilly went to work. During the early parts of the interview, Roy and Lilly describe the first years of their marriage as very happy. Lilly's parents died when she was young, and she was happy to be adopted into Roy's family. He was an only child and she liked his parents very much.

When the family becomes emotional during the discussion about Grandpa, the therapist asks each person for their reflections and memories; the therapist models differentiated (calm) behavior that is empathic but not reactive to their level of emotion. When they express anger toward each other over current conflicts, the therapist does not take sides but seeks understanding of each point of view, allowing each member to confirm or correct the therapist's understanding (multidirected partiality). As each side of the conflict is clarified, the therapist begins to ask questions intended to diffuse emotional reactivity and to help each member listen to the others. Throughout the session, the therapist engages in continuous self-monitoring to manage personal anxiety that might allow triangulation to occur. Triangulation is the tendency for two people who are in conflict to involve a third person in order to reduce the stress in the dyad. When Paul begins to accuse his parents of being unfair, the therapist is most interested in having Paul express his thoughts and feelings, not in discovering all areas of the parents' perceived unfairness. Since Paul is actually talking to the therapist, he is able to develop some emotional distance from the problem instead of engaging in the same repetitive interactions with his parents. Roy and Lilly are given the opportunity to listen to Paul with some distance instead of having to respond to him in direct interaction. In this manner, the process provides opportunities for the therapist to help family members differentiate, and the actual content of their discussions is less important.

As this session comes to a close, the therapist has received an overview of the Nelson family history, of their emotional evolution with each other, and of the significant events that may have influenced their current lack of differ-entiation. In Bowenian therapy, this overview might require several sessions. Eventually, family members are given assignments such as gathering more family history, writing letters (to the living or the dead) that will be reviewed with the therapist, visiting relatives, or visiting the cemetery. With the Nel-sons, the therapist decides to ask them to plan a hypothetical family vacation, since they have not had one in 5 years. Now that Paul is in a residential facil-ity, the weekly telephone call to his family can be used in vacation planning so that his views are represented. Paul is also asked to write a letter to Grandpa. In subsequent sessions, reviews of the assignments provide useful information to help detriangle relationships and help the family discuss their unresolved is-sues; the therapist coaches family members with their assignments so that emotional reactivity decreases as each issue is addressed.

Experiential Family Therapy

Experiential family therapists focus on subjective needs of the individual in the family and work to facilitate a family process that addresses the individual-ity of each member. They are similar to intergenerational therapists in their focus on the subjective; however, they place more value on emotional expres-sion as part of the growth process. They also resemble structural and strategic therapists in their emphasis on present interactions. Carl Whitaker and Vir-ginia Satir, though very different in personal style, best represent the distin-guishing characteristics of an experiential approach. These clinicians believe that all individuals have the right to be themselves; however, family and social needs may often suppress the individuality and self-expression by which a per-son becomes fully understood and known in the family. As parents are the ar-chitects of the family (Satir, 1972), it is incumbent on them to provide sufficient structure and nurturance so that the individuality of each child can be fostered.

In the Nelson family, communication is rigid and focuses mainly on su-perficial topics that do not reveal vulnerabilities, hurts, hopes, fears, and dreams. Lilly can be affectionate with her children but spends most of her time nagging Paul about his problems and preaching to Ed about his predica-ment. Roy is often silent. When he begins to talk about himself, he launches into long monologues about the men he works with on the assembly line at the meat-packing plant; he describes the pranks they pull on each other to break the monotony of the work. In experiential family therapy, this family would be thought of as lacking enough creativity and flexibility to adapt to the transitions that challenge them. Their restricted range of emotional expression prevents family members from feeling loved and accepted for who they are.

In exploring the climate for personal growth in the Nelsons, the experiential therapist discovers that Ed dropped out of school with his parents' permission. He felt discouraged about his school performance and did not want the continued humiliation of failure. He never had a behavior problem at school or at home. However, as the family discussed ways in which they tried to help Ed with his studies, it emerged that both Lilly and Roy had no understanding of the math techniques being taught at the high school, and they felt intimidated and helpless in the process. They would usually become angry and embarrassed when he received his report card, telling him to ask his teachers for more help. When Ed announced that he wanted permission to drop out of school, Roy had little to say and Lilly was relieved.

Currently, the Nelsons exhibit the same sense of alienation from each other. When discussing Ed's present attempts to earn enough money to support his forthcoming child, the conversation moves quickly away from the hurt that the parents are feeling; Roy shrugs his shoulders in confusion and Lilly sermonizes. Experiential family therapists would view the Nelsons as needing more nurturance. With empathy and support from the therapist, the parents come to accept their own emotional experience, thereby becoming more intimate and caring. As self-awareness increases, the quality of communication improves, fostering self-esteem and growth in family members.

Lilly and Roy manifest their low self-esteem through the embarrassment and helplessness they feel regarding their children's struggles. By fostering self-acceptance, the experiential family therapist helps parents become who they want to be. Roy and Lilly can learn to forgive themselves for not being perfect parents. As they do this, they can also risk more intimate self-expression with each other. As they learn to tolerate intimacy (and the accompanying risk of conflict), their acceptance of themselves and each other generalizes to their children. Interactions become opportunities for family members to be heard and understood rather than contests to control or judge.

Therapeutic Process   An experiential session with the Nelsons includes the entire family. The therapist employs self-disclosure, revealing feelings and experience relevant to therapeutic goals. By modeling good communication, the therapist begins to teach the Nelsons how to tolerate honest emotional expression. Meeting each family member, the therapist makes a gesture or expression that personalizes the therapeutic experience and helps each family member feel accepted. At the same time, the therapist demonstrates self-acceptance through having the courage to admit mistakes and fallibility. As introductions proceed, the therapist looks for opportunities to demonstrate frankness and candor, commenting on some aspect of each individual that normally might be ignored in typical communication. In addition to modeling and teaching, the therapist facilitates the family's process during the session so that effective communication can occur. Ed is asked, "How do you know when your dad is feeling good toward you? What does he do to show his love?" Roy is asked, "Do you love Ed? What are the ways you prefer to show your love?" As the family squirms at such uncharacteristic openness, the therapist models respect for their fears and discomfort. Through encouragement, the therapist develops rapport with the family through empathy, questions, and directives. The therapist also models genuineness by disclosing fears, embarrassments, fantasies, and foibles. In so doing, experiential family therapists trust the universality of human experience to help family members identify with them.

Compared to other practitioners, experiential family therapists are less systematic in their use of specified interventions because of their emphasis on spontaneity and creativity. Consistent patterns of intervention usually stem from the therapist's style. For example, if Carl Whitaker were meeting with the Nelsons, he would focus first on Roy and address the alienation that keeps him from being a more nurturing father. He might also become argumentative with Paul to encourage the honest expression of the anger that conceals his pain (Napier & Whitaker, 1978). If Virginia Satir were meeting with the Nelsons, she might start by asking Paul to help her construct a live sculpture of his family by placing members in physical locations that represent the degree of emotional distance present within the family. As the sculpture is constructed, she would use the resulting scene as a catalyst for honest communication about family relationships. Satir emphasizes nurturance, whereas Whitaker makes liberal use of confrontation and modeling with frankness.

As treatment continues in experiential family therapy, the Nelsons find each session to contain some opportunity for emotional experience and interaction with each other through the therapist's directives and various techniques borrowed from Gestalt psychotherapy. Experiential practitioners believe that change occurs through increased intimacy and through interactions that help family members resolve their hurt and anger toward each other with warmth and respect. Central to this process is the therapist's ability to model the confrontation of difficult issues with courage and humanity.

❄ INTEGRATIVE MODELS

The history of integration within marriage and family therapy began during the early years of the field. For example, Jay Haley, after participating with the MRI group, continued his work in collaboration with Minuchin at the Philadelphia Child Guidance Clinic (Simon, 1992). These experiences became the foundation for what he called strategic family therapy. This mode of family therapy incorporates elements from each of Haley's previous settings. His focus on cross-generational coalitions provides a structural means of assessment. His preference for giving a series of directives became the distinguishing characteristic he referred to as strategic.

Stanton (1981) coined the term *structural-strategic* and then applied that model with Todd in their groundbreaking work on drug addiction (Stanton, Todd, & Associates, 1982). This term is now used frequently to describe those who attend to structural themes while using strategic interventions. In an additional move toward integration, Stanton (1992) developed the use of a "Why now?" question into his structural-strategic approach. This question incorporates elements of family history into the process that might be overlooked by a more present-focused orientation. We can see from these examples that integration, just like family process, often happens in stages.

Other models of practice have been developed by those who made further innovations based on their own experience. These integrative models combine the best elements from other approaches and also account for structure, gender, race, culture, transitional issues, and individual experience. In addition, leaders such as the Milan team from Italy and Michael White from Australia brought ideas that are now considered part of the movement in family therapy toward constructivism. As these family therapists began to introduce concepts related to the uniqueness of each person's worldview, others joined these discussions and introduced further concepts related to social construction theory.

Constructivists argue that traditional approaches to family therapy represent many different ways of viewing the same case. The question of which view is correct becomes irrelevant. Instead, they ask which view is most helpful to the family. They also suggest that the family's view of the problem may be the most important to consider, since it may be restraining them from more effective solutions (White, 1986). They emphasize Bateson's idea that, if brought forth, information that provides a contrast to the family's dominant (or negative) mode of thinking is information that begins the change process.

Thus, as Goolishian and Anderson (1992) point out, individuals are thought of as a "storehouse of maps and lenses" (p. 11). Constructivists try to capitalize on this human capacity for change by shifting attention to alternate ways of thinking.

In contrast to constructivism, social constructionists consider a person's view to be the product of conversations, dialogues, and interactions. The meaning a person gives to a situation comes through social process, not an isolated internal process. Thus,

> The self that emerges in the social constructionist vision is a self that exists only in and through the coherence that we construct across the changing webs of meaning and the first-person narratives that span our lives in our changing conversations with each other. (Goolishian & Anderson, 1992, p. 11)

This view of the therapeutic process places more emphasis on developing collaborative dialogues with and among clients rather than searching for a given reality that is assumed to be flawed. Language is also highlighted as a critical element in therapy. Social constructionists often encourage the use of words based in human experience (i.e., stories, conversations, etc.). This comes in contrast to constructivists who may continue with language that comes from concepts of science and power (i.e., intervention, structure, feedback loop). The integrative models of the Milan team, Michael White, and Harlene Anderson are examples of constructivism and social constructionism applied to family therapy. Their differences represent a range in the degree to which a therapist actively intervenes and strategizes versus the adoption of a reflective, collaborative stance.

An additional integrative model, cognitive-behavioral family therapy, while not associated with social construction, is presented here to illustrate how models coming from different traditions develop over time to include elements shared with others. Coming from the early traditions of behavioral marital therapy, Christensen, Jacobson, and Babcock (1995) have developed a model for close relationships (e.g., gay, lesbian, married, and common law) that addresses the issue of "acceptance" in working with couples. This model of family therapy attempts to balance traditional behavioral methods for change with an equivalent emphasis on acceptance of elements that cannot be changed (e.g., developmental histories, traditions, values).

The Milan Systemic Approach

In 1967, Mara Selvini Palazzoli organized the Milan Center for Family Studies. Selvini Palazzoli was joined by Luigi Boscolo, Giuliana Prata, and Gianfranco Cecchin. This group developed a systemic approach for treating the families of anorexic, encopretic, and emotionally disturbed children. Their book *Paradox and Counterparadox* (Selvini Palazzoli, Boscolo, Cecchin, & Prata, 1978) provides the most comprehensive description of their early therapy, although the team eventually split into two interest groups, each emphasizing different aspects of their earlier work. Before this split, however, the entire team developed systematic practices such as circular questioning, hypothesizing, and neutrality (Selvini Palazzoli, Boscolo, Cecchin, & Prata, 1980a).

In their early strategic work, the team pursued research and practice in the area of cross-generational coalitions. They developed the invariant prescription, which is a standard directive given to every family. The directive instructs the parents to continue coming to therapy secretly without their children. Their early research suggested that when parents did this successfully, symptoms in the children remitted. However, if the secret was broken, symptoms recurred (Selvini Palazzoli, Cirillo, Selvini, & Sorrentino, 1989).

Following some of Bateson's earlier work in communication and knowledge systems, the Milan team has also pursued a less direct model that emphasizes changes in thinking. They developed a method of interviewing called circular questioning to assess family interactions, the historical evolution of the problem, and emotional issues still influencing the family. *Circular* was used as a synonym for systemic because early pioneers in the field spoke of "circular causality." This term refers to cycles of interactions, perceptions, and experiences that make up the relational pattern associated with a certain problem. Circular questions illuminate these *cycles of interaction* by searching for *varying opinions* about the problem, *typical reactions* to the problem, and the *sequences* in which these thoughts and behaviors occur. Then they look for opportunities to provide a positive connotation for problematic behaviors. Each family member is often provided with a positive connotation not only for the behavior of the identified patient but also for any behavior that is thought to be maintaining the problem. Going beyond the strategic idea of positive labeling, these clinicians use positive connotation to elucidate how and why family members may be covertly cooperating with the problem (Boscolo, Cecchin, Hoffman, & Penn, 1987).

Therapeutic Process   The Milan team would initially assume that Paul is in a secret coalition with one parent. Upon detecting Lilly as the most likely part of the alignment, they might move to sessions with Roy and Lilly alone. Their main goal is to help Lilly maintain different boundaries with the children and to help Roy become a more involved partner with Lilly.

In a session with the Nelsons, Milan therapists might spend most of the session asking circular questions that compare different points of view. Who first noticed the problem? What was happening in the family at that time? Who agrees and disagrees about what the problem is and what the solution should be? What is the next most important problem in the family after these concerns about Paul? Who is in the most pain in the family? The least pain?

After learning about the correlation of the problem with significant events in the family history, the therapists might tell the Nelsons that it is important for Paul to continue his behavior because the alternative of having him grow up before the family fully recovers from Grandpa's death might result in a greater void in the family. Thus, it is wise to slow the process down. In addition, Roy is being a dutiful husband by keeping his distance so that Lilly can have closeness with her children as a way of filling the void that Grandpa left for all of them. In addition to this in-session intervention that targets changes in thinking, the Milan team might also create a ritual for the family (see Chapter Nine for a description) or prescribe other interactions to help the family reorganize their behavior so as to accommodate developmental transitions.

By drawing on the family's generational and structural history and incorporating strategic interventions, the Milan team integrates key elements of other models. A focus on a developmental history of how the problem has evolved progresses toward a focus on present behaviors and future goals within the family. Behavioral and cognitive changes are addressed simultaneously by eliciting systemic information in session about multiple points of view within the family and by assigning rituals or tasks out of session to help change interaction patterns.

As part of the constructivist movement in family therapy, the Milan team remains open to multiple interpretations of any problem. They consider indirect interventions to be the most appropriate for difficult cases because they are more respectful of the client's reality and minimize resistance to change by making paradoxical arguments for no change. These arguments indirectly legitimize client ambivalence toward change and provide an atmosphere that is accepting and respectful of these client dilemmas. By providing the Nelsons with the paradoxical suggestion that it might not be the right time for Paul to grow up, the therapists acknowledge hardship and adversity in the family; they hypothesize that the symptoms have developed accidentally from coping patterns that have evolved. In this way, family members are provided with a face-saving way to begin the change process. No one is blamed for the problem and everyone's positive intentions are acknowledged.

Narrative Approaches

Narrative approaches are characterized by a language to describe the change process that is rooted in stories and literature. As one of the first to introduce narrative ideas to the field, Michael White has continued the constructivist trend in family therapy. These stories most commonly address themes of oppression and liberation. Just as constructivism asserts the validity of alternative points of view when addressing social problems, the playful interventions of White also spring from a variety of theoretical tracks. In working with the Nelsons, White would assume that the dominant view held by much of the mental health system has led to their depersonalization and oppression. He would also assume that the family is feeling oppressed by their problems. By using social theory regarding oppression and liberation, White would help the Nelsons notice their expert knowledge to recognize when the problem did not interfere with their lives. In helping the Nelsons develop their expert knowledge, he uses a concept developed by Bateson (1972) and looks for small exceptions to their negative experiences (so-called *unique outcomes*). He uses this increased awareness of successes to help the family develop a new life story of victory, competence, and leadership.

White emphasizes the importance of characterizing the problem as some force or entity that is outside the identified patient and outside the family. In the case of the Nelsons, a "truant lifestyle" might become the label for the problem. This process of externalization, based on the integration of sociological theories about oppression, is one of White's distinctive contributions to family therapy. He applies these concepts in redefining the role of the therapist.

Therapeutic Process   A session with Michael White might consist of a progression through various sets of questions. The family might first be asked about the problem and how it influences or defeats them. Then the therapist might ask Lilly and Roy to describe instances when things go well with Paul, even though they are few and far between. As they describe these times, White elaborates on these few experiences as examples of the family's expert knowledge of how they have influenced and controlled the problem.

When Paul fails to recognize anything positive about the exceptions, White uses his own observations of Paul to begin creating a picture of competence and cooperation. One of the ways he accomplishes this is to use strategic questions that provide a benevolent confrontation with present destructive cycles while pointing toward a hopeful future. He might ask Paul, "Which description would you prefer? Paul as a fellow who is being held hostage by a truant lifestyle, or Paul as a fellow who has battled the influences of a truant lifestyle and won?" He might ask Lilly and Roy if they would like to feel victorious over the oppressive influence of this lifestyle and then illustrate how the exceptions they have described are the first steps toward freedom.

The Nelsons would find that White adapts easily to their own subculture. He carefully notes their words and their language, incorporating them into his analysis and into their story of liberation. As therapy proceeds, they are invited to think about their lives and problems as an old story that they are rewriting together. He is the audience, director, and editor of the emerging work of art. The Nelsons are the authors and principal characters in the production. His playfulness demedicalizes and depathologizes family problems by placing them in an alternative knowledge base (literature and sociology). He prefers thinking of solutions in those terms rather than adopting the dominant language of traditional mental health practice. The goal is to liberate the Nelsons from their own oppression and from that of larger systems that stereotype, label, and objectify them.

As work progresses with the Nelsons, White uses sessions as a time for the family to report on their successes. When difficulties occur, they are compared to situations that were even worse to help the family maintain their sense of momentum. For example, Roy and Lilly might report discouragement arising from an episode in which they began to lecture Paul, falling back into old patterns. White might quickly ask them how they managed to lecture him for only 5 minutes instead of the usual 10 minutes, like in the old days. He would focus his questions on how they were able to stop the old pattern so quickly and what they thought made the difference. If they remained discouraged, failing to see any progress, he might comment on how quickly they became aware of the old trap. Further questions might be, "What difference do you think it will make in your future if you are able to continue this type of awareness? What does it say about you as parents if you are able to continue exercising this type of awareness?"

White has successfully integrated the search for competencies with an analysis of interactional cycles and playful interventions. Probably his most famous example of playfulness is cited in the protocols he developed for working with encopretic children, externalizing the problem as sneaky poo and enlisting family members in a game to outsmart sneaky poo (Epston & White, 1992). Although his therapeutic process is quite different from that of the Milan team, he is also successful at helping families find a face-saving way out of their present difficulties. However, he is quick to discourage stereotyping his interventions. In describing their work, Epston and White (1992) observe:

We have been steadfast in our refusal to name our work in any consistent manner. We do not identify with any particular "school" of family therapy, and are strongly opposed to the idea of our own contribution being named as a school. We believe that such a naming would only subtract from our freedom to further explore various ideas and practices, and that it would make it difficult for others to recognize their own unique contributions to developments in this work, which we regard to be an "open book". . . However, we are drawing attention to the fact that one of the aspects associated with this work that is of central importance to us is the spirit of adventure. We aim to preserve this spirit, and know that if we accomplish this our work will continue to evolve in ways that are enriching to our lives, and to the lives of those persons who seek our help. (pp. 8–9)

Collaborative Approaches

Collaborative approaches are often characterized by the conversational models of Lynn Hoffman (1998), the late Harry Goolishian, and Harlene Anderson (1992). Frustrated by the concept of intervention taken from cybernetics, the proponents of collaborative approaches see models of family therapy based on constructivism as too focused on the doing of therapy to a client rather than being with a client in a helpful way. They consider the emphasis on technique and outcome to hinder the caring quality of their relationship; hence, it reduces opportunities for change. These clinicians generally emphasize the elements of social construction theory that define therapy as a helpful conversation. Inherent in these conversations is the use of language that distances the therapist from the role of "expert."

In this model, since the therapist is no more an expert on the problem than the client, the therapist is likely to be more interested in clients' thinking and views on what needs to change and how. Rather than using a language of techniques, they use a language of stories, possibilities, and dialogues. Thus, in constructing their conceptual map, they begin with a therapeutic relationship of respect and equality. Next, they determine who are most involved or affected by the problem. All those who perceive a problem (problem-defining system) might be invited to discuss it together.

H. Anderson (1991) suggests that collaborative approaches are rooted in hermeneutics, the methodology of interpretation. Thus, collaborative family therapists are concerned with conversations that inspire multiple interpretations. These interpretations become a dialogue that is encouraged so that communication leads to shared understanding. The process leads to a sense of discovery for those included in the dialogue.

Therapeutic Process   In the case of the Nelsons, the therapist attends to their story and attempts to give it shape with conversational questions. The therapist reflects on each family member's comments. Therapeutic opinions or ideas are offered tentatively and respectfully. The therapist may collaborate with the family to generate solutions if the family wishes. The therapist is always careful not to understand the Nelsons' story too quickly so as to help the family provide full meaning to their experience. Through modeling and "modesty," Anderson (1991) would seek to create an environment where family members can dialogue in a sustained way. The issue of who should be talking with whom is addressed flexibly and inclusively, allowing the final direction to emerge from the participants who are present. The staff of the residential facility might be included with parents if all are comfortable with the idea. Listening and mutual understanding are given as much value as speaking. The Nelson parents might be asked, "Who are the people with whom you talk most about the problem? Who is the most concerned?" When they respond that Roy's mother has been very close to them, they are asked whether it would be helpful to include Grandma in the discussions. Care is taken not to imply that anyone is the cause of the problem. Instead, all are valued for their unique perspective.

Collaborative family therapists might describe themselves as organizers of information that participants provide. This organizing might take the form of looking for connections between various perspectives. The purpose is to provide an atmosphere of reflection in which creative solutions emerge from the clients themselves, not from the therapist. If Mr. and Mrs. Nelson express opinions about Paul's behavior, the therapist listens for any statements that might stifle conversation for others and considers them carefully until the speaker feels understood and respected. Those who might have been stifled are encouraged to provide another point of view. The conversational process also includes speculation and curiosity about any given train of thought, seeking others' opinions, and expanding the number of possible views about any one idea.

A collaborative approach to the Nelsons' situation would assume that creative and respectful solutions evolve from an atmosphere of caring and curiosity. As participants dialogue and share their perspectives, they change with each other through these thoughtful, questioning conversations. As they change with each other, the original problem "dis-solves," and the need for a facilitator of conversations disappears.

Cognitive-Behavioral Family Therapy

Cognitive-behavioral family therapy (CBFT) has developed primarily from the work of psychologists whose backgrounds in research led them to design programs that yield quantifiable results. This approach developed as a variation of behavioral family therapy practiced by Jacobson (1991), Alexander and Parsons (1982), and Falloon (1991). These family therapists combined social learning theory with systems theory to address couple problems, delinquency, and adjustment to schizophrenia. The behavioral approach has traditionally focused on the behavior of individuals and the environmental events that trigger, shape, and maintain their behavior. The consequences of behavioral patterns are considered goals and reinforcements to them. These sequences are identified through a functional analysis of relationships relevant to the problem.

The most obvious influence in the early development of behavioral family therapy was the social learning approach used to modify children's behavior. As behavioral therapists began to consider the cost effectiveness of their treatment of children, they paid increased attention to employing the child's parents as agents of change. Typically, treatment would involve parent training in which both parents were instructed to identify and record appropriate behaviors of the child and then systemically intervene using social learning principles (e.g., modeling, time-out, and extinction) to eliminate the problem.

As behavioral therapists began to help parents with their children's behavior, they also noted the interactional patterns of other family members. Research began to shift from investigating the child's inappropriate behavior to studying patterns of interaction between family members (i.e., how two family members influence each other to maintain the behavior). When parent training was ineffective, parents often reported marital difficulties that contributed to the child's problem. Thus, marital discord and other factors such as peer relations are also seen as contributing factors to the child's behavior, and the same operant principles used to modify children's behavior also apply to the behavior problems of couples.

The social learning approach views family dysfunction as the result of infrequent positive reinforcement between family members (i.e., not enough rewards for positive behavior). Often an aversive stimulus, or punishment, is used by one family member to control the behavior of another. For example, a wife's criticism is thought to trigger a husband's drinking, and vice versa. Social learning theory views family conflict as the use of aversive control rather than the use of positive reinforcement. The eventual outcome is a low rate of positive reinforcers exchanged over an extended period of time. Each person begins to feel less attracted to the other.

Recently, behavioral family therapists have emphasized cognitive dimensions (e.g., thoughts, expectations, images, etc.) that influence behavior

(Jacobson & Christensen, 1996). Of particular interest have been therapists' assessments of how thoughts and attitudes serve to both trigger and maintain behavior. This has led to the term *cognitive*-behavioral. Cognitive-behavioral therapists help family members self-monitor their thoughts and attitudes to understand how these influence behaviors of family members.

To cognitive-behavioral therapists, a person's internal process affects behavior (e.g., unspoken self-talk influences what one does). Unrealistic expectations of another (spouse, child) often produce undesirable behavior (e.g., anger, criticism). These behaviors may be viewed as a response to the expectations and not necessarily to the behavior of others. In such cases, the spouse or parent may need to develop more realistic expectations to adjust to the situation. Baucom, Epstein, Sayers, and Sher (1989) list five types of cognitions that influence the interactions of couples: (a) selective attention, (b) attributions, (c) expectancies, (d) assumptions, and (e) standards. Cognitive- behavioral therapists often use self-report inventories to assess the effects of these cognitions on a couple's relationship. For example, one spouse may think the other is trying to control him or her, and this may lead to arguments over who controls the finances or who should clean the house. Thus, it may not be the area of disagreement (finances, cleaning the house) that is the problem but the underlying thought (control) that is the major issue.

Cognitive-behavioral therapy has demonstrated its effectiveness in improving couple relationships. Baucom, Sayers, and Sher (1990) found that cognitive restructuring produces meaningful changes in the way couples view their relationship and improves marital adjustment. It appears that when spouses alter their cognitions as well as their behavior, positive change in the relationship is more likely.

Therapeutic Process   The role of the cognitive-behavioral therapist is both active and directive, providing structure to the session (Baucom, Epstein, & Rankin, 1995). During assessment, the therapist evaluates: (a) the strengths and weaknesses of a couple's interactional pattern, (b) relationship themes that are essential to helping the couple change, and (c) each spouse's subjective view of the relationship. In addition, the cognitive-behavioral therapist assesses the couple's ability to solve problems and spend time in pleasurable activities.

In a session with the Nelsons, the cognitive-behavioral therapist assesses Roy and Lilly's interaction patterns. As these patterns become evident, the therapist assesses the strengths and weaknesses in their relationship and attempts to identify cognitive themes that influence their behavior. For example, when Lilly states that "Roy is too hard on Paul," the therapist needs to focus on this belief. The therapist likely discusses with Lilly how her beliefs affect her relationship with Roy in both a positive and negative way. The therapist also addresses Roy's beliefs and discusses with him the combination of these two beliefs, how they influence their relationship, and how that might affect Paul's behavior. The therapist might also assign Roy and Lilly a task in which they are asked to interact with each other in a new way. Ultimately, the therapist's role is to help alter counterproductive thoughts held by one or both spouses and to improve their relationship with each other and their children.

Cognitive-behavioral family therapy and other approaches share many properties. First, several approaches share a functional view of problem behaviors and interactional sequences. This means problems are seen as serving some function within the family and as being maintained by family members' behavior. Like structural and strategic family therapy, CBFT focuses on the present interaction of family members rather than on past history. The goal of therapy is to alleviate the presenting problem by restructuring family interaction through cognitive or behavior change. Finally, this approach also employs cognitive restructuring and assigns tasks to facilitate behavior change at home.

❄ SUMMARY

The models presented in this chapter have discussed the Nelson family from many different perspectives. While each model provides somewhat different concepts and language, we think the therapist's ability to integrate the family's reality with a given theoretical reality may be at the heart of successful family therapy. As the field of family therapy has developed over the past several decades, the movement toward distinct schools of thought has given way to integration of these major modes of thinking. While early pioneers spoke of their particular approach as a certain type of truth, the trend toward constructivist thinking has led toward greater acceptance of the family's unique reality (truth) and a flexible inclusion of contrasting points of view. Representative of such integration is Minuchin's (1987) reflection on the factors influencing his practice:

> *Recently, I was working with a family with three adult children whose mother committed suicide 20 years ago. . . . I surprised myself by asking them to watch family movies and to mourn the mother's death. I thought Norman Paul might be proud of me. Another day I was seeing a family with an anoretic child. . . . I found myself remembering some of the writings of*

Hilde Bruch. I didn't know she was one of my voices, but so it seems. Natu-
rally pulling many voices together usefully demands an organizing frame.
Briefly, the business of family therapy is change. . . . Within this framework
the possibilities are many and varied, as are the voices that speak to me . . .
Within the possibilities open to us, the best in us always learns from the best
of others. I am pleased to acknowledge that when I say to a man, "When did
you divorce your wife and marry your office?" it is Carl [Whitaker]'s voice
speaking. He might not recognize it in my accent, but it is there, as are all the
others. (pp. 13–14)

It is interesting to see that Minuchin shifts from his own tradition when the
family's context requires a different lens. We can only imagine that, if his early
career had brought him in contact with hundreds of midlife families whose
mothers had died tragically, he would have pioneered a therapy different from
his structural approach. On the other hand, we might also imagine, in the latter case, that his personal style, insight, and caring would still inspire us today.

Thus, we see that family therapy has a history of diversity and integration. Its leaders also have their own history of development and growth. The
models presented in this chapter and summarized in Table 1.1 are samples of
the past, present, and future of the field from our perspective. As one scans
down the list of concepts from each model in Table 1.1, there is an evolution
from more technical to more human terms. In the list of unique interventions,
there is a pattern starting with strategy and evolving toward reflection and
questioning. One irony in the list is the fact that some integrative models have
become more respectful of clients' personal wisdom and the "intuitive" side of
therapy (i.e., collaborative, narrative), whereas others have developed from
sophisticated research (i.e., cognitive-behavioral). We think this is a sign of
maturity in the field.

The old phrase "All roads lead to Rome" suggests that there are some
general outcomes that can be achieved in a variety of ways. In the world of
families and relationships, this is especially true. For example, the emphasis on
social construction and family therapy has brought renewed interest in the
importance of the therapeutic relationship and in the client's own wisdom.
This view has introduced the notion that the therapist is as much on a journey
of discovery as the client and must be open to shifting directions as new information comes forth from clients. This trend invites the family therapist to become humbler, less strategic and more caring, less directive. This direction is
difficult for some because anxiety often accompanies the uncertainty that pre-
cedes discovery. However, we think it is possible to become a family therapist
by adopting a spirit of discovery while still keeping the seat belt on! Thus, the
integrative approach that we encourage focuses on common elements from

these approaches and research on psychotherapy outcomes. We hope this helps the beginning practitioner develop a sense of direction without sacrificing the sense of discovery that helps each of us solve our own private mysteries.

With respect to keeping the seat belt on, the next chapter reviews common themes in family process that are represented in family therapy's history of diversity and integration. We think these themes provide conceptual anchors to help beginning clinicians grasp the complexity of family relationships. When these themes are pursued during the therapeutic encounter, they provide flexibility and stability in pursuing the problem-solving process—just like a seat belt when driving a car.

Chapter Two

INTEGRATION OF THEORY: COMMON THEMES

GENDER
When to Focus on Gender
Implications for Treatment

RACE AND CULTURE
When to Focus on Race and Culture
Implications for Treatment

INTERGENERATIONAL RELATIONSHIPS
When to Focus on Intergenerational Relationships
Implications for Treatment

TRANSITIONS AND DEVELOPMENT
When to Focus on Transitions and Development
Implications for Treatment

STRUCTURE
When to Focus on Structure
Implications for Treatment

INDIVIDUAL EXPERIENCE
When to Focus on Individual Experience
Implications for Treatment

As shown in Chapter One, the field of family therapy has many conceptual models that guide the practitioner, but this diversity can often be overwhelming for the beginner. The structural therapist might assess the boundaries, coalitions, and hierarchy of a family (Minuchin & Fishman, 1981). The intergenerational therapist might focus on family beliefs, conflicts, and losses transferred from one generation to another (Framo, 1981; Paul & Paul, 1975). The Milan team might search for different points of view related to a symptomatic impasse in family interactions (Selvini Palazzoli, Boscolo, Cecchin, & Prata, 1978). While theoretical models offer practitioners a way to organize their thinking, trainees must often incorporate concepts and techniques from various schools. This can be confusing because different theoretical models use different terms to describe similar concepts. For example, Bowen's concept of differentiation is similar to Minuchin's concept of boundary. Likewise, certain techniques have proven useful in a number of schools of family therapy. For example, several approaches (structural, strategic, and experiential) clarify communication, direct enactments, and describe the symptom (M. Nichols & Schwartz, 1991).

These overlapping concepts can be confusing, but the pursuit of conceptual purity has pitfalls of its own. We think the adoption of a rigid theoretical framework may limit a family therapist's effectiveness; there may be a tendency to distort observations so as to conform to theoretical precepts. For example, if practitioners are interested in assessing structural boundaries, they may only attend to specific interactions (e.g., when family members talk for each other). Practitioners who utilize this approach can easily organize their observations, but they may miss some important information merely because it does not fit within that framework (e.g., an important issue raised even though members are talking for each other). To use an old cliché, a person with a hammer starts to think everything is a nail.

In a review of family therapy approaches applied to later-life families, Hanna and Hargrave (1997) found most early models of family therapy to be lacking in their pure form:

> *Structural Family Therapy tends to ignore longitudinal changes over time with a family, thus ignoring historical factors that play heavily into the development of legacies. Bowenian Family Therapy does not offer enough pragmatic thinking to intervene in crises brought on by chronic illness. Behavioral Family Therapy does not have a framework for addressing the phenomenology of losses experienced by elders. Experiential Family Therapy may be too direct for some families who prefer to cope with changing family roles in silent, persevering ways. (p. 27)*

While this critique is given in light of the needs of later-life families, we have seen similar shortcomings appear with minority families, court-ordered cases, and families who are not "therapy wise." Given that the early approaches came from clinicians socialized according to certain norms in the culture of psycho-therapy, it is not difficult to understand how those first approaches became the foundation, but not the entire structure, of the family therapy movement.

The majority of practicing family therapists do not draw from a single theory or school of techniques (Quinn & Davidson, 1984). Even therapists who have been trained in a single theory eventually incorporate other theo-ries and techniques (Todd & Selekman, 1991). Therapists integrate their own blend of methodologies based on training, personality, and the population of families they are serving. Thus, we think of integrative practice as that which moves away from separate family therapy theories toward a systematic combi-nation of models. Broderick and Schrader (1991) write:

> Although there are still strong networks of therapists loyal to one or another pioneer, particularly in the areas of family therapy and sex therapy, the enor-mous majority of marriage and family and sex therapists today are trained in secular settings. That is, in programs that impartially have them read a wide range of current textbooks rather than those representing only one view. Perhaps, the university or agency will invite Haley or Bowen or Satir or Stu-art or Masters for a special workshop, and for a period of weeks everyone is a convert to that philosophy. These men and women are charismatic and ar-ticulate, but after a series of such appearances, learning from such special-ized workshops tends to become integrated into the therapist's own views. (p. 34)

The integration spoken of here comes from reviewing the range of thinking available in the field and combining these perspectives into a useful method of practice. Each of the early approaches provides an assessment of family functioning in relationship to problems (theory). These models also make suggestions about what is considered appropriate therapeutic function-ing (practice). In addition, later contributions to the field have added ideas about gender, race, and culture missing from earlier models. Thus, we begin this process of integration by identifying major themes that provide ways of thinking about relationships, interactions, and problems.

These themes can be organized along a continuum that proceeds from larger to smaller spheres of observation. These differences are sometimes re-ferred to as macro- versus microviews of family process. The macroview in-cludes broad social factors that affect interpersonal process such as the influence of gender, race, and culture. As the view narrows slightly, intergenerational and extended family relationships become additional influences on the problem. In the immediate relationship, it is possible to look at relational transitions and structural interactions. Finally, individuals can be studied as systems in their own right—as a combination of thoughts, feelings, behaviors, intentions, and in tandem with their psychodynamics, as a collection of biological subsystems that operate at all times. Like a camera with a zoom lens, the family therapist must maintain a flexible viewpoint to make an assessment from different angles and about multiple levels of process. Sometimes the problem must be viewed from a macrolevel of observation. At other times the microlevel reveals important information. In addition, the problem-solving system may comprise formal family relationships, friendships, or other important associates who may be resources in problem solving. The following discussion focuses on common conceptual themes and when it might be useful to explore them.

❄ GENDER

At the most general level, all families are influenced by patterns of socialization that lead to rules and roles governing family process. Gender-related roles and rules are the most fundamental of these patterns. Goldner (1988) argued that gender is not a special topic in family therapy but is "at the center of family theory" (p. 17). Because gender influences structure in the family, it should be a fundamental element in family assessment.

In a pioneering article on the subject, Hare-Mustin (1978) offered suggestions for implementing gender-sensitive family therapy:

> My purpose in what follows is not to analyze family therapy techniques, per se, but rather to consider certain areas of intervention in which a feminist orientation is important. These areas are: the contract, shifting tasks in the family, communication, generational boundaries, relabeling deviance, modeling, ownership and privacy, and the therapeutic alliance with different family members. (p. 185)

Of the areas cited by Hare-Mustin, the contract is an important element discussed in Chapter Six. The following questions pose possible hypotheses that address each of the other areas:

1. Could role inflexibility regarding tasks be related to the problem?
2. Are communication styles disempowering to the females in the family?
3. Have generational coalitions developed as a result of disempowerment in the marriage?

4. Can disempowering stereotypes ("nag," "passive-aggressive") be re-labeled to account for the context of powerlessness?
5. Can the female therapist model more egalitarian relationships with males in the family and can male therapists affirm female strength within the family?
6. What are family rules around females' personal development and autonomy outside the family?
7. What does each family member need from the therapist to feel understood and accepted?

As family therapy proceeds from the initial interview to the assessment process, these questions can be considered by the therapist as the definition of the problem is explored in greater depth. Then, during the assessment process, it may be useful to explore each person's point of view regarding gender development and how they arrived at their current position. An initial set of questions posed to clients might be:

1. What are some of the differences between how you each grew up as a female or male in our society?
2. How does your family address the differences between females and males in our society?
3. Are there certain traditions in your family that are more closely related to either women or men?
4. How do you feel about these traditions and practices?
5. Are there any ways you think these ideas and traditions might be related to _____ (the presenting problem)?

Such a line of questioning acknowledges gender differences in a neutral, exploratory way. While the ultimate goal may be to correct gender imbalances, beginning with neutral questions allows families to describe themselves without feeling any pressure to change. As exploration continues, family therapists can decide which issues might be targeted for change later in the process.

Some clinicians provide suggestions for therapeutic dialogue that combines assessment and intervention. For example:

1. "What best explains your not wanting to tell me too much: that I am white, female or highly educated?" (Goldner, 1988, p. 29)

2. "Should you accommodate to prescriptions for men's greed and expediency or defy these prescriptions and insist that wisdom influences your decisions?" (White, 1986, p. 15)
3. Would you prefer a life where you are a slave to tradition, or would you prefer a life where you are free to develop new views of people and relationships? (White, 1990)

While these questions are generally employed after extensive groundwork to establish the relationship and develop empathy, they illustrate the creative use of questions that not only assess readiness for change but motivate families to consider change.

When to Focus on Gender

General questions about gender differences should be incorporated into all assessments. Each person's experience should be heard. In cases of marital conflict, gender differences are often the core issue and should be identified. For example, Jacobson, Holtzworth-Monroe, and Schmaling (1989) found that women often complain more than men about their current relationship. Indeed, women often desire greater involvement and closeness from their husbands, whereas husbands prefer to maintain the status quo and create greater autonomy and separateness for themselves. Moreover, women are more likely to seek therapy and push for an egalitarian relationship, whereas men are less likely to seek therapy and are inclined to maintain traditional gender roles.

When any family member exhibits extreme masculinity or femininity, this can become an opportunity to explore issues of gender socialization. Although therapists always have subjective views from their own socialization, it is possible to engage clients in discussions about their subjective gender experiences while acknowledging one's own biases. Such modeling on the part of the practitioner can provide a new environment from which a person may explore unacknowledged influences. In discussing gender issues with men who manifest extreme masculinity, Frank Pittman (1991) notes that a therapist must remember three things:

1. A hypermasculine display indicates the man is frightened of his own inadequacy. The show of hypermasculinity is an effort to scare off whoever is coming to measure his shortcomings.
2. Men who suffer from hypermasculinity cannot tolerate female anger; they will wet their pants and run away, or do something

hypermasculine, as if they think every angry woman is their mother come back to take their puberty away.

3. Hypermasculinity is armor, just a protective coating, a shell—like mussels, or clams, or lobster, or shrimp. Just beneath the shell the meat may be sweet. It's there you'll find the beautiful, vulnerable boy. (p. 23)

Hypermasculinity often contributes to domestic violence and child abuse. In such cases, it is critical that both survivors' and perpetrators' beliefs and traditions about gender be explored in detail. Current trends in the treatment of abuse suggest a focus on both perceptual and behavioral change. Exploring beliefs and attitudes about gender differences is an important step toward identifying which beliefs and behaviors are ultimately targeted for change.

Implications for Treatment

The client's understanding of how gender relates to the presenting problem should dictate whether the therapist addresses gender directly or indirectly. When families are not ready to address gender differences directly, the practitioner should refrain from confrontation and address the issues in more indirect ways. For example, child and adolescent problems may be an opportunity to explore the impact of gender on developing children, thus introducing parents more indirectly to their own limitations.

Sheinberg and Penn (1991) list four categories of gender questions:

❋ The first category examines the "norm" the man or woman aspires to and the relational consequences of changing it . . .

❋ These questions can be followed by hypothetical questions: ideas about the relational consequences of changing these norms . . .

❋ Questions that identify norms to which the couple's parents aspired: how those affected both the couple and their parents . . .

❋ Once the family considers different possibilities of gender behaviors, future questions address the potential for establishing new norms as well as altering how the problem continues. (pp. 36–37)

Marital partners may be highly sensitive to discussions regarding gender if they feel criticized. For example, men may be sensitive to the label "chauvinistic" and women may be sensitive to the label "just a housewife" when a therapist begins to explore issues of sex-role stereotypes. Practitioners should maintain a curious but hopeful position as they explore and identify patterns of thought and behavior related to gender differences. A lack of readiness on the part of families to discuss gender directly suggests the need for a more thorough assessment of the family's experience before choosing an intervention strategy. Then, the therapist can develop indirect ways of addressing imbalances.

❄ RACE AND CULTURE

While gender is undoubtedly the first element that distinguishes human beings from each other, race and culture must rank second. Although race is similar to gender in that both are biologically determined, it is considered with culture in this discussion because of its influence on social and family groups.

Family therapists who have reviewed ethnicity in a broad way include McGoldrick and Giordano (1996) and their survey of diverse ethnic groups in terms of history, values, and other distinguishing cultural characteristics:

> *Italians rely primarily on the family and turn to an outsider only as a last resort. Black Americans have long mistrusted the help they can receive from traditional institutions except the church. . . . Puerto Ricans and Chinese may somatize when under stress and seek medical rather than mental health services. . . . Likewise, Iranians may view medication and vitamins as a necessary part of treating symptoms. (p. 2)*

In addition, these authors explored the process of family therapy for each group with particular attention to ways in which therapy could be respectful of cultural norms and values. Often, a family's cultural heritage is overlooked as an important resource and strength that may be at the center of the family's ability to overcome their current difficulties.

The social class and background of therapists can be critical factors in how they draw conclusions about the family. Spiegel, in McGoldrick et al. (1982), summarizes some typical therapeutic values:

> *Middle-class therapists, no matter what their ethnic origins, have been socialized in terms of mainstream values. The therapist will be future oriented, expecting clients to be motivated and to keep appointments punctually. He or she will also expect families to be willing to work on therapeutic tasks (Doing), over reasonable periods of time (Future), with the prospect of change before them (Mastery-over-Nature). All this is to be done while taking a pragmatic view of moral issues (Neutral), and at the very least the therapist will expect to help clients to distance themselves from any*

*overwhelming moral burden or intense feelings of shame. And clients will
be expected to separate themselves from enmeshment in the family structure and to develop increased autonomy (Individual). (p. 46)*

Thus, ethnicity—a sense of shared identity that has developed over
many generations—can be a critical variable in understanding client families
and mobilizing their strengths. If clinicians are not aware of differing world-
views and values, they are apt to be critical rather than complimentary of differences exhibited by families out of the mainstream.

In addition to acknowledging differences between cultural groups, it is
also important to avoid stereotyping. The practitioner's intent should be to
strike a balance between understanding the common ground of general patterns and clarifying distinctions and variations within the larger group. Boyd-
Franklin provides valuable help in this area with African American families,
summarizing the fundamental premises of her book *Black Families in Therapy*
(Boyd-Franklin, 1989) as follows:

1. There is a great deal of cultural diversity among Black families that is
   often overlooked or misunderstood.
2. Black Afro-American culture represents a distinct ethnic and racial
   experience that is unique for a number of reasons, including: history;
   the African legacy; the experience of slavery, racism, and discrimination; and the victim system.
3. The illusion of color blindness or the "class not race" myth needs to
   be challenged as both misguided and counterproductive.
4. There are many myths about Black families in the social science literature that have painted a pejorative, deficit picture of Black family
   functioning.
5. There is a need to clarify and understand the strengths of Black
   families, which can serve as a foundation for therapeutic work. (p. 5)

When family therapists serve minority families, they can prepare by referring
to Boyd-Franklin (1989), McGoldrick et al. (1982), or Diller (1999) for helpful specifics related to many minority groups in the United States.

The questions in Box 2.1 may be used to develop an assessment process
that accounts for the effects of culture. Whatever questions the practitioner
chooses, it is important to acknowledge and respect cultural differences between the family and therapist. Then, families can be invited to teach therapists about the significant parts of their cultural identity. As clinicians pursue
this type of assessment, their role is similar to the anthropologist who lives

with the people and understands them while being a participant in their culture. Such a role is in contrast to the physician or scientist who analyzes, categorizes, and treats people from a distance.

A critique of the social service system by Minuchin (1984) illustrates that cultural conflicts can often be central to the definition of a problem. In reviewing selected court cases from British Social Services, he describes the plight of Mrs. Obutu, a Ghanian mother rearing her family in London. After her daughter, Sylvia, was arrested for shoplifting, Mrs. Obutu was summoned to the police station and was observed beating her daughter with a stick. Court proceedings determined that Sylvia should not return to the family home. After the mother's poignant objections, Minuchin (1984) provides this commentary:

> *The magistrates return, looking upset. Not because Mrs. Obutu roared in pain; in their many years on the bench, pain has become a frequent witness in the chamber and they have learned how to deal with it. . . . No, they are upset because their sympathies are with Mrs. Obutu. They understood, because all of them are parents, that Mrs. Obutu is a Ghanian mother trying her best with her English daughter. Cultural gaps are familiar to them. But they were caught in their own legal structure. Nobody protected Mrs. Obutu from giving evidence against herself. Nobody defended her because*

BOX 2.1
Questions for the Assessment of Racial and Cultural Factors

1. How does your racial/cultural/religious heritage make your family different from other families you know?
2. Compared to other families in your cultural group, how is your family different?
3. What are the values that your family identifies as being important parts of your heritage?
4. At this particular time in your (family's) development, are there issues related to your cultural heritage that are being questioned by anyone? What and by whom?
5. What is the hardest part about being a minority in this culture?
6. When you think of living in America versus the country of your heritage, what are the main differences?
7. What lesson have you learned about your people? About other peoples?
8. What have you learned about disloyalty?
9. What are people in your family really down on?
10. What might an outsider not understand about your racial/cultural/religious background?

*she wasn't accused. . . . Nobody represented Mr. Obutu. And certainly it
didn't occur to anybody to have Mrs. Obutu and Sylvia talk to each other in
the court to put in evidence for the magistrates the conflicting sets of loyalties, affection, care, frustration, and rage that characterized their relationship. Just as in all families. (p. 130)*

When to Focus on Race and Culture

As the preceding example illustrates, cases that involve families of an immigrant or minority culture invariably have cultural issues to which the clinician
should attend. With these families, the focus on culture is an important part
of the joining process. As clinicians invite families to teach them about their
culture, the opportunity to join emerges in a context that is familiar and comfortable for the family. In this way, the family becomes the expert and the
therapist becomes the learner.

If the joining process does not evolve into a comfortable collaboration,
family therapists are encouraged to invite a native consultant to the sessions.
This individual can provide support for the family and clarify the cultural differences between therapist and family (Waldegrave, 1990). This consultant might
be a bilingual extended family member, a professional from the native culture,
or anyone else of the family's choice who could serve as a bridge between cultures. Such an effort on the part of the practitioner nonverbally communicates
an acknowledgment of differences, a respect for his or her limitations, and a desire to tailor the therapeutic process to the family's unique circumstances.

With respect to families who appear mainstream, it is recommended
that family therapists still ask one or two basic questions about culture, race,
or religion because many subcultures in the Western Hemisphere are not set
apart by physical or biological characteristics. For example, military families
form a subculture in the United States characterized by certain patterns of
mobility and a degree of patriotism not found in many nonmilitary families.
In addition, certain religious groups have histories of persecution that may
leave members with a heightened sense of alienation from the dominant culture. While on the surface such families might appear to be white, middle-
class, and Protestant, questions about the effects of military life or religion
could alert the therapist to the family's uniqueness and relevant cultural differences.

Implications for Treatment

As mentioned earlier, therapist inquiry into culture facilitates the joining process. When specific personalities clash or the clinician is having difficulty join-

ing, attention to culture can overcome difficulties that might arise at the microlevel of the therapeutic relationship. This is because an inquiry into the world of the family moves the therapist away from a hierarchical position ("Do what I want you to do") and into a collaborative position ("Teach me what is important for me to know about you"). This exploration shifts practitioners into a macrolevel of experience, and the new information broadens their perspective about the interpersonal impasse.

Constructivist therapists such as White (1990) use gender and culture as concepts to define the problem so that the family can be helped to externalize blame and minimize shame while assuming more responsibility for solving the internal experience. These practitioners come to understand interpersonal dynamics through the lens of socialized cultural practices.

In addition, as therapists learn details of the client's culture, then rituals, tasks, directives, and their rationale can be couched in language and practices that are comforting and empowering. Very often, seemingly mainstream clients feel alienated from some part of their world on account of the problem that brings them into therapy. This alienation may be addressed as a cultural problem to acknowledge the family's pain and isolation. As treatment proceeds, the family therapist can assist the family in feeling more connected to their world by a process known as normalizing (helping them see their similarities with others). One way of accomplishing this task is to explore intergenerational patterns.

❄ INTERGENERATIONAL RELATIONSHIPS

The family is not only the usual vehicle for socialization within a given culture, but it also evolves more specific traditions, roles, rewards, and obligations that bind family members together. Each family's history shapes unique patterns of belief and interaction analogous to cultural practice. These patterns often take the form of nonverbal rules (what people should do) that shape attitudes, communication, and intimacy.

Many family therapists have recognized previous generations as a major influence on family life in the present. Bowen (1978) conceptualized multigenerational transmission as the process by which dysfunctional patterns of coping are passed from one generation to the next. Boszormenyi-Nagy and Spark (1973) focused on loyalties or transgenerational obligations, suggesting that these were represented by symptoms in various family members. Ferreira (1963) discussed the significance of family myths, those beliefs that go unchallenged within the family and enable members to maintain a certain image of themselves. Other family therapists applied object-relations theory to family life, theorizing that we unconsciously attempt to change intimate relationships on the basis of those in our past either by making them familiar or by making them fit our fantasies of idealized relationships that would compensate for past rejection or abandonment (Framo, 1976; Jacobson, 1984; Sager, 1981).

Trends in intergenerational family therapy include a wide range of issues. Williamson (1981) focuses on how an individual can develop a sense of personal authority within the family of origin. Kramer (1985) resolves generational conflicts through an emphasis on acceptance of differences rather than approval or agreement on the issues. Boszormenyi-Nagy and Spark (1973) assist family members to explore their invisible loyalty or debts and to find appropriate tasks by which to balance the ledger of indebtedness to the previous generation. Anderson and Bagarozzi (1989) explore family and personal myths on the grounds that they give meaning to the past, define the present, and provide direction for the future. These developments represent attempts at integration that work to resolve historical conflicts in multigenerational families.

In assessing intergenerational dynamics, the therapist might ask questions regarding past family issues, current extended family relationships, and future hopes and expectations for these relationships:

1. What stories from your own life would best describe your development in your family of origin?
2. What stories from your family's history still influence the thinking of family members?
3. Which family members have strong feelings about this situation?
4. Are there family members who have tried to help you with this situation?
5. Does this situation seem similar to any other situation that you recall in your family of origin?
6. Have other family members had experience in resolving a similar situation for themselves?
7. With which extended family members do you feel most comfortable? Least comfortable?
8. What are the emotional debts in the family?
9. What are the issues of loyalty?
10. What past experiences trigger current problems?

For interviewing couples, Wamboldt and Wolin (1989) developed a structured interview that incorporates questions such as:

1. How did you meet?
2. What is the state of your relationship now?
3. What are some of the important challenges that the two of you have made it through?
4. What are some of the most important similarities and differences between you and your family members?
5. What do you most want to conserve from your family background?
6. What do you most want to change from your family background?
7. Given the family you grew up in, is there a reason that your partner is a particularly good or meaningful choice? Is your partner ever too much that way? What is that like?
8. What do your parents think about your relationship? How do they react?
9. Is there anything I haven't asked that you think is important?

When to Focus on Intergenerational Relationships

Unattached adults who are not in significant relationships can benefit from intergenerational exploration because the intensity of family-of-origin relationships has not been diminished by relationships in a family of procreation. For clients whose goal in therapy is to understand some aspect of their lives, an intergenerational assessment often lays a foundation for later discussions of self-understanding. Additionally, adults who would normally seek individual counseling for the healing of traumatic childhood experiences can benefit from an intergenerational perspective, which encourages reflection on past experience as a springboard for future change.

Frequently, clients seek family counseling for a marital or child-rearing difficulty. In these cases, questions about present extended family relationships may alert the therapist to historical family issues that may be restraining the change process in some way. For example, the therapist might assume that the family member has an internalized critical voice that keeps saying, "I am incapable of changing this problem or my perception of the problem." In addition, problems related to aging and the elderly must often be put in the context of relationships that have evolved through the generations to assist adult children in making necessary transitions with their parents.

Implications for Treatment

Erickson and Rossi (1979) suggest that change can be brought about in individuals by facilitating "an inner resynthesis of past experience." Analogously, it is also possible for families to change their views and behavior toward each other by identifying restraining myths, exploring unconscious patterns of communication, and detaching from their current experience to develop a broader and more hopeful perspective with positive possibilities.

Durrant (1988) illustrates such a case in which intergenerational messages are identified for a female client and used as an externalized influence over which she was helped to triumph. Because the intergenerational process was used as the definition of the problem, blame was not personalized to any one person, but was assigned to tradition. In this way, motivation for change is facilitated, and clients do not need to feel disloyal to parents. Even in cases of painful abuse, an intergenerational perspective can often help families and individuals explore the historical issues without becoming weighed down with unproductive introspection. Because intergenerational therapy maintains a focus that is interpersonal, clients can be helped to focus on interactions rather than internal pain alone and to discover important insights while also claiming the necessary strength to heal. By addressing stories, myths, rules, and roles from their family of origin, clients can also gain a sense of moving through time, just as the generations of their family have evolved. This opportunity for a sense of temporal movement can be enhanced by reflecting on family transitions that may have influenced the development of intergenerational dynamics.

❈ TRANSITIONS AND DEVELOPMENT

The critical timing of traditional nodal events or transitional periods for each stage of life was first undertaken by Evelyn Duvall (1977). She conceptualized the family as passing through eight stages, with developmental tasks for each stage. While there are many variations to Duvall's eight stages, all emphasize nodal events: entering and leaving the family, birth, parenthood, children leaving home, retirement, and death (Carter & McGoldrick, 1989b). Hiebert, Gillespie, and Stahmann (1993) have paid particular attention to stages of marital relationship and the interactional and psychological nuances that occur during each of the important nodal events.

Nodal events often require a reorganization of rules and roles for the family to remain functional. This reorganization can be thought of as a set of developmental tasks for each stage. Box 2.2 outlines assessment questions that can be used to understand family functioning at each stage of life. For some cases, questions from the current stage are all that is needed. For other cases, a complete review, with a sampling of questions from each stage, may be required to fully understand the family's experience.

All couples have the task of solidifying their commitment and placing friends and family of origin second to their relationship. When this task is not negotiated successfully, in-law conflicts may be chronic. In the next stage, many families may renegotiate rules and relationships to allow for the entry of children. Parenting roles may be established, and the relationship with the extended family may be redefined to include parenting and grandparenting. For couples without children, this stage may involve the establishment of shared values, interests, or goals that provide a sense of unity and identity for both partners. If children were desired, this stage may also be a time to resolve grief in order to create alternate stages of growth and development.

The adolescent stage begins when the first child enters puberty. The primary task during this stage involves increased autonomy for adolescents in the household. Parents must continually alter their relationships and rules to allow the adolescent to move in and out of the family system. At the same time, the parents are facing midlife decisions and emotions. The ways in which critical tasks of communication and boundary negotiation have been resolved in previous stages affect the resolution of challenges in this stage.

To the degree that previous developmental tasks have been mastered, the family can move into the launching stage. At this stage, the parents and the adolescent are ideally in a position to attain greater independence from one another. Parents must develop adult relationships with their children and renegotiate their marital relationship without children. Stress occurs when parents are alone for the first time in many years and must renegotiate their time, new careers, and other issues.

If couples do not have children, stages four and five may still involve interpersonal tasks related to structure, discipline, dependency, and autonomy. However, they may surface in a variety of situations such as work, friendships, and the development of personal identities and competence through family and community relationships.

The later-life family must deal with its declining health. Family members must reassess their life structures and explore new ways of living. At this stage, they may have to deal with the loss of a parent or spouse or the loss of vitality and fears concerning senility and death—both their own and others'. These developments affect all members of the system.

BOX 2.2
Questions for Developmental Interviews

I. Stage One: Forming Relationships
When did you meet? What year?
Who introduced you to each other?
Who initiated further dates?
Were you dating other people at the time?
When did this relationship become exclusive?
What did you like about each other?
What did you discover? How were you different from each other?
What didn't you like?
How did your families react to each of you during dating?
When did each of you say on the inside, "You're for me"?
When did each of you say to the other, "You're for me"?
When did you get engaged? How did that happen?
Did the relationship change after the engagement?
How did you determine the wedding date?
How did you determine who was to attend the wedding?
Were you sexually involved prior to marriage? Were you able to talk about sex?
Did you have any serious disagreements before marriage? How did each of you know the other was angry?

II. Stage Two: Commitment
How did the wedding go? What were your expectations?
How did the honeymoon go? What were your expectations?
When did the first difference of opinion come about?
What kind of social life did the two of you have at the beginning of this relationship? Who initiated it?
How were decisions arrived at in regard to what you would do?
Who were your friends? His, hers, both?
How did the two of you decide to handle your money? Who decided that?
Did anybody have veto power?
How much could each of you spend without asking the other?
When did the two of you begin your sexual relationship? Did you discuss it before it happened?
How did you each experience the first time?
Who initiates it now?
How did each side of the family feel about the marriage?

(continued)

BOX 2.2 *(continued)*

What were early relationships like between each of your families?
How were disagreements handled between in-laws in the early years?
How did you each define happiness?

III. Stage Three: Parenting, Values, Goals
How did the two of you decide whether to have children?
Did you talk about contraception and family planning?
What were your different attitudes and ideas about it?
How did your husband react to the pregnancy?
How did your wife react to the pregnancy?
How did the pregnancy go? How was the delivery?
What kind of changes took place after the child was born?
Did you notice any differences developing between you after the birth of the child? How did you resolve these?
What attitudes from your families of origin have influenced your child-rearing relationships?
What percentage of your time is spent taking care of your marriage as opposed to taking care of your children?
Who do the children turn to for support? If they want something fixed? If they want to play?

IV. Stage Four: Adolescence
Who do the children think is stricter, more lenient, moodier, and so on?
How do Mom and Dad feel about school? Friends? Other issues?
What privileges do your teenagers have now that they did not have when they were younger?
How do you think your parents will handle it when your younger sister wants to date?
Will that be different from when you wanted to date?

V. Stage Five: Launching Children
How did your parents help you leave home?
What is the difference between how you left home and how your children are leaving home?
Will your parents get along better, worse, or the same with each other once you have left home?
Who, between your Mom and Dad, will miss the children the most?
Did you confide in one or more of the children if you were having difficulties with each other?
What effect did the children's leaving home have on your marriage?
Have either of you thought about goals for yourselves after the children leave home?

(continued)

BOX 2.2 *(continued)*

What type of support do you need from each other to adjust to the children being away?

Are there any unresolved issues between you that can be traced back to an earlier stage of development?

Have you discussed this time as an opportunity to resolve those issues?

VI. Stage Six: Legacies

As you see your child moving on with a new marriage, what would you like your child to do differently than you did?

If your parents are still alive, are there any issues you would like to discuss with them?

When you look back over your life, what aspects have you enjoyed most? What has given you the most happiness?

About what aspects do you feel the most regret?

What was the one thing you wanted but did not get from the children?

Have there been any changes in the way you and your children relate since they have become adults?

How does your family deal with the effects of illness and advanced age?

How do you maintain a zest for life as you get older?

Have you discussed issues such as death, living wills, and life supports with your children and each other?

Do you have a plan for resolving conflicting feelings over any of the foregoing?

Source: Adapted from Hiebert, Gillespie, and Stahmann, 1993.

The divorced or remarried family goes through additional stages of development. Box 2.3 contains interview questions for divorced and remarried families. Like other stages of family process, the stages of divorce and remarriage include developmental issues that can guide the clinician and family toward the most beneficial adjustment. It may be more difficult for divorced and remarried families to complete developmental tasks than it is for the original nuclear family. Remarried families may have role models for parenthood but lack such models for single parenthood or stepparenthood. While society focuses on the joys of family living through advertising and television, divorced and remarried families have difficulty adjusting to this pattern.

BOX 2.3

Questions for Divorced Family Development Interviews
Have you accepted your inability to continue this relationship?
How do you and your ex-spouse deal with the issue of custody? Visitation? Finances?
What do your parents think about the divorce?
What do you miss from your old family?
How are things different for you now?
What do you like about your new life? What don't you like about it?
Do you ever wish you were back together?
Have you developed any new relationships? Activities?
What kind of relationship do you have with your ex-spouse?
How did you tell your children about the divorce?
What have you learned about yourself in this process?
What kinds of problems are your children having?
How are you responding to those problems?

Questions for Remarried Family Development Interviews
When did your last marriage end?
Do you think you had enough time to finish your first marriage?
What kind of communication do you have with your ex-spouse?
How are each of your children getting along?
How do each of them feel about your marriage?
How often do they see their mother/father?
How do your children get along with your spouse?
What do you do to help them get along with your spouse?
Which of your children has had the most difficulty with the new marriage?
How do your children get along with their stepbrothers? Stepsisters?
Do your children accept your spouse?
How do you expect your spouse to relate to your children?
Who is mostly in charge of the children?
What kind of help do you get from your spouse for your parenting role?
Are each of you responsible for disciplining your own children?

Moreover, at the time of remarriage, spouses must deal with many of the issues unresolved in the previous marriage.

In addition to the traditional transitions and tasks that have been conceptualized for white middle-class families, each family and individual also has a particular developmental path that evolves from the different settings where development occurs (Falicov, 1988). Nodal events such as untimely deaths, chronic illnesses, or other unusual circumstances may affect the course of life and the completion of various stage-related tasks. In addition, many other types of transitions may occur for unmarried adults, gay and lesbian couples, adoptive families, and family groups from nonmajority cultures.

The level of stress is much greater for families today than for those of past generations. The increasing divorce rate, the women's movement, and sexual and technological revolutions have had a profound impact on family development. The vast amount of change produced by these events puts a great deal of stress on families today. Job loss or divorce often precipitates a crisis that sends the family to therapy. However, if therapy focuses only on the symptom or the interactional patterns at the time of crisis, the therapist may be missing information from a macroview that will help normalize the current difficulties, thus making them easier to overcome.

To trace a family's or individual's development over time, the family therapist must understand traditional and alternative patterns of evolution. Carter and McGoldrick (1989b) do this by enlarging upon Duvall's work and discussing stages of divorce adjustment and remarriage. Howard (1978) researched related and nonrelated family groups, discovering that high satisfaction was related to the following aspects of family life:

1. Good families have a chief—someone around whom others cluster.
2. Good families have a switchboard operator—someone who cannot help but keep track of others.
3. Good families are hospitable.
4. Good families deal squarely with directness.
5. Good families prize their rituals.
6. Good families are affectionate.
7. Good families have a sense of place.
8. Good families find a way to be involved with children.
9. Good families honor their elders.

In diverse and nonrelated family groups, these aspects can be considered as developmental tasks that lead to relational satisfaction over time.

Landau-Stanton (1986) uses a practice known as "transitional mapping" to pinpoint the impact of social and cultural changes that may be transforming a family. Such issues as migration, changes due to illness, and shifts from rural to urban society have important effects on the family. They begin as an event, such as a geographic relocation, but evolve as a gradual process of adaptation and change. Families can track their process in retrospect and begin to capture the complexity that contributes to their dilemmas.

In mapping transitions, the practitioner becomes aware of sequences and processes that evolve. The result is a perspective that identifies family and individual problems according to their developmental place in time:

1. What stage of relationship is the family/individual in now? What other major life transitions have they lived through? What is the next stage?
2. How did things come to be the way they are now?
3. Has the problem always been this way? When did it change?
4. When were things better than now? When were they worse?
5. Does the family view their current life situation as part of a temporary stage or part of a permanent problem?
6. Does the family therapist have a view of the problem that uses time as a dimension of hope or as an indictment of despair?
7. Does the use of parental control fit the developmental needs of the individual?
8. Does consideration of differences allow developmentally appropriate growth?
9. Are there signs that tasks of previous stages have not been successfully accomplished?
10. Is each person in the family attaining his or her needs in a fashion that helps the parents maintain control?

When to Focus on Transitions and Development

Many family therapy theorists focus on developmental issues in some way (Haley, 1980; Hoffman, 1983; Minuchin, 1974; Selvini Palazzoli et al., 1978). Most commonly, client populations with children, adolescents, and elders are best served by focusing on these issues because common life transitions can be easily implicated as part of the problem. In addition, individuals and nontraditional family groups can benefit from an assessment that helps them identify and label their unique developmental progression, giving them a sense of movement through time, which helps create a positive context for targeted changes.

Implications for Treatment

The advantage of a developmental perspective is that it offers the family therapist increased options for defining the problem. Rather than seeing a problem as a permanent condition, the therapist is able to view behavior and symptoms as a response to a unique transition in the person's life (Haley, 1980). If a couple's marital conflict became serious after the birth of their first child, that developmental stage can be explored for circumstances that might have prevented the couple from developing problem-solving strategies. These developmental circumstances (e.g., isolation, poverty, or in-law interference) can be labeled as the problem, and the couple can then be invited to join together to overcome this problem rather than blaming each other and remaining adversaries (White & Epston, 1991).

When a person or a family does not proceed through traditional stages, the problem brought into therapy can be thought of as an opportunity for clients to pioneer a new societal pattern or as an opportunity for the therapist and the clients to collect information from their unique experience to share with others. In a developmental interview, the family therapist might ask participants to talk about what they perceive as the major stages of their life thus far and, more specifically, to reflect on perceptions of self and others and also the challenges and abilities that characterized each stage. By focusing on developmental milestones in family and individual history, the family therapist can conduct an assessment that invites the process of change to begin with affirmations of strength and resilience.

As the therapist assesses the developmental process, information begins to emerge about the interactional process between family members—that is, the microprocess that accounts for small, specific behavioral sequences in families, such as who started the fight or who stole the last cookie from the jar. Interactional process within the family is generally assessed as an indicator of family structure.

❄ STRUCTURE

The study of family structure is primarily concerned with interactions within the family that determine its organization. According to Minuchin, this organization must be modified to meet the developmental tasks for each stage of the family life cycle. He used the concepts of hierarchy, boundaries, subsystems, and coalitions in describing family structure.

The structural approach to family therapy evolved from the work of Salvador Minuchin and associates with families of delinquent boys at the Wiltwyck School in New York. These practitioners began to theorize that patterns of delinquency are related to the degree of disorganization in the family (Minuchin, Montalvo, Guerney, Rosman, & Schumer, 1967). This disorganization is characterized in terms of hierarchy—the pattern of leadership and power manifest in the family. Within families, hierarchy is often expressed by the pecking order, by shared perceptions of who the boss is, and by interactional patterns that indicate who gets the last word.

The family organism, like other social organizations, functions through an internal organization of subsystems (couple, parental, and sibling). When the functioning of subsystems breaks down, the family is unable to provide support and autonomy to meet the developmental needs of individual members. Thus, the family therapist must ask: "Does the family's structural organization at this time, in this particular social context or culture, sufficiently meet the needs of all its individual members?" Families who are not able to meet these needs often lack models for sufficient functioning and thus seek treatment.

A breakdown in the parental subsystem occurs, for example, when one parent joins in a coalition with one or more children against the other parent. Such a coalition is often indicated if the therapist notes critical discussions about a parent who is absent, if one parent confides in a child about marital discord, or if one parent openly sides with a child against the other parent. In structural terms, parent–child coalitions are thought of as a violation of the boundary between the parental and sibling subsystems because they change the role of the child from one of dependent to one of confidant or emotional peer.

In addition to Minuchin's pioneering concepts related to structure, other family therapists have refined these ideas. Breunlin, Schwartz, and Mac Kune-Karrer (1992) refer to family organization, with related concepts of leadership, balance, and harmony. Their work illustrates the trend we noted in Chapter one, that of marital and family therapy moving toward concepts that are more human and less mechanistic. As this trend continues, it provides greater clarity for those who are learning to think systemically. Well-functioning systems have some form of leadership. Effective leaders use their influence judiciously in person-to-person interactions. As influence is exercised, members of the system have their needs addressed in tandem with the needs of the group. The intended outcome of these interactions is harmony.

Questions to assess leadership, balance, and harmony include:

1. How much time do you spend with each other? Who does each family member spend the most time with and what things do they do together?

2. How do you decide what gets accomplished within the family? What is the process of decision making and who is involved?
3. Who is close to whom? Who is most alike and most dissimilar in the family?
4. How are the mother and father different from each other?
5. How is each sibling different from the others?
6. Who agrees and disagrees with stated views about the problem?
7. Do you feel your spouse doesn't care what is going on?
8. How do you decide the rules for your children?
9. Do you feel your spouse is too easy with your children?
10. Who seems to be most upset by this problem?
11. What are some things you have tried to do to solve this problem?
12. Which of these seem helpful to you? How are they helpful?

The therapist assesses family interaction by observing various kinds of behavior. Useful nonverbal clues include tone of voice, facial expression, or eye contact with other family members. It is important to take careful note of who speaks for whom and when. The therapist may also probe other family members to assess their view of the family problem. Using these data, the therapist formulates hypotheses about the family problem and the underlying organization of the system.

When to Focus on Structure

It is a basic practice in family therapy to assess the pattern of leadership in each family and to develop a collaborative relationship with the family members who have the greatest ability to influence family life. Thus, a structural assessment is recommended for all cases because treatment is maximized when it is aligned with the family's primary leaders. In addition, information about balance in relationships is important to assess specific interactions in the family and who is actually involved in problematic sequences.

Implications for Treatment

While structural assessment is most closely associated with the clinical work of Minuchin, Haley's strategic therapy also makes use of structural concepts in defining child and adolescent problems. Structural-strategic forms of family therapy routinely emphasize the goal of strengthening the parental subsystem and addressing parent–child coalitions. These goals are often pursued by tracking interactional sequences in detail and intervening in these interactions to change a targeted relationship. In addition, the Milan team and other practitioners have developed circular questions designed to elicit information about family structure and family politics: Who is close to whom? How did the family come to their conclusions about the problem? Whose opinion has the most influence? What purpose might the symptom be serving? What is the exact sequence of events when the problem is occurring? As these questions are answered, the therapist can describe the structure of the family and note, in particular, how family interactions are influenced by the personal dynamics of each individual.

❄ INDIVIDUAL EXPERIENCE

Despite the tendency in the field of family therapy to deemphasize the analysis of intrapsychic dimensions within the individual, many approaches provide very helpful information related to how a family therapist would address individual concerns. In fact, even approaches that may overtly discourage attention to psychodynamics eventually reveal that they have not totally thrown the baby out with the bathwater. For example, although Watzlawick has long been an advocate of analyzing failed solutions, rather than analyzing people (in the traditional psychoanalytic sense), he suggests that in finding solutions, "the tactic chosen has to be translated into the person's own 'language'; that is, it must be presented to him in a form which utilizes his own way of conceptualizing 'reality'" (Watzlawick, Weakland, & Fisch, 1974, p. 113).

Thus, without a framework facilitating empathy for each person's position, the family therapist is likely unable to successfully elicit trust and cooperation from the significant parties involved. The following review illustrates the variety of views related to understanding individuals from a systems perspective.

Self-Esteem   Experiential family therapy focuses primarily on individual growth. As an extension of this emphasis, experiential theorists have conceptualized self-esteem as the result of interpersonal processes. Virginia Satir (1972) was particularly interested in teaching others about the impact of family functioning on individual self-esteem. Satir was noted for therapeutic interventions in which she adopted a nurturing role with clients while coaching them toward more honest, open, and accepting communication with each other. In a statement that she called "My Declaration of Self-Esteem," Satir (1972) envisions the potential of every person to become an aware, self-responsible, growth-oriented person.

Satir also influenced other personal growth theorists who were interested in interactional models based on self-awareness and communication. One such model (Miller, Nunnally, Wackman, & Miller, 1988) integrates the study of interpersonal interaction with humanistic psychology and family studies. Known as the Couples Communication Program, this approach begins with five basic elements of self-awareness that can be taught to a student or family member to enhance the self-awareness and communication skills needed for personal satisfaction in relationships. In family therapy, they can guide the practitioner toward an understanding of individual experience as it relates to significant relationships.

1. Senses   Information from the five senses is the initial link between the individual and the outside world. Sensory information is present at the beginning of all human life and continues to the end as part of an interactional cycle. Sensory data are regarded as factual; carefully assessed, they yield a limited but verifiable truth. For example, if a wife hears her husband's voice raised, this is an objective fact distinguishable from her subjective response, which may be the thought, "He's angry." Only her husband can really verify what his emotion is at that moment, even though family members commonly consider their subjective information to be fact.

2. Thoughts   This category includes interpretations, assumptions, opinions, beliefs, and the conclusions that an individual makes in response to sensory information. Often the result of history and experience, thoughts become a frame of reference that influences a person's actions, feelings, and intentions. In addition, assumptions are distinguished from objective facts in that they are constructed by the person in response to sensory data. If a wife says, "I think you're angry," the statement legitimately communicates a fact about what she is thinking and distinguishes her thought process from what her husband's emotion might really be. In addition, self-esteem in individual family members is often related to their beliefs or thoughts about themselves as well as what they perceive to be the beliefs of others about themselves.

3. Feelings   This category encompasses the physiological and behavioral responses associated with feeling a certain emotion. Common feelings include sadness, anger, happiness, fear, shame, and hurt. However, there are hundreds of words in the English language that label an even wider range of emotional states. Self-awareness entails individuals' ability to label their emotions, whether pleasant or unpleasant, and to accept them as part of being human.

Self-esteem involves an acceptance of emotions as important information about the self and an ability to act responsibly on those feelings. When individuals are not able to tolerate their fears or anxieties, they develop controlling or addictive behavior intended to numb unpleasant emotional states.

4. Intentions   These are personal and general goals, hidden and open desires, short-term and long-term needs, motivations, dreams, and hopes. They can involve both the self and others and are related to an individual's thoughts and feelings as they evolve. Behavior is viewed as always having a purpose; thus, intentions provide a personal context for actions. For example, when family members wish to please others as much as possible, they may develop behavior patterns that consistently accommodate others and do not assert on behalf of self. In other cases, intentions may underlie symptomatic behavior that serves a function in the family, as in the case where a child's problem interrupts parental conflict. While the intention in young children may not be conscious, adolescent and adult family members are often able to identify their systemic intention when the therapist asks, "How might this problem actually be preventing something worse from happening in the family?"

5. Actions   These are behaviors that can be communicated with verbs. We suggest that an individual can increase self-awareness by becoming aware of actions. Sitting, smiling, talking, shifting eye contact, listening, shouting, initiating, waiting, breathing, and walking are examples of actions that are related to the individual's feelings, intentions, thoughts, and senses. When the clinician begins to track interactional sequences, it is helpful to focus on actions because family members often move quickly to their subjective experience before weighing the facts related to another's actions:

> *Therapist:*   Tell me exactly what happened.
>
> *Client:*   He was trying to get me to do his homework for him. [a statement of assumption—thoughts]
>
> *Therapist:*   No, I mean what was he actually doing when you had that thought?
>
> *Client:*   Well, I guess he was sitting on the couch, watching TV. [sensory data—"I saw him sitting"]
>
> *Therapist:*   What else was he doing that made you think he was trying to get you to do his homework for him?

Client: He doesn't have to do anything else! He knows that if he hasn't already started working on his homework before I get home, then I will do it when I come in! [statement of assumption—thoughts]

Therapist: Now, how do you think he knows that?

Client: He knows because I've told him time and time again that I want his homework done before I get home so I won't have to worry about it. [action statement]

Therapist: So, aside from what your son may think, you have a desire that you put into action when you walk through the door. Is that right?

Client: Yes, I want to know if he's done his homework, and if he hasn't, I want him to get busy right then. [statement of intention]

Therapist: Is this pretty predictable behavior for you? I mean, does it happen nearly every night?

Client: Well, lately, yes, because he's been getting so bad. [statement of perception—senses]

Therapist: Well, we might want to start by seeing if we can help you to become more "unpredictable" in your son's eyes! Sometimes, surprising behaviors help kids change their minds about things.

Taken together, the five elements of self-awareness represent the individual as a system of interrelated parts. These parts interact with each other to form an individual's contribution to a relationship, regardless of whether the relationship is with self or others. Interactional patterns are comprised of sequences that use all five elements:

ACTIONS: Wife is fixing dinner in the kitchen.

SENSES: She notices her husband coming up the driveway.

THOUGHTS: I wonder if he's still thinking about the argument we had this morning.

INTENTIONS: I hope he isn't still mad at me.

FEELINGS: I'm afraid he won't be happy.

ACTIONS: Husband comes in the door. He is frowning.

FEELINGS: He is tired and embarrassed about a traffic ticket just issued to him on the way home.

INTENTIONS: He wants to save face; he wants his wife to think well of him.

SENSES: Wife sees his frown.

ACTIONS: She asks, "Are you still mad about this morning?"

THOUGHTS: He thinks, "She's criticizing me and belittling my feelings."

ACTIONS: Husband says, "Why do you always think you can read my mind?"

By paying attention to all five dimensions of experience, the clinician is able to track a sequence while also understanding the individual's experience as it evolves in the interaction. Then, as the therapist helps the couple clarify and accept both their own and their partner's emotions, they are able to increase intimacy by understanding each other's intentions and emotions—especially their particular sensitivities. If each person had begun their part of the interaction with a statement of intent (e.g., "I want you to be happy" or "I want your approval") or with a statement of feelings (e.g., "I'm afraid" or "I'm embarrassed"), the interaction might have taken a different turn. When family members feel most vulnerable, their intent is to protect themselves from anticipated psychological or emotional hurt.

In addition to experiential family therapists who focus on communication and self-esteem, social constructionists focus on communication and personal belief systems. These new theoretical frameworks have been greatly influenced by theorists such as Jean Piaget, George Kelly, and Kenneth Gergen (1985). They posit that personal belief systems are an evolving set of meanings that continue to emerge from interactions between people. However, unlike traditional psychologists, who view the individual as a reactive being, the social constructionist asserts that personal meaning (beliefs) derives from the individual's perception of what occurs in interactions with others (Mahoney, 1991). For example, if a young unattached man characterizes himself as "weak" and "independent," this may be because he has neglected those aspects of his life that are incongruent with his self-image of helplessness. The individual may have ignored times when he was able to overcome his helplessness. Likewise, through his interactions with his family, he may allow them to describe him as helpless, which likely influences the way they interact with each other. In this case, personal narratives become an internalized set of conversations ("I must depend on others for help") that are consistent with our behavior (acting in ways that elicit help from others).

Thus, for social constructionists, the meaning that family members attribute to an event determines their behavior.

Related to this view, the influence of Milton Erickson has brought a new understanding of the unconscious. For Erickson, the unconscious was an untapped reservoir of positive resources, not a complex stockpile of repressed anguish (Erickson & Rossi, 1979). As he put his own belief system into operation, he was able to help his patients begin to use their perceived deficits as strengths and assets. Some of his techniques relevant to the practice of family therapy are reviewed later in this book.

Although the terms were not widely used in family therapy literature until the later 1980s, we think Erickson was a constructivist and a social constructionist. Evidence of his similarities with these orientations can be seen in the way he views the formation of individual or family problems:

> *Patients have problems because of learned limitations. They are caught in mental sets, frames of reference, and belief systems that do not permit them to explore and utilize their own abilities to best advantage. Human beings are still in the process of learning to use their potentials. The therapeutic transaction ideally creates a new phenomenal world in which patients can explore their potentials, freed to some extent from their learned limitations. . . . As the therapist explores the patient's world and facilitates rapport, it is almost inevitable that new frames of reference and belief systems are created. This usually happens whenever people meet and interact closely. (Erickson & Rossi, 1979, p. 2)*

Thus, Erickson considered the importance of the belief system of the patient and the meaning attributed to the ongoing flow of the person's life to be a critical factor in problem formation. He then paid particular attention to the dialogues he shared as a part of problem resolution.

An intergenerational approach that addresses personal beliefs in a slightly different way is the contextual family therapy of Ivan Boszormenyi-Nagy (Boszormenyi-Nagy & Krasner, 1986). In this approach, exploring a person's beliefs about the give-and-take in relationships helps the clinician understand how an individual experiences fairness and equity within the family. These family therapists suggest that human beings carry a subjective family ledger consisting of personal beliefs about how much they have contributed to family members and how much they are entitled to receive in return. According to Boszormenyi-Nagy and Krasner (1986), this concept of relational ethics is based on the premise that there is an innate sense of justice or fairness within people. This approach suggests that dysfunction occurs within families when relational imbalances lead to a lack of trustworthiness or the development of "destructive entitlements" that involve individual symptoms (actions) developed in response to beliefs (thoughts) about unfairness within the family.

When to Focus on Individual Experience

Although many family therapy models address behavioral change before perceptual change, cases that do not respond to behavioral interventions most likely need a greater focus on personal dynamics that may be restraining behavioral change. Therefore, cases where behavioral interventions are not successful can benefit from a shift to an exploration of personal dynamics (self-esteem, self-awareness, personal beliefs, or feelings of entitlement). In addition, when the joining process seems stalemated or the practitioner begins to notice subtle power struggles with clients, it is very important to step back from the normal operating procedure and explore personal dynamics to understand and affirm clients' beliefs about their process and about the process between therapist and clients.

Too often, clinicians forget to focus on their own personal dynamics. How is their work related to their sense of self-esteem? Are they aware of their own hidden agendas that may be incongruent with what clients have stated as their priorities? Do clinicians have certain beliefs that may lead them to harbor critical or condescending views of their clients? Is their sense of entitlement such that they pursue unrealistic goals for their clients in family therapy? A focus on individual elements on both sides of the therapy experience often helps the clinician develop goals and expectations that match the developmental level of the family.

It is also appropriate to focus on individual dynamics when the client goal is more process-oriented than problem-oriented (e.g., "I need help getting over the death of my daughter"). When the client goal is related more to coping, growth, or adjustment to some transition, focusing on individual dynamics also fits better with client expectations of the therapy experience.

Implications for Treatment

While many models of family therapy have deemphasized traditional Freudian views of individual psychodynamics, all models use some newer understanding of personal dynamics. Whether it is the structural therapist joining with the family, the strategic therapist looking for a directive that the client will accept, or the intergenerational therapist who seeks to help family members with unfinished business, the ability to understand personal dynamics is a clinical imperative in the practice of family therapy.

Falloon (1991) takes a strong position by suggesting that the individual goals of every family member should be targets for treatment:

At times, these goals may be highly personal and inappropriate for intergenerational problem solving. For example, the resolution of sexual difficulties between parents, obsessive-compulsive rumination, or prophylactic drug therapy for schizophrenia. Such problems may be addressed in an individual or a marital context, where this seems most appropriate. (p. 79)

There seems to be increasing evidence that individually oriented strategies work best within a systemic framework. This is particularly so when the presenting problem involves major mental disorders, such as phobia, severe depression, or schizophrenia (Falloon, 1991).

Returning to the continuum of macro- and microconcepts of family process, an emphasis on microdynamics facilitates therapeutic effectiveness as a complement to all other levels of assessment. By starting with a larger view of life and evolving to an exploration of personal dynamics, family therapists are able to fluctuate between macropositions that minimize personal shame and blame and micropositions that liberate clients to think of themselves and their relationships in new ways.

Each conceptual theme presented here can be thought of as a different reality or lens from which to view families who seek treatment. Each lens has its own set of issues and questions that range from larger societal views of human problems to smaller dissections of personal and interpersonal process. The beginning family therapist can learn flexibility by using different lenses to view panoramas or get to the heart of the matter, depending on clients' needs and the type of problem. Taken individually, each level provides a sense of direction that is informed by theories of family functioning and social process. Sluzki (1992), drawing from narrative ideas, makes these observations about how any given model becomes a catalyst for effective family therapy:

In order for new stories . . . to consolidate themselves in the therapeutic conversation, they must evolve from and yet contain elements of the old, "familiar" stories. The transformed stories are usually a recombination of the components of the old story to which new elements—characters, plot, logic, moral order—have been introduced either by the therapist, by the patient, or by the family . . . (p. 220)

The next chapter explores common themes of practice that have developed in the field. In contrast to theories about families, practice themes center on theories of change as they relate to therapeutic process and those factors related to positive therapeutic outcomes. While a great deal of family therapy practice has evolved from the major approaches reviewed in these first two chapters, evidence also suggests that family therapists often continue their tradition of innovation by adding other modes of thinking quite apart from family theories. These additional directions often provide a curve in the therapeutic road or a new breathtaking vista. Therefore, as we settle into the seat of family process with our seat belts fastened, we now look toward the actual driving.

Chapter Three

INTEGRATION OF PRACTICE: COMMON ELEMENTS

KNOWLEDGE AND CONCEPTS
Naturalistic Change
Therapeutic Change
Perceptual, Behavioral, and Relational Change
The Therapeutic Relationship

PERCEPTIONS AND ATTITUDES
Perception of Client Competence
Therapist Flexibility

BEHAVIORS
Questions
Tracking Interactional Sequences
Reframing
Directives

Driving a car is a process that involves a collection of actions, thoughts, certain knowledge, and ideas. The territory one drives through may be as different as Africa and England; nevertheless, there are certain aspects of the activity that are always the same. In addition, driving is a series of separate but related activities (e.g., watching the road, estimating distances, steering the vehicle), and each activity may occur in situations other than driving. However, when driving is the task at hand, one must coordinate these activities in a certain way.

Integration can be thought about in the same way. For many contemporary practitioners, integration begins at an early stage of training. Our integrative approach attempts to focus on similarities between approaches and to identify common elements of the change process that can guide the practitioner. For example, some literature on family therapy training divides therapist skills into three categories: conceptual, perceptual, and executive (Tomm & Wright, 1979). These refer to how the family therapist thinks, observes, and behaves as a facilitator of change. The intent of such authors is to identify general guidelines that are not theory-specific. Other theoreticians consider change from a more universal perspective (a metaperspective), discussing how problems and solutions develop or whether humans can indeed change (Watzlawick, Weakland, & Fisch, 1974). However, even without addressing specific theoretical biases, a family systems approach to facilitating change can still be complicated. Therefore, we have attempted to limit the array of options to those that seem most important for a beginning clinician.

With integration as our primary objective, the important questions are: What type of knowledge must every family therapist have to be therapeutic? What are the specific skills, attitudes, and ideas that are common to this area of practice? In answering these questions, we have found that some categories of learning are shared by all forms of family therapy practice. Those categories include knowledge as well as expertise and attitudes as well as specific concepts. Because these elements are central to most theories of family therapy, we believe that the practice of family therapy can be based on a synthesis of key principles across multiple models. Just as driving a car has some universal elements regardless of the roads, territory, or destination, it is possible to think of systems and relational therapy in the same way. The remainder of this chapter reviews our assessment of key elements that should be considered in family therapy practice. They are related to (a) knowledge and concepts, (b) perceptions and attitudes, and (c) behaviors. In addition to the theoretical themes reviewed in Chapter Two, there are crucial elements of practice that can be applied across models of family therapy to develop a workable starting point for beginners.

❄ KNOWLEDGE AND CONCEPTS

With respect to our task of integration, the most important knowledge about family therapy and its diverse models may be the knowledge that most models fail to supply. For example, many approaches fail to include a discussion of ethical considerations. As a starting point, we think all marital and family therapists should have a working knowledge of the code of ethics published by the American Association for Marriage and Family Therapy (1991). We have included this in Appendix A. From here, practitioners should become aware of how these issues might emerge differently with different approaches. If a client is hesitant to involve certain family members, how does the clinician work systematically without becoming coersive? When seeing couples, what is the marital therapist's responsibility for confidentiality in the event that each partner is seen alone? These are examples of questions that are commonly addressed in typical family therapy programs.

In addition to knowledge about ethical issues, a critical study of current approaches in family therapy prompts these questions: What really works? What criteria should be used to choose models or judge outcomes? How are various assumptions derived? In answering these questions, certain information comes to mind. Scholars who study psychotherapy have conducted outcome research for many years (Pinsof & Catherall, 1986). Repeated studies show that 40% of the variance in psychotherapy outcome is related to client attributes and factors outside the therapy process, 30% of the variance is related to the therapeutic relationship, 15% is related to the client's sense of hope, and another 15% is related to specific techniques and models of the therapist (Bergin & Garfield, 1994; Lambert & Bergin, 1994). Thus, when we as family therapists discuss our explanations for certain outcomes, these perceptions may not be shared by our clients. This information from quantitative research can also be verified with examples of qualitative research from the field of family therapy (Newfield, Kuehl, Joanning, & Quinn, 1991).

In reviewing this research on psychotherapy outcomes, Miller, Duncan, and Hubble (1997) argue that many psychotherapists spend little time learning how to incorporate client factors and environment into the therapy process, even though these comprise the largest single influence. We agree with their suggestion that many therapists become caught up with their own familiar model, sometimes at the expense of achieving a better outcome.

Family therapists have not conducted extensive research on outcomes; however, these data on psychotherapy outcomes are persuasive. We think integration should include the development of guiding principles that relate to the process of change. Practitioners need knowledge about theories and research on how change occurs. The various theories used by family therapists can be grouped into two categories. Some address the occurrence of change outside of therapy in the natural world; others address the necessary elements of change within a therapy session. In addition, some prefer behavioral change, whereas others emphasize perceptual change.

Naturalistic Change

In family therapy, models that focus on development, narratives, and information flow within the family often use the natural occurrence of change in relationships. Developmental theory implies that change is an inevitable part of family life. In other words, the passing of time brings about a natural change in the family through the growth of its members. This perspective also suggests that family life is a continual sequence of periods of change, followed by periods of stability, followed by periods of change, and so on. For the family therapist who uses this theory, a problem brought to therapy would be placed in its developmental context to investigate the possible relationship between the onset of the problem and the developmental tasks that are normally associated with a given stage of life. If a client described the problem as chronic, ongoing depression, then the family therapist would explore what life stage the person was in during the onset of this depression and how the onset might be related to an unfinished task from an earlier developmental stage. Perhaps the onset of depression came at the death of a loved one and has been intermittent since that time. Perhaps the depression was noticed as children were leaving home or during the early stages of recovery in an alcoholic spouse. In this way, the family therapist tries to relate the onset of a problem to developmental transitions in family life.

Many times, just as problems are related to developmental changes, solutions may be related to other developmental changes. For example, many parents of high school seniors become frustrated with the tension and conflict sometimes present in their relationships with their children. Often, the tension disappears as the child prepares to leave home and become independent. A family therapist would use naturalistic theories of change by anticipating and expecting that changes can occur spontaneously within family life. This assumption could likely lead the therapist to look toward the future and help family members generate possible solutions to their problem as part of anticipated future events.

Another naturalistic theory of change within the field follows the notion of Bateson (1979) that change comes about from "information that makes a

difference" (i.e., comparative information). For example, a son's voice changing at the onset of puberty might signal his growth and influence his parents'
behavior toward him. Or if a husband says to his wife, "I'm not sure I married
the right person," this communicates information that makes a difference; it is
comparative information about how he has changed in the marriage over
time. If the wife was unaware of his changes, the new information would likely
make a difference in her behavior, thoughts, and feelings. In this approach,
then, comparative information is evolutionary information, and eliciting information about change in a system is thought to bring about other changes.

To utilize this type of naturalistic theory in their practice, therapists ask
questions that focus on transitions within the family in an attempt to find resources and strengths that the family has overlooked: How long has this been
a problem? When did things change? What was your relationship like before
the problem began? Very often, such questions serve a dual purpose as both
assessment and intervention: By eliciting information before and after, the
family begins to step back and gain a new perspective. This new view may pre-
cipitate spontaneous change within the family.

Other applications that focus on the natural flow of family life may explore the stories clients use to describe their evolution. These stories become a
foundation for therapeutic responses that encourage the development of new
stories or new views of existing stories. These narrative applications are related to Bateson's suggestion that change occurs from variations in the natural world that become "amplified" or firmly established over time. Drawing on
theories of biology and evolution, he suggested that permanent changes begin
as mutations or exceptions to the rule. Narrative approaches to family therapy
follow this logic. They rely on the assumption that there are always exceptions
occurring in the problematic patterns identified by family members. These patterns can be amplified by developing narratives about the old situation that encourage the exceptions with greater frequency. For example, family members
often say, "I can't trust him" or "he never does what I ask him to." The clinician
can help family members identify incidents when someone did not lie, did not
create a problem, or was different from before. Then an exploration of these instances gives each family member an opportunity to understand what made
that exception possible. The assumption is that if an exception can occur
once, it can happen again in similar circumstances. In a similar vein, those
who adhere to solution-focused models also search for naturally occurring instances when the person or relationship was problem-free.

As noted earlier, none of the early writers of family therapy explicitly incorporated elements of change studied in the general field of psychotherapy.

However, in light of the research on psychotherapy outcomes, those models of family therapy that acknowledge naturalistic change seem more likely to consider the existence of outcome factors described as "extratherapeutic," or client variables and environment outside the therapy process (Lambert, 1992). Miller et al. (1997) provide an excellent summary of how a therapist might be more aware of these very important factors. Their suggestions include:

> *listening for and validating client change whenever and for whatever reason it occurs during the treatment process . . . highlighting the contribution to change made by the client . . . recognizing client competence, working within the client's world view and utilizing client strengths. (p. 80)*

These suggestions can be seen operating in many integrative approaches to family therapy and reflect the growing trend that we have observed in which family therapists attend to the natural context of the client. This context may be significant relationships or events. It may be daily routines or hobbies. It may be a history of challenges and successes or detailed descriptions of what life is like when family relationships are going well. Since many therapy services are offered outside the family's natural world, it is important for the family therapist to obtain a clear picture of life outside the therapy room. People, places, activities, thoughts, and so forth are important outside factors to ask about, especially as they contribute positively to change.

Therapeutic Change

In contrast to these ideas about naturalistic change, other approaches focus solely on how change occurs in a family therapy session. Structural, strategic, and behavioral models emphasize that behavioral change can be brought about without insight or cognition by attending to interactional sequences and interrupting those that become associated with the identified problem. This is usually done within the session, focusing on present interactions. Intergenerational models, by contrast, focus on the emotional nature of out-of-session interactions and the clients' reactions to them. The tools that the therapist uses are modeling and questions aimed at fostering interactional and intrapsychic insight.

In the early literature of the field, explanations about how change was brought about through these models were either too vague or too complicated for beginning family therapists to emulate. For example, Haley (1967) wrote:

> *Therapeutic change comes about through the interactional processes set off when a therapist intervenes actively and directively in particular ways in a family system. (p. 7)*

On the mechanisms of change in structural therapy, Aponte and Van Deusen (1981) wrote:

> *Change in structure produces change in functioning . . . the therapist will intervene in transactions that are manifestations of the problem-bearing structure in such a way that the system will internalize the structural changes and operate differently as a result. . . . Structural change in treatment is induced by the maneuvers of therapists of all orientations. . . . This approach serves as a framework for a broad range of therapeutic techniques, structural and otherwise. (p. 337)*

In addition, Bodin (1981) described the principles of change used by the Mental Research Institute (MRI) Brief Therapy Center in this way:

> *These principles include an emphasis on observable behavior in the present rather than on historical genetic factors, since intrapsychic insight is not regarded as the royal road to change, although it may follow as an epiphenomenon or ex post facto rationalization as a result of change instigated through any of a number of techniques for reframing or behavioral prescription. (p. 303)*

Similarly, Kerr (1981), who taught intergenerational family therapy, described the therapeutic process in this way:

> *The early sessions were devoted to trying to help the spouses, through the therapist's questions, describe the nature of their emotional interaction . . . A successful session is one in which one or both spouses have been able to think about the emotional process . . . instead of just continuing to react emotionally to each other. . . . Objectivity and emotional detachment are reflected in the way the therapist sits, how often he talks, in the absence of preaching, in his tone of voice, and sense of humor. . . . The therapist's main task is to help people recognize and deal with their lack of objectivity when applying the concepts to their own situations. . . . It is usually difficult for families really to see that one generation's problems are related to the previous generation's problems, but placing a three or four generation diagram on the blackboard and asking questions about it can be a step toward helping the family gain that kind of perspective. (pp. 255–259)*

While all four of these descriptions provide the therapist with an emerging picture of what the therapist does to bring about change in the system, there is some variation in focus between behavioral and perceptual change. For instance, intrapsychic insight is considered unimportant. On the other hand, intergenerational insight or systemic insight may lead to success. In addition, this early literature focused on the distinguishing characteristics of the models, leaving the beginning clinician without a systematic model for integrating these differences. Therefore, we will pursue integration with a dual focus on behavioral and perceptual change to identify some common themes in family therapy practice.

Perceptual, Behavioral, and Relational Change

A contemporary review of family therapy can argue that earlier theories actually focused on both perceptual and behavioral change. For example, reframing, as reviewed here, is a technique aimed at facilitating perceptual change (i.e., changing how a client views some aspect related to the problem). Structural, strategic, and brief therapy models employ reframing to change relationships in some way. Accordingly, despite the argument that intrapsychic insight is not "the royal road to change," many interventions in these models address the importance of the client's view or perception of the problem. While this is not the same as intrapsychic insight, it does involve an internal process of the client. Similarly, intergenerational therapies have had a greater emphasis on perceptual changes within the therapeutic session that are akin to insight, and yet much of the coaching toward objectivity takes the form of motivating and directing the client toward different interactional patterns with family members. Thus, these major schools, while claiming their distinctions, have some important similarities that eventually serve as a guide for the practitioner.

Two integrative models illustrate how the clinician might address both perceptions and behavior in the practice of family therapy. The Milan team makes use of questions and reframing to bring forth new information, as well as directives and tasks to bring forth new behaviors. The therapy of Michael White also integrates these elements by asking questions that bring forth exceptions and by assigning tasks that amplify these exceptions into sustained and changed behaviors. The identified exceptions are often begun by a strategic reframing of some typical behavior that describes it in a new light. As the exceptions are named and encouraged, White asks the family for reports of new behaviors that support the change. In addition, cognitive-behavioral family therapy addresses a spouse's experience to understand relational themes that may require "acceptance." As these themes are addressed, the therapist also helps couples increase positive behaviors with each other.

Brief and solution-focused therapists also address behavior and perceptions. These newer variations of Ericksonian models describe therapy as changing "the viewing" or "the doing" (O'Hanlon & Weiner-Davis, 1989).

These models recognize the therapist's role in assisting a family to identify its resources, to build on what is working, and to manage their problems. They do not see problems as signs of failure but rather as an inevitable part of family development. The relationship between the therapist and the family becomes less hierarchical and moves closer to a collaborative problem-solving relationship. Such a therapeutic stance is thought to help clients adopt a more hopeful attitude about solving their problem. These perceptual changes are related to the assumption that unnecessary time is wasted, and therapeutic relationships weaken by discussions of problems and deficits. Families often become defensive when discussing the problem, particularly if a family has a previous history with public agencies from whom they have felt criticism. Because solution-focused therapists work at normalizing problems, perceptions about the problem and about helping professionals begin to change. This does not mean that therapists normalize violent or abusive behavior; rather, the practitioner acknowledges the problem from the family's point of view and addresses problem behavior within the context of the family's perceptions. As this hopeful and collaborative pattern continues, behavior change occurs from a discussion of behaviors related to exceptions.

As the family therapist begins to understand types of change, whether naturalistic, therapeutic, perceptual, or behavioral, these are applied to relationships and to family process. As mentioned in the preceding chapter, the models of change in family therapy are not always rooted in a theory of family process. Sometimes they come from Ericksonian or social construction theories. Standing alone, we do not consider them to be marriage and family therapy. However, when integrated with theories of family process, and a focus on the importance of interpersonal relationships and social process, they become important components of the integrative approaches found in the field today. Table 3.1 illustrates our definition of the practice of family therapy as it combines theories of family process, communication, and relationships with theories of change.

Table 3.1

Conceptualization	+	Implementation	=	Marital and Family Therapy
Theories about relationships		*Theories about change*		*Approaches that fit*
Family process		Naturalistic		Client
Relational process		Therapeutic		Setting
Communication		Perceptual-behavioral		Clinician

In addition to having a knowledge about the processes of change, we think a family therapist's success depends on one's ability to apply information about the importance of the therapeutic relationship. Among early family therapists who debated the mechanisms of in-session change, Satir (1972) may have been the most direct in emphasizing the relationship between client and therapist. Current outcome research suggests that in spite of the proliferation of psychotherapy models, client perception of the therapeutic relationship still accounts for 30% of the variance. Because of these data, we consider it important to review various concepts related to this crucial variable.

The Therapeutic Relationship

The therapeutic relationship is one of the most critical factors in the effectiveness of treatment (Pinsof & Catherall, 1986). In an interesting study conducted at an agency emphasizing solution-focused brief therapy, researchers found that the espoused model had little to do with clients' reported experience (Metcalf, Thomas, Duncan, Miller, & Hubble, 1996). Miller et al. (1997) describe their final results:

> *while therapists tended to attribute therapeutic success to the use of solution-focused techniques (e.g., specialized interviewing techniques, miracle questions), the clients consistently reported a strong therapeutic relationship as the critical factor in treatment outcome (e.g., therapist acceptance, non-possessive warmth, positive regard, affirmation, and self-disclosure). (p. 85)*

Thus, we think the therapeutic relationship should be reemphasized as a critical factor that organizes integration. Research in this area of effectiveness has been reliable for many years. As beginning family therapists critique each model, they should ask: How does this model contribute to a positive therapeutic relationship from the client's point of view? To answer this question, we advise students to learn as much about people as they do about models. As one learns more about people, it is also important for the practitioner to learn more about self in relationship to others. Perhaps more than in any other mental health profession, we consider as the hallmark of a competent family therapist the ability to develop a positive relationship with diverse people, some times in conflict with each other. Add to this the challenge of engaging these diverse, conflicted people all at the same time, all in the same room! This unique aspect of family therapy is a significant test for professionals entering the field. However, like many of life's obstacles, when mastered, we have reaped some of our greatest rewards. As mentioned in Chapter Two, some models of family therapy encourage an exploration of personal phenomenology. Given the research data on the importance of therapeutic relationships, we make a case for stronger emphasis on personal process during the training experience of a family therapist.

Learning about others from their point of view can be done in a number of ways. We often recommend movies that may expose students to a world different from their own. In a multicultural environment, it is not difficult to find movies that portray life in other cultures. For example, producer Spike Lee has become well-known for his illustrations of African American issues. Fiction and nonfiction also provide trainees with views of the world that can be examined apart from professional jargon and scientific terminology. Exposure to diverse professions and cultures provides insight about others from their perspective.

The challenge of helping diverse people is also related to how family therapists respond to their own and others' conflicts. We encourage students of family therapy to explore their own patterns of thought and emotion in the face of interpersonal conflict. Identify those coping strategies most often chosen and critique them for their usefulness in professional settings. As one begins to gain awareness of this personal process, the next step involves exploring how these personal patterns may or may not fit with the inclinations of a given client group. An interesting example of how personal process interacts with client process comes from a study by Gonzales, Hiraga, and Cauce (1995). In observing mother–daughter interactions in African American and Asian American families, they discovered that non–African American coders rated the level of conflict higher for African American mothers and daughters than did the "in-group" coders or the mothers and daughters themselves. In applying this research to family therapy, it is possible that the practitioner's experience may be quite different from that of the family. We think learning to account for these differences and developing the ability to step back from them to "go with the flow" of a family are defining elements of competence.

For beginning practitioners, it is important to have a knowledge of the change process and the ability to personally relate to diverse people. We think each of these elements interacts to form a foundation for effective family therapy. Understanding the importance of extratherapeutic factors in the process of change leads the clinician toward a metaview of people's lives. This view provides perspective from which to creatively incorporate perceptual and behavioral change. This perspective also requires sensitivity to the unique aspects of a person's life that can become resources. These unique aspects are discovered through the therapist's ability to relate comfortably to individual differences. To help with this task of becoming "relationally versatile," we now review information on perceptions and attitudes useful in reaching this goal.

❄ PERCEPTIONS AND ATTITUDES

The personal characteristics of the therapist determine how a particular intervention is delivered. Therapists must be able to utilize skills that fit their own personality. Lebow (1987) explains:

> *Training in integrative models should not merely teach technique and theory, but explicitly accent the generation of a therapeutic stance by the therapist. The ability to feel and be hopeful, empathic, assertive, confrontative, and focused are all a part of being a therapist. To the extent possible, such skills should be directly taught, supplemented by personal therapy, to help overcome obstacles to attaining a therapeutic position. Each therapist ultimately needs to find a mode (or modes) of operating that is (are) comfortable and blends successfully with the theory, strategies, and techniques utilized. (p. 8)*

The therapeutic position described here is multidimensional, encompassing the behaviors and attitudes of the therapist. These two dimensions find a number of similarities across the various models of family therapy. In a survey, Figley and Nelson (1989) asked family therapy supervisors to list the most basic skills that should be taught to beginning family therapists. Their results might surprise some:

> *While the questionnaire asked the respondents to nominate generic skills, it is quite interesting that a large number of personal attributes were nominated. We had been thinking of behaviors in the context of therapy that could be taught to beginning therapists—behaviors that could be demonstrated, explained, and measured in some way. . . . Our fellow educators/trainers seem to believe, based on these data, that the person of the therapist is as important, if not more so, than the skill of the therapist. . . . It is probable that our respondents were aware that, for therapy training to be effective, a foundation of abilities, values, attitudes, and other traits is essential for effective family therapy. (p. 362)*

In their survey, 5 of the top 16 ranked items were "possess integrity," "desire to learn," "intellectually curious," "flexible," and "take responsibility for mistakes." Although the authors saw these as personal attributes that could not be measured with behavioral methods, it is possible that even these qualities could be "demonstrated, explained, and measured in some way."As the role of the family therapist has become more active and involved, there has been an accompanying shift in attitudes. Implicit in the more traditional doctor–patient relationship was the assumption that the therapist was the expert and authority who would pursue a cure for the client's distress. However, as interventions such as positive connotation have become popular, the therapist–client relationship has become more egalitarian. A focus away from deficits to strengths has also become prevalent. The Milan team suggests that the therapist's stance should be "hopeful and curious" (Tomm, 1984). Piercy and Sprenkle (1986) describe experiential family therapists in the following way:

> *Experiential family therapists participate actively and personally in therapy sessions; they do not attempt to hide behind a therapeutic mask. This means at times being vulnerable with family members and at other times being angry and upset. If the therapist expects the family to have the courage to be real, the therapist must also demonstrate that courage. (p. 53)*

While there is debate in the field regarding which of these attributes is essential to the process of facilitating change, there is generally a consensus that certain personal qualities are likely to enhance therapeutic effectiveness. Lankton, Lankton, and Matthews (1991) write:

> *We can make some generalizations about two qualities of the therapist that are important variables in therapy. The first is that it is desirable that therapists have a great pragmatic understanding of people and of coping with life's exigencies. The second quality is an ability to step outside of oneself into the world of another person while at the same time retaining an awareness of that pragmatic understanding of coping with life. These two qualities are operational aspects of what is usually called empathy and sympathy. An excitement about learning is visible in the most successful therapist. And finally, the ability to articulate, especially the differences between one's own experience and that of the client, is highly valuable. (p. 274)*

This list of desired therapist qualities exemplifies the variety within the field, and it is possible to select certain contemporary trends from the myriad of suggestions. These trends, while not exhaustive, are considered here as the best starting point for the entry-level family therapist. They include an ability to perceive client competencies and to shift from one view to another.

Perception of Client Competence

Many family therapists use language that describes and labels competencies in clients. For example, Michael White (1986) suggests that clients can become experts about themselves. This highlights client strengths and downplays the authority of the therapist. Brief therapists such as O'Hanlon (1987) have elaborated on the Ericksonian technique of referring to positive possibilities. For example, a brief therapist, after listening to a description of the presenting problem, might ask the client to describe the times when things are going well. This is representative of a trend toward competence-based treatment in which strengths and successes are systematically investigated and highlighted as central elements in the treatment process.

More traditionally, this same element can be found in structural and experiential family therapy. Minuchin and Fishman (1981) outlined their emphasis on client strengths as they integrated their values with other leaders in the field:

> *In every family there are positives. Positives are transmitted from the family of origin to the new family, and from there to the next generation. Despite mistakes, unhappiness, and pain, there are also pleasures: spouses and children give to each other in ways that are growth-encouraging and supportive, contributing to each other's sense of competence and worth . . .*
> *The orientation of family therapists toward "constructing a reality" that highlights deficits is therefore being challenged. Family therapists are finding that an exploration of strengths is essential to challenge family dysfunctions. The work of Virginia Satir, with its emphasis on growth, is oriented toward a search for normal alternatives. So is the work of Ivan Nagy [Boszormenyi-Nagy], with its emphasis on positive connotations and his exploration of the family value system. Carl Whitaker's technique of challenging the positions of family members and introducing role diffusion springs from his belief that out of this therapeutically induced chaos the family member can discover latent strength. Jay Haley and Chloe Madanes' view that the symptom is organized to protect the family and Mara Selvini Palazzoli's paradoxical interventions all point toward family strengths. (p. 268)*

In a different way, Whitaker (1982) considers the goals of family therapy to be an increased sense of competence and self-worth. Symptoms are considered an attempt toward growth. While each model may execute this objective in a different way, the trend toward a more positive, affirming mode of practice appears to be gaining considerable momentum. Partly on account of the influence of social construction in mental health circles, this competence-based approach is a key element found across many models. A second attribute essential to the family therapist's repertoire is flexibility.

Therapist Flexibility

In defining therapist flexibility, it may be helpful to return to the research of Figley and Nelson (1989). Some of the attributes that family therapy supervisors regarded as important include "nonjudgmental," "respectful of differences," "understanding that one reality doesn't work for everyone," and "meet clients 'where they are.' " These characterize a family therapist who has learned to be flexible.

If beginning family therapists recognize their limited view of the world, it is easier to experiment with different perspectives. However, if beginning practitioners believe that there are few other ways to view a problem besides their own, it may be difficult to learn the art of reframing. In developing a greater sense of flexibility, constructivist views have encouraged practitioners to reconsider some assumptions that may limit flexibility and narrow the possibilities for creativity. Duncan and Parks (1988) elaborate:

> *Simply stated, reality, like beauty, rests entirely in the eye of the beholder; there is no objective reality or truth inherent in a given situation. Reality, therefore, is constructed by each individual in each circumstance. The process of construction is based in complex sociocultural interaction between the ever changing larger society, the family, and the biologically/psychologically developing individual. The constructivist position is central to a selective integration model. In the absence of a specific view of reality, the therapist is free to entertain the "reality" of any content that seems applicable in a given clinical situation. Rather than imposing the therapist's theoretical reality on the client, a theoretical language or specific content is chosen because it best matches the client's conceptualization and presentation of the problem. (p. 156)*

Similarly, Milton Erickson, who has had a primary influence on MRI, strategic, and Ericksonian models of therapy, stated that he invented a new theory for each individual (Lankton & Lankton, 1983).

In addition to such theoretical flexibility, it is important for the family therapist to learn a type of "political" flexibility that requires the clinician to adopt a cooperative and hopeful stance regardless of the family's own idiosyncrasies. For example, in research conducted on the treatment of adolescent substance abuse, the Purdue Brief Family Therapy model (the PBFT model) listed the following curative factors related to successful change (Lewis, Piercy, Sprenkle, & Trepper, 1991):

1. The family feels the therapist is "with them" or "on their side."
2. The therapist engenders hope.
3. The therapist diminishes the family's fear of change.
4. The therapist avoids resistance.
5. The therapist respects the family's uniqueness.
6. The therapist mobilizes the family's resources. (p. 41)

These curative factors, shared by the models that the PBFT model integrates, begin to describe in greater detail therapist attitudes that are associated with successful outcomes in family therapy.

To summarize, knowledge about the change process sets the stage for the beginning clinician to focus on the therapeutic relationship. This can be maximized when the therapist is active in promoting competencies and flexible in accepting differences. As these perceptions and attitudes are internalized and become second nature, specific interventions become entwined with these basic processes. We now review selected behaviors used as a starting point for the clinician's skill development.

❄ BEHAVIORS

Historically, family therapists focused on the etiology (i.e., cause or origin) of the problem. Practitioners who emphasized the role of the family considered the goal to be the treatment of mental illnesses such as schizophrenia. For these therapists, the goal of therapy was healing, and the treatment of choice was the involvement of family members with the symptomatic person. This placed the therapist in a traditional doctor–patient relationship but with a more active, directive role than traditional psychoanalysis, which encouraged the therapist to remain aloof and detached. This change in therapist behavior toward more activity is illustrated by the following models.

Bowen (1978) became noted for his work with individual family members, coaching them toward a more rational perspective vis-à-vis their family of origin. Instead of remaining passive, he took an active, involved role in facilitating change. His intergenerational approach to family therapy was characterized by information gathering about the nuclear family, each spouse's family of origin, and the relationship of nodal events over time to the development of the symptom in question. Then, with this family story in place, he would coach the client into developing a strategy that could be executed over time outside of sessions.

Minuchin, as he developed his model of structural family therapy, characterized his role as that of a director, actively moving in and out of involvement with the family during a treatment session. As a director, Minuchin guides interaction between members in a session, develops rapport with hesitant members, or assigns tasks for the family to perform in the session. While the directives given to the family are diverse, the clinician plays the specific role of a pragmatic stage manager who enacts old and new dramas that help the family reorganize their relational difficulties.

Communication theorists such as Watzlawick, Weakland, and Fisch (1974) introduced the "gentle art of reframing" into the repertoire of family therapists. In developing strategic family therapy, these authors defined reframing as a reconceptualization of some context that keeps the clients from exercising other options in solving their problem. These practitioners attempt to reconstruct their clients' view of the problem in a way that produces new options. Therefore, they generate multiple meanings for various problem behaviors. They found that, when they could help their clients assign a new meaning to an old problem, new attitudes brought forth new options for problem solving.

Experiential models such as those developed by Whitaker (1976) and Satir (1972) generally consider personal growth and self-responsibility as the goals of therapy for both the therapist and family members. These therapists believe that the use of self to foster family members' flexibility and range of choice facilitates growth and increased self-esteem. Although these clinicians have different personal styles, they are both noted for their dramatic and impactful interactions with clients. Both believe that, when the therapist is open and spontaneous, family members learn to behave openly and spontaneously. Satir describes a therapist as a resource person and a model of congruent communication. The therapist helps family members clarify and alter their values so they can communicate openly with one another. The therapist teaches family members how to observe discrepancies between the intent and impact of their messages. The therapist becomes a standard by which family members can evaluate themselves and the effectiveness of their communication. Experiential family therapists refrain from emphasizing specific therapeutic techniques; however, their use of questions, empathic responses, clarification, and directives facilitates effective communication in the family. Family members learn to solve their own problems. The therapist trusts that the family finds a creative solution to their problem within the therapeutic relationship.

The Milan team developed a style of conducting family therapy based on "hypothesizing, circularity, and neutrality" (Selvini Palazzoli, Boscolo, Cecchin, & Prata, 1980a). In this model, the therapist gathers information about the family through a continual series of questions. The intent of such questions can range from the exploratory ("Has it always been this way? When have things been different?") to the provocative ("When did you first realize that your father needed your support in dealing with your mother?"). When the intent is exploratory, the Milan team emphasizes the usefulness of questions that draw comparisons, whether between people, between points in time, or between definitions of the problem. When questions are provocative, they are used as an indirect way of making some implicit family dynamic explicit and verbalized.

Michael White focuses on "exceptions to the rule." Emphasizing the work of Gregory Bateson (1972), White looks for small positive exceptions to a negative pattern and amplifies this new reality. Convincing the family that change has already occurred, he promotes a strategy that expands this newly discovered improvement. This information or insight about exceptions, discovered in session through persistent interpretations, becomes the basis for therapeutic directives and "experiments" (White, 1986) that lead to out-of-session changes for individuals and families.

Certainly, these models illustrate the diversity within family therapy, and the therapist's active and involved role is evident in all the examples. That role can be operationalized into four main interventions found in all of the major schools of family therapy: the use of questions, the tracking of interactional sequences, reframing, and directives.

Questions

Someone once said that wisdom is not in having the right answer but in asking the right question. Although all models of family therapy use questions in some part of their practice, the Milan team, Michael White, and Murray Bowen rely heavily on the use of questions as interventions. The literature has emphasized the use of questions in family therapy (Fleuridas, Nelson, & Rosenthal, 1986; Penn, 1982; Tomm, 1984). Family therapists make systematic use of questions to elicit information that brings about change. Numerous accounts of the Milan team's questions began to surface in the literature in the 1980s (Tomm, 1984). These authors coined the term *circular questions* to refer to the line of questioning that they used in family interviews. The questions are of four types: problem definition, sequence of interaction, comparison/classification, and intervention. In addition, they reported an evolution from present-oriented questions to past-oriented questions to future-oriented questions in the course of the therapeutic process.

In the work of Michael White, questions are used for two primary purposes. First, the family therapist can ask questions as a way of looking for exceptions to the stated systematic behavior. For example, "When are the times that you are not fearful?" or "When are the times that the two of you are getting along?" Second, the family therapist can use questions to gain the specifics of family interactions. White refers to this as "relative influence questioning." Basically, these questions ask how the client is influenced by the problem and how the problem is influenced by the client. For example, if a couple comes to therapy complaining about their conflict, the therapist might ask, "How does conflict affect you? What do you do when you are being influenced by conflict?" The therapist actually personifies conflict and states the questions as though there is an interaction between conflict and the person (externalization). Another set of questions is, "What do you do that seems to overcome conflict? How do you have an influence on conflict?" In both instances, attention focuses on specific behaviors. What do the family members do? The family therapist must be able to visualize how people act and what people say when they are overcome by conflict and when they are overcoming conflict.

Such questions yield a clear picture of the present while providing a hopeful direction for the future. In keeping with a Batesonian perspective, these questions also introduce new information in the form of contrast. Very often, clients come in with perspectives that are distorted by their own pain; they fail to see the positive possibilities that lie in their own circumstances. Through the use of questions, family therapists help uncover and emphasize small moments of progress that can become new patterns of relating. The choice of questions that call the clients' attention to new information keeps the family therapist active and directive; it is a fundamental skill in family therapy. In addition to circular questions and relative influence questions, these models focus on interactional patterns that unfold in family life over time. This focus, shared by virtually all models, is a basic skill for the beginning practitioner and merits detailed consideration.

Tracking Interactional Sequences

Structural and strategic models define the therapeutic goal as structural or interactional change within the family system. Both models are chiefly interested in how family members interact with each other: Do family members speak for each other? When a child speaks, does Mom or Dad interrupt? Do parents agree about how to solve the problem? Is the symptom a metaphor for something else in this family? How is the symptom maintained by the system and how does the system maintain the symptom? What system function could these symptoms serve? From these questions, the therapist attempts to understand the sequence of interactions surrounding the presenting problem. By determining the sequence of interaction, the therapist gains information useful in developing an intervention to alleviate the problem.

Although structural and strategic approaches emphasize the interactional sequence, each treats it somewhat differently. Strategic family therapists are more symptom-focused than structural therapists, and both are more symptom-oriented than intergenerational therapists (Stanton, 1981). For instance, strategic therapists focus on dysfunctional sequences of interaction that contribute to the problem. Structuralists center attention on how family members interact to carry out specific functions within each subsystem (marital, parental, and sibling). For both models, the emphasis on interactional change corresponds to a focus on behavioral change, even though each model may focus on different aspects of behavior. In these models, assessment and intervention are based on observations of interactional sequences.

Ericksonian and brief therapies also have a strong emphasis on tracking interactions with clients (Lankton, 1988; O'Hanlon, 1982). In these models, the therapist gathers very specific information about what a client does when depressed and what the client does when less depressed, or what a child does when a parent behaves in a certain way and what happens to the child's behavior if the parent behaves in an unexpected way. Interaction sequences that are nonproblematic are elicited by such questions as, "What is different about the times when you are less depressed?" or "How do you get that to happen?" Specific interventions are designed to interrupt or change the behavioral patterns that appear to be the family's response to a presenting problem.

Regardless of the school of thought, much of the activity of a family therapist is focused on gathering interactional and behavioral information about the family. Box 3.1 summarizes examples of how to track behavior and communication in interactional sequences. This information, in turn, becomes a foundation that enables families to make behavioral changes. In general, change is behavioral, perceptual, or both. The next skill is aimed at perceptual change in families.

Reframing

The term *reframe* (or *reframing*) is commonly used in contemporary psychotherapy as well as in family therapy. It is possible that Watzlawick et al. (1974) were the first family therapists to use this term. Subsequently, Minuchin and Fishman (1981) promoted an intervention called *relabeling,* and later the

BOX 3.1

Questions to Track Interactional Sequences
Who did what when?
What did he or she actually say or do?
What was happening right before this?
When he or she said or did that, what happened next?
And then what happened?
Then what did they do?
While this was going on, where were _____ , _____ ,
_____ (other family or household members)?
When he or she does that, then what happens?

Questions to Clarify Meanings and Messages
What was actually said?
What were you thinking when he said that?
When you said _____ , what were you thinking?
When you thought _____ , how did you come to that conclu-
    sion? (Where did you get that idea?)

Milan team introduced the idea of *positive connotation*. Stanton (1981) has reported using an intervention called *ascribing noble intentions*. Because these
terms have similar meanings and uses, we limit our discussion to reframing
and positive connotation, which adequately represent the important aspects
of this general intervention.

Reframing is a reinterpretation of the problem or symptom. For example, if two adolescent brothers are engaging in rough and physically aggressive
wrestling, their parents may conceptualize their behavior as "fighting." If
these parents want their sons to quit this behavior, an attempted solution may
include telling them to "stop fighting." However, when this solution doesn't
work, it becomes tempting to try the same solution over and over again. If the
family seeks the help of a therapist to solve this problem, a possible intervention would be for the therapist to reframe the behavior known as fighting and
refer to it as "the way in which they love each other." If their behavior is seen
in this new light, it would encourage parents and others to point out how
much these two young men love each other when their wrestling is a problem.
The rationale behind this reframe is that two adolescents trying to be "manly"
would find the idea of open expressions of love to one another as "sissy"; consequently, the new label for their behavior might make them feel embarrassed
rather than enjoying the attention, which in turn might encourage them to

stop the behavior. The principle behind this strategy is that a new meaning attached to old behaviors produces new behaviors that are associated with the new meaning.

After the concept of reframing was introduced to the family therapy profession, the term was generalized to refer to a relabeling or a new understanding of a problem. For example, if a wife becomes concerned that her husband's lack of communication connotes rejection, she may label his behavior as "distant" and label her own response as "feeling rejected." A family therapist may use reframing to help the wife consider other factors outside the relationship that might explain her husband in a different way: Perhaps he has recently lost his job; perhaps one of his parents has recently died; perhaps he has recently sustained a serious injury. Any of these circumstances might help this woman define her husband's behavior as "pain" or "sorrow" rather than distance. Another possible explanation for this man's behavior might lie within the marital relationship. Perhaps they have recently had a child, and the wife is preoccupied with her new responsibilities as a mother. Thus, her husband may be feeling the effect of this change in their family system; the behavior that she interprets as rejection or distance may be explained by his feeling "left out" or "insecure." Very often, such feelings are difficult to communicate. In reframing, the therapist's ultimate goal is to help clients see the problem behaviors of their family members in a new light. In this example, the wife's new perception of the situation might change her behavior, transforming her criticism into reassurance.

In learning how to reframe a problem, the family therapist must understand how the reframe will facilitate change. The therapist's own limited way of defining a certain problem may prove an obstacle to reframing. For example, if the family therapist has the same view of the problem behavior as the client, sincere use of reframing may be difficult. However, as the beginning practitioner comes to understand how many interpretations of human problems are possible, it becomes progressively easier to develop more flexible and multiple views of every situation. In addition, the most effective reframes, though they may be expressed in dramatic language, usually involve a relabeling of the problem that has some truth to it in the sense that it fits with the client's point of view or experience. For example, in the case of the adolescent brothers, if their behavior was truly reinforced because of the attention they were receiving and not because of some deep-seated resentment for each other, this suggests a fundamental bond between them that is ultimately positive rather than a chasm. Speaking of their behavior in terms of love, while dramatic, would be a movement in the right direction. However, if their behavior stemmed from serious hostility or some other unrecognized issue, the reframe might have to address their attempts to communicate deep hurt.

Another way to begin experimenting with reframing is to consider several new terms for the problem behavior and decide which one might be most consistent with the client's experience and goals rather than with what the therapist thinks is the most accurate definition of the problem. If a certain reframe seems to strike an effective chord with the client, even though the therapist doesn't actually believe it, the therapist should consider that what is most important is what fits the client, not what fits the therapist. Beginning family therapists often struggle with the dilemma of sincerity when new definitions are awkward and untested. We encourage readers to conceptualize the training process as an experiment with different maps of the world and with learning how to identify the client's map before their own. It is also useful to note that it is possible to learn how to reframe the problem simply by using new language. A therapist's choice of words can be powerful regardless of the personal conviction behind it. These new words, when effective, not only facilitate new options in clients but also transform a therapist's view of reality.

In some cases, negative problems can be relabeled to have more positive meaning. For example, "jealousy" could be relabeled as "caring," and "anger" could be relabeled as "desiring attention." Positive labels often provide family members with new ways to think about solving the problem (Stanton, 1981). For example, Madanes (1981) describes a woman whose "hysterical paralysis" was relabeled as "muscular cramp," and a man whose "depression" was relabeled as "irresponsibility." In each case, the problem was relabeled in less severe terms so that it was within the client's control to change.

The Milan team coined the term *positive connotation* as they worked with families who had psychotic and anorexic young adults. They found their work to be more effective when they identified a positive aspect of some family member's problematic behavior. Examples of positive connotation include when a therapist may describe a benefit of a daughter's anorexia by suggesting that she is doing the family a service by giving them an opportunity to come together. In turn, the Milan team might reframe the family as being terrified of growing apart. By reframing one behavior and positively connoting another, they found that family members respond between sessions with some meaningful change in their behavior patterns. Another example involves an adolescent male who was deaf from birth. The young man was of great concern to many people because he persistently cross-dressed, wearing his sister's or other female clothing. When the consultant on the case discovered that the young man and his father were both first-born sons with younger female siblings, both were detached from their fathers, and the father was also detached from his mother and sisters, it was suggested that the boy's behavior could possibly be a message to his father about how to relate to women: "If you can't beat 'em, join 'em." Surprisingly, the parents found great comfort in such an interpretation. It provided them with a less shameful analysis of their son's problem. It was also more hopeful than labeling his behavior as a dysfunction.

Selvini Palazzoli (1986) suggests that rigidity in families can often be addressed through positive connotation. Because she believes that much rigidity is the expression of intense shame, positive connotation helps bypass client shame in the service of developing new patterns for relating. In the foregoing example, the positive connotation for cross-dressing provided an alternative view of the young man's struggle by avoiding the shame of transvestism and the shame of having a deaf child who could not communicate in conventional ways.

While there are some similarities to the skills of positive connotation and reframing, the main difference is suggested by their names: Positive connotation is always intended to be positive from the client's perspective; conversely, reframing can be experienced by the client as either positive or negative and still be effective. The similarities between positive connotation and reframing are generally found when a therapist uses either skill to depathologize a presenting problem and relate it to normal occurrences such as family transitions, the identified patient's ordinal or sibling position, some significant event prior to the development of symptoms, ethnic factors, or some other circumstance in the client's background. In any case, reframing and positive connotation are used to bypass shame and blame, to create a hopeful acceptance of client characteristics, and to introduce multiple views of the presenting problem.

While the techniques already considered attempt to change family perceptions, the last skill to be discussed focuses on behavior change.

Directives

This category of interventions is usually associated theoretically with strategic family therapy. Madanes (1981) states that the directive is to strategic therapy "what interpretation is to psychoanalysis" (p. 10). However, considered more broadly, directives are found in all the major schools of family therapy, whether as an assigned task or ritual to be completed outside of the session or as one of the many maneuvers within the session that the therapist uses to direct interaction, clarify communication, or change behavior. In structural family therapy, the term "restructuring" refers to tasks aimed at changing some aspect of family organization, such as the balance of power or the nature of some coalition. For example, a mother who confides in her child regarding her marital difficulties might be directed to discuss some marital issue directly with her husband. A mother who favors one child over another might be asked to sit next to the less favored child. Through simple directives aimed at changing some behavioral pattern, the family therapist creates new possibilities by directing new interactions that the family does not initiate independently. Once begun, the in-session change is expected to have out-of-session influence.

Experiential family therapists often encourage increased self-disclosure or influence the direction of communication flow within the family. For example, Satir (1972) directs family members to follow three rules for effective communication: (a) Family members should speak in the first person and express what they think and feel (the therapist might ask, "I want to know how you feel about that"); (b) family members are asked to take responsibility for their feelings ("Tell me how you feel when he ignores you"); and (c) family members are required to level with each other ("Tell your son what you want him to do when he gets home"). Such directives shift the responsibility for communication as well as the content.

Other schools such as intergenerational family therapy generally use directives as assignments or projects that a client may incorporate into his or her long-term strategic plan for improving family relationships. For example, a young married woman told her therapist that her father had sexually abused her when she was an adolescent, after the sudden death of her mother. She was directed to explore all extended family members for the person most likely to respond sympathetically to her disclosures on the matter. She was able to identify an aunt whose memory had remained positive despite years of distance and no contact. The family therapist encouraged her to reestablish contact with the aunt and explore possibilities for an adult-to-adult relationship in the present. The aunt proved to be a source of comfort, and the woman soon planned a vacation with her husband and children to visit this aunt who lived 1000 miles away. In this case, directives helped the client entertain and explore possibilities for increased satisfaction within her natural environment.

Directives can be direct or indirect depending on the skill level of the therapist. Indirect interventions include paradoxical prescriptions and the creation of rituals. Some guidelines for these strategic interventions are reviewed in later chapters.

While this discussion of therapist behaviors does not claim to be all inclusive, it is intended to help the beginning family therapist identify basic skills needed in clinical practice. In mastering these four interventions—questions, tracking interactional sequences, reframing, and directives—the clinician will realize that these form the basis for more advanced skills. Table 3.2 summarizes the important elements discussed in this chapter. It is interesting to note that the role of the therapist is evolving. In the early models, the therapist is focused more on behavior and less on phenomenology. In later models, the roles of cognition, personal experience, and individual meanings emerge as a critical factor in the process of change. Nevertheless, interesting parallels also remain. The structural therapist and collaborative therapist are both active in directing behavior. However, collaborative activity is directing the thoughts of one person toward another or guiding a group toward a creative brainstorming process. Thus, we maintain our stance that certain activities remain universal in family therapy, even though the destination or purpose of the journey may vary. We see these activities as the foundation for a therapeutic style that is effective in working systemically and relationally. Most important, the family therapist must have a knowledge about the different ways change occurs and be willing to recognize the varied influences on the change process. In addition, the clinician must make a personal decision to respect and esteem diverse people. In particular, the client's perception of the therapeutic relationship is an important factor related to successful outcomes.

In the next chapter, we review the basic stages in the process of family therapy and provide a framework for integrating the themes of theory and practice that have been reviewed to this point. As we start the car and begin to move, we take our knowledge, perceptions, attitudes, and skills. We circle the parking lot—many times—and begin to see how each component interacts with the others, sometimes overlapping, sometimes proceeding in order. These movements and cognitions become entwined as stages and interactions in the process.

Table 3.2

Type of Therapy	Theoretical Distinction	Role of Therapist
Structural	Subsystem Boundaries Hierarchies	Stage manager
Strategic	Parental hierarchies Cross-generational coalitions	Formulates directives
Intergenerational	Extended family patterns, myths, rules	Coach or guide
Experiential	Developmental environment for human growth	Modeling
MRI	Attempted solutions	Identify myths Identify successes
The Milan team	Role of symptoms in family Extended family relationships	Hypothesizing Positive connotation of the symptom

Narrative	Influences on the presenting
	   problem that are outside the
	   family
		Finds and emphasizes
		   exceptions to the problem

Collaborative	Problem-defining system Influence of conversation	Collegial partner
Cognitive- Behavioral	Interaction between individual cognition and behavior	Active and involved

Primary Intervention	Type of Interactional Sequences
Track sequences Reframing Directives	In-session sequences
Track sequences Reframing Directives	Parent–child sequences
Questions Track sequences Directives	Emotional sequences with family of origin, spouse, children
Track sequences Directives	Sequences between therapist and client
Track sequences Reframing Directives	Sequences related to problem solving
Questions Track sequences Reframing Directives	Developmental sequences of how symptoms formed over time
Questions Track sequences Reframing Directives	Interactions related to successes
Collaborative questions Active listening Conversation that promotes dialogue	Interactions leading to dialogue and collaboration
Track sequences Restructure sequences through cognitive and behavioral change directives	Couple sequences

Chapter Four

Preparing to Practice: Sequences and Interactions in the Process

The Referral Process

The Joining Process

The Therapeutic Contract
Levels of Communication
Intentions
Goals

Data Gathering
Content Versus Process
Past, Present, Future

Hypothesizing

Specific Interventions

Evaluation

In-Session Stages of Family Therapy
Negotiate Structure
Explore Client Experience
Address Relationships
Develop a Shared Direction

Thus far, the basic elements of practice have been identified across the various models of family therapy. Some of these elements relate to skills, attitudes, or qualities of the therapist, and others relate to specific concepts. We have attempted to integrate areas of similarity among the theories studied. In this chapter, we continue this integration process by reviewing the common interactional elements of these models in problem or symptom resolution. These elements are presented within a sequential framework in which the therapeutic process is characterized as interactional, circular, and evolving. We outline this framework in the form of sequential steps to help the beginning family therapist manage the complexities of direct client contact. However, several of these processes can also occur simultaneously in microsequences of therapist–client interaction. First, there is a review of interactions we believe span the entire life of a clinical case. Then, we introduce integrative microstages that can be used as a format for planning each treatment session.

Family therapy can be thought of as an interactional and perceptual process. One person, called a therapist, and one or more persons, called clients, interact together. Efran, Lukens, and Lukens (1990) suggest that:

> If psychological assistance is to be effective, it must take place in the very same space in which our living and our problems are enacted—in meaningful conversation. In other words, that which we have labeled "psychotherapy" must begin to be seen as a specialized form of dialogue—not as a medical treatment analogous to administering inoculations, performing surgery, or dressing wounds. (p. xv)

This evolves through many different stages, some of which may be limited to a certain order, whereas others repeat over time to form a pattern. These stages, which we believe are found in every therapy experience, are:

1. The referral process
2. The joining process
3. The therapeutic contract
4. Data gathering
5. Hypothesizing
6. Specific interventions
7. Evaluation

While not every family therapy model addresses each of these processes consciously or explicitly, we suggest that each one occurs either simultaneously or consecutively as an influence on the larger process of therapy. These interactional processes, when combined with therapist skills and attitudes, form a macro-framework from which to apply the other skills taught throughout the remainder of this book.

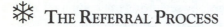 THE REFERRAL PROCESS

Referral is the process by which a client enters family therapy. The context of referral is an interactional process in which, generally speaking, someone decides that a problem exists and someone initiates the idea that therapy is a possible resource and should be sought. Important questions to ask are:

> Who first thought there was a problem?
>
> Whose idea was it for you to seek therapy?
>
> When you began to think about seeking help, who or what gave you the thought that therapy might help?

With the increasing frequency of court-ordered therapy in the United States, it is important to explore and understand the step-by-step sequences of interaction that led the client to schedule an appointment or inquire by phone. At the very least, the family therapist obtains information about who has taken the initiative. Ideally, the family therapist obtains crucial information about the family's level of motivation, their influential external relationships, and whether therapy is even appropriate in such circumstances. Obviously, a court-ordered case has implications for the motivation of the client to do therapy.

If one spouse is more motivated than the other to pursue marital therapy, the following questions might be asked:

> When you thought about coming to counseling, how did you talk to him or her about it?
>
> When he or she talked to you about counseling, what was your reaction?
>
> Were you dragged here against your will?

In this way, differences in motivation may be addressed during early stages of the therapeutic process. By asking these questions and tracking the perceptual and interactional process, the therapist gains information for subsequent use in developing mutually satisfying goals that are sensitive to individual needs.

In addition to court-ordered cases or public agency referrals, there are circumstances in private-practice settings where relatives, family members, clergy, and service providers have recommended or even initiated counseling while excluding themselves from the process. For example, the parents of a young married couple may send them to marriage counseling and even pay for it. The Milan team has consistently addressed the referral process in the case where therapy was initiated by someone who claims to be uninvolved in the life of the problem, such as a member of the clergy or a sibling (Selvini Palazzoli, 1985; Selvini Palazzoli, Boscolo, Cecchin, & Prafa, 1980b). They found that examining the relationship between the referring person and the family must take precedence over traditional therapy—that is, over merely examining relationships within the family or even exploring the problem itself.

In addition to the Milan team, O'Hanlon and Weiner-Davis (1989) address a similar concern by establishing who the "customer" of therapy is—that is, Who is actually requesting that a change be made? Questions such as these can aid in identifying the customer:

Who first noticed that this was a problem?

How was it brought to your attention?

Do you agree or disagree with them that this is a problem?

On discovering that someone besides those in attendance actually developed the definition of the problem, the family therapist's goal is to clarify the relationship between the family and the parties who have defined the problem. This remains the focus of treatment until the appropriate role of the family therapist is clarified with the parties involved. As the Milan team discovered, when the problem is being defined by a sibling, in-law, or service provider, that party should be included in the session to properly define what the problem is. Since the family may disagree with the person's opinion but still initiate therapy, the family may define the real problem as a difference of opinion with this outside influence.

In court-ordered cases, it is appropriate to involve caseworkers or probation officers until the problem can be defined in a way that mobilizes the client's motivation (e.g., "As family therapist, my job is to help you develop a plan that will get the court system off of your back"). While other models rarely address this aspect of the therapeutic process, our opinion is that the be-ginning family therapist will encounter puzzling superficiality or courteous compliance without personal involvement unless the influence of the referral process is ruled in or out as a major issue.

❄ THE JOINING PROCESS

First used by Minuchin (1974) as he developed structural family therapy, join-ing is probably the most universal—or the most borrowed—of family therapy terms. As we discussed in Chapter Three, the personal rapport or empathy that therapists develop with those they are trying to help remains the single most proven variable determining the effectiveness of psychotherapy (Gar-field & Bergin, 1978). However, when a family therapist begins to grapple with this process from a larger systemic framework, the number of people in-volved may make this a significant challenge.

Minuchin and Fishman (1981) view joining as an attitude:

> *Joining a family is more an attitude than a technique, and it is the umbrella under which all therapeutic transactions occur. Joining is letting the family know that the therapist understands them and is working with and for them. Only under this protection can the family have the security to explore alter-natives, try the unusual, and change. Joining is the glue that holds the thera-peutic system together. (pp. 31–32)*

In contrast to the referral process, which can be thought of as an interac-tional and political event to be explored at the outset of therapy, the joining process can best be conceptualized as an interactional pattern that is repeated throughout the entire course of family therapy. When a family therapist first becomes acquainted with the family, a certain formal stage may exist, but later stages of therapy require an understanding that is continually expanded as new information challenges the original perceptions of therapist and client alike. Therefore, it is helpful to think of joining as a process that pervades all the other stages discussed here. For example, by attending to the referral pro-cess described in the previous section, the family therapist may successfully join with the family through an astute sensitivity to political issues that are of-ten overlooked by other therapists.

The following exemplify how each school of thought in family therapy can also contribute to the therapist's ability to join with family members:

Theories regarding the importance of ethnicity help a family therapist join through an appreciation of the family's language, customs, heritage, and beliefs.

Theories regarding development help a family therapist join through identification with clients' age, empathy with their stage of life, or understanding of the dilemmas they face as various transitions approach.

Intergenerational theories help a family therapist join through a recognition of significant family members who may not be present in the session. Their nicknames, circumstances, and impact on present family members may lead the family therapist into the clients' private world.

Structural and strategic theories help a family therapist join through assessing the family's hierarchy and making sure that those in authority are sufficiently engaged.

Contextual theory encourages multidirected partiality, which is the art of consecutively siding with each member to develop trust and fairness in relationships (Bemal & Flores-Ortiz, 1991).

Ericksonian and social construction theories often encourage humor and playfulness. They also accept resistance as a helpful message about the client's uniqueness.

While these are not exhaustive, they are meant to stimulate the reader's creativity to find spontaneous and endearing ways of relating to family members that contribute to trust and rapport. Many family therapists find it useful to join through the use of metaphoric comparisons from the client's world. For example, a therapist who routinely constructs a genogram and a relationship history provides a rationale to each client for the necessity of these procedures. A young couple who likes to go boating was given this rationale for an assessment:

> *In order for me to help you, it is important to get to know you and to understand something about the important people and events in your life. Marriage counseling is often like teaching someone how to sail. By gathering information on your extended family, I learn something about what kind of boat you have, from the type of sail that it comes with to its size and shape. Your families equip you with many skills for sailing through the waters of life. In addition, some of the family experiences you have help you develop certain strengths. By learning about your relationship history, I learn about the*

weather conditions that you have sailed through in the past and present. The direction of the wind and the speed of the currents are important for the sailor to know about. A good sailor must learn to take many different factors into account while planning the journey. Once I understand something about the gusts of wind in your life and the many directions that your boats have taken you, I can help you to fine-tune your sailing skills for the current waters and your future life together. Your present complaint may be the result of a coincidence between several of these elements, just as a storm might come up in the water and you must struggle to learn and master some new sailing technique.

In this example, the therapist took into consideration the couple's stage in life; this was a young couple in the first stage of married life. If the couple had been married for 20 years, a different metaphor might have been more appropriate. A later stage in life would suggest that these people have been struggling with the same problems for a longer time. What they may need is some new way to address their conflict if the old ways have not worked in 20 years. Thus, a more appropriate metaphor for such a couple might involve a new mode of transport: learning to canoe or deciding to take the train.

The process of joining is closely related to therapist flexibility. Is the clinician a person who can modify his or her style to match that of the family? If they are boisterous, can the therapist join with them rather than convey subtle disapproval? Has the clinician been influenced by theories that encourage stilted jargon, or is there room for a wide range of interactions (e.g., playfulness, empathy, firmness, and humor)? The chemistry between the therapist and the family depends, in part, on the ability of the clinician to become comfortable with a wide variety of people.

During a period of training, it is sometimes most helpful for the trainee to spend as much time as possible with nontherapists to remain connected to the broader culture. In addition, the academic world can sometimes become an obstacle to the trainee's attempts to remain balanced and versatile. It may seem an ironic paradox, but nonprofessional leisure activities can often be the best teacher in providing a trainee with exposure to a variety of people, cultures, languages, and metaphors. The use of metaphor is especially effective when clients differ dramatically from the therapist in age, values, economic level, and ethnic background, to name a few. If the client is a farmer, the family therapist might want to be compared to the county extension agent. If the client is a physician, the family therapist might want to be compared to a medical specialist, perhaps a cardiologist. If the client cares a great deal about physical appearance, the therapist might want to be compared to a hair stylist. By searching for metaphors and analogies that come from the clients' world, the therapist attempts to join clients in their world rather than expecting them to fit into the prescribed world of the therapist.

❄ THE THERAPEUTIC CONTRACT

Although some schools of therapy never mention an explicit agreement between family therapist and family, our belief is that all therapeutic interactions are part of a spoken or unspoken therapeutic contract. This contract consists of expectations and goals transacted at two levels of communication: content and process. How clearly goals and expectations are communicated affects how cooperatively therapist and clients work together.

Levels of Communication

To use Bateson's (Ruesch & Bateson, 1951) terms, all communication has report (content) and command (process) levels. The report level is the verbal information transmitted; the command level is the nonverbal manifestation of how the sender is defining the relationship. Therefore, the family therapist and family each define the nature of the relationship, but neither may be communicating their expectations to the other. For example, the family therapist may have chosen a role as neutral negotiator vis-à-vis the family. Meanwhile, the family may have defined the therapist as a referee or even as an ally. As these implicit expectations unfold through nonverbal behaviors (process), the implicit conflict may interfere with explicitly stated goals (content). Once the implicit information is brought forward, roles can be clarified in a way that enlists cooperation more fully. It may be helpful to think further about the therapeutic contract as it relates to expectations and goals. As we discussed in Chapter Two, intentions are an important part of exploring individual experience. These expectations and goals are examples of intentions that relate to our thoughts, feelings, and behavior in the therapeutic process.

Intentions

The family therapist and the family each bring a set of intentions to the therapy hour. These relate to each party's role, the procedures that are followed, and the conditions that each party expects the other to meet. Perhaps the family has a media-related stereotype of a counselor, therapist, or social worker. Perhaps the family therapist has a desire to maintain a certain image with the family. What if the two sets of expectations don't match? For example, a woman once sought help from a family therapist that evolved into a pattern of bringing a different problem to therapy each week. Puzzled and frustrated that she was of no help, the therapist wondered about how the woman might be defining the role of the therapist. In the next session, the therapist inquired about the pattern and what it could mean. With prompting from the therapist, the woman was able to explain that involvement was more important to her than problem solving. She thought that if she didn't bring some problem to talk about each week, the therapist would discontinue involvement with her. Having clarified the relational aspect of her communication, they could decide a better way to structure the course of therapy. With this added information, the therapist could help the woman feel more in charge of therapy and how long it continued. Once the problem of involvement was solved, they could move on to more important issues.

Very often, families have unrealistic hopes regarding what a therapist can actually do for them. Sometimes they hope for a miracle; other times they may have hidden agendas that they are unable to make explicit. For example, an unfaithful spouse may come to marital counseling simply to assuage his or her guilt, having already decided to leave the marriage. Without ever intending to salvage the relationship, this client may hope that the therapist becomes someone for the abandoned spouse to lean on. However, the client may be unable to disclose that intention unless the family therapist raises the possibility first. Here, the hidden agenda has a great influence on the course of therapy, especially if it remains unknown to the family therapist. If it can become known, it may become the focus of therapy, since it is actually the primary motivation for seeking services. In another case, a single parent may seek family therapy for his or her child when the parent is still grieving the loss of the marriage. Here, the hidden agenda may not greatly affect the course of therapy, since divorce adjustment work could be done in a way that simultaneously benefits parent and child, but it might be helpful for the therapist to understand the implicit expectations to intervene in a broad enough way.

In addition, families often have ideas regarding who will actually be seen in sessions (the child alone, each spouse separately, etc.), how the problem will be defined, and what topics will or will not be discussed. While it is difficult to second-guess all the possible expectations, the therapist can try to join sufficiently so that families feel comfortable in disclosing even their most sensitive agendas (e.g., "I'm hoping you can tell me if my marriage is worth saving"). Sometimes it may help to make some tentative guesses about what clients may be expecting; other times it may only be necessary for the family therapist to provide a comfortable atmosphere for sharing all possible re-sponses. When the therapist suggests an acceptance of the most unusual, the family will be more forthcoming with hidden agendas.

Deciding whom to include in sessions is often difficult for the beginning family therapist. While some pioneers were noted for their insistence on see-ing the entire family (Boszormenyi-Nagy & Framo, 1965; Napier & Whitaker, 1978), others were noted for seeing individuals (Bowen, 1978). With such ap-parent diversity, the following questions may be helpful to the reader:

❋   *Who is defining the problem?*   If it is a spouse or parent not in at-tendance, involving that person is a priority.

❋   *Is the client living with significant others in the household or de-pendent on others in significant ways?*   If so, involving them as sources of in-formation and support should be strongly considered. It is important to engage spouses for such problems as depression, anxiety, and eating disorders. Many times, they are willing to come, but it simply did not occur to them. At other times, they may need to know they are not being blamed but rather are considered a positive influence on the healing process.

❋   *Does the client explicitly name others as a legal, psychological, fi-nancial, or relational part of the presenting problem?*   To ensure a peaceful resolution, the client must believe that the therapist can remain on his or her side while also engaging the other party. If convincing the client of this proves to be beyond the skill level of the clinician, working systemically may involve playing devil's advocate, developing interactional strategies, or asking ques-tions that provide multiple points of view.

❋   *Has the person definitely decided on a divorce?*   If not, informed consent could involve the information that individual sessions may contrib-ute to further distance in the marriage. Many times, one spouse who is reluc-tant to involve the other can clarify her or his own fears over including the husband or wife. Addressing these fears can become a preliminary goal until the person is assured that the therapist is able to conduct conjoint therapy in a manner that is comfortable for the reluctant spouse. The skill level of the therapist may be a factor in this issue, and later chapters address basic skills for conducting conjoint sessions.

❋   *Are there significant others who appear to have ongoing knowledge of the day-to-day occurrence of the problem?*   If so, a preliminary goal of gathering multiple points of view is important, even if those other parties are unwilling to attend. Many times, however, parties who are involved but not necessarily perceived as part of the problem may be willing to attend as consultants. When expectations can be addressed and respected, it is possible to involve a number of people as sources of information or support, as long as the clinician respects their position as nonclients (i.e., someone who is not asking for help or change).

❋   *If others were involved in sessions, would the person seeking help become more or less alienated in the process?*   Situations of violence, emotional abuse, and extreme alienation may be contraindications for involving other parties on whom the client may be dependent. The clinician's skill level, the client's goals, and other contributing circumstances need to be explored in total to determine the most beneficial course.

In clarifying intentions and making recommendations for the structure of therapy, it is important to remember C. Whitaker's (personal communication, 1986) assertion that "there is no such thing as a person without a relationship." However, in deciding on issues of structure, it is also important that the expectations of the client be fully known at the beginning to negotiate effectively without coercion.

Goals

Each individual (including the clinician) not only has personal expectations about the process of family therapy, but also brings both stated and privately held goals. Although similar to expectations, goals concern the actual problem that becomes defined and mutually understood as the focus of the therapeutic process. While expectations can often involve personal needs related to the nature and structure of the process, goals relate directly to what problem or issue is addressed and what is to be accomplished.

In the early years of family therapy, setting goals was a continual struggle. Clients came in asking for help with a child's behavior or their own predefined mental illness, but family therapists, anxious to convert their client–families to systemic thinking, were quick to persuade families to think of their child's behavior as a family problem or their mental illness as a marital problem. This approach only served to communicate blame to other family members, even though the intent of the family therapist was to develop a shared goal.

Today, many social constructionists speak of co-creating the definition of the problem (O'Hanlon & Weiner-Davis, 1989), and integrative models such as the PBFT model speak explicitly about avoiding resistance and respecting the family's uniqueness. By asking families to clarify what they would like to see happen in family therapy, therapists have the opportunity to rid themselves of any hidden agendas that might prevent the negotiation of mutually agreed-upon goals. Many times, families come to counseling with a definition that has been co-created by others in the system. As the therapeutic contract is negotiated, the therapist may be able to influence the definition of the problem away from a pathologized view. Sometimes families are relieved at this and are able to express their hopes and fears. However, if families feel strongly about a certain view of the presenting problem, family therapists must negotiate a cooperative relationship above all else rather than one that unwittingly becomes subtly adversarial. If the family's definition of the problem becomes an issue for the practitioner, he or she must take care to understand fully the importance of their views before designing interventions for later stages of therapy that might influence their perceptions. Consequently, in making the initial contract, the therapist explicitly accepts the family's definition of the problem while implicitly exploring possibilities for future change. In these instances, the therapist must be flexible and trusting enough to grant the clients a certain wisdom that demands further understanding. The clinician can often gain this understanding by engaging in more systematic data gathering.

❄ DATA GATHERING

The process of data gathering can occur in many formal and informal ways. Schools of family therapy provide a wide variety of distinctions regarding what type of information to gather and how to gather it. However, in keeping with our integrative theme, the goals of perceptual, behavioral, and relational change may be incorporated into the process of data gathering. From a systemic perspective, perceptual and behavioral change may be related to the levels of communication discussed previously: Perceptual data could be considered content; behavioral data could be considered process. Relational data could be considered as any of the common themes in Chapter Two. Therefore, data gathering can be conducted through observations and through questions that elicit information on micro and macro levels of experience. In addition, the clinician must decide whether to gather such information from the past, present, or future.

Content Versus Process

When family members come to therapy, they usually focus on the content of their concerns. Parents may say that their child does not come home on time or is hyperactive. A couple may describe their relationship as empty. The therapist listens to what family members say about each other (content) and is interested in how family members interact with each other (process). A distinguishing characteristic of family therapists is their interest in relational process rather than content alone. Therefore, the beginning practitioner must begin to gather data on multiple levels. Through observation, in-session interactions can reveal the nature of intrafamily relationships as well as the nature of the therapist–family relationship. Through questions and sequence tracking, the clinician also learns about out-of-session relationships and personal perceptions. As information is gathered regarding perceptions, behaviors, and relationships connected to the problem, the therapist may begin to develop hypotheses about which area of change is the most appropriate to target.

Communication theorists at the Mental Research Institute often look for myths or patterns of thought that may hinder problem resolution in the present. One of their concepts—the utopian syndrome—refers to problems that are defined as due to a client's idealistic view of how the world should be. For example, a widow hoping to cure her depression through therapy is helped to see that her depression is a natural response to loss and not a problem to be solved. It may actually be her response to her own grief that is the problem. Only in a utopia would humans fail to feel the impact of death and loss. To integrate with other dimensions, we can see that change might occur as a result of exploring the content of the client's thoughts and providing her with a new reality. This reality would then be a basis for helping her address her isolation from others.

Another concept—the solution becomes the problem—suggests that some presenting problems grow out of proportion when an attempted solution has an exacerbating effect. In this instance, the therapist can discover this phenomenon by tracking interactional sequences between people and gathering specific behavioral information about attempted solutions for the original problem. On the basis of these concepts, therapists help the client analyze the content of thoughts and the process of problem solving in the present so as to discover alternative solutions that were previously overlooked. Whether the clinician targets behavioral or perceptual change is often a matter of skill level and preference.

The Milan team's model balances attention to content and process. Their approach is based on the Batesonian concept that information regarding differences or comparisons within the family can bring about change in family life (e.g., the therapist might ask, "How are Mom and Dad different from each other?"). Some questions were designed as interventions to bring forth information (content) regarding the systemic functioning (process) of family members that was new or different from the family's normal way of viewing the problem (i.e., to reframe the situation). Informational interventions can be thought of as eliciting systemic insight into the therapeutic arena so that a family can view itself from a distance. This metaperspective, as articulated by the Milan team, often includes data gathering regarding family roles, rules, and beliefs that may be related to the life of the presenting problem. This information then becomes the basis for hypotheses and directives that affect out-of-session relational changes in a family.

Past, Present, Future

Among the many decisions a family therapist must make in conducting a session is whether to focus on the past, present, or future. Fleuridas, Nelson, and Rosenthal (1986) suggest that within each of these categories the therapist may examine "(a) differences or changes within the family between relationships, between beliefs or behaviors of family members, or between their family and other families; (b) agreements or disagreements between members; and (c) explanations of why relationships and interactions proceed as they do and the intended or perceived meanings of certain behaviors" (p. 119).

For many years, psychotherapy tended to focus primarily on the client's experience of the past. However, as family therapy began to offer new ways of thinking about mental and emotional problems, data-gathering strategies leaned away from focusing solely on past experience. Similarly, other therapists, such as Haley and Minuchin, recognized the importance of information regarding the family's current stage of life and focused their observations on present in-session behavior.

More recently, the historical approach has been expanded to include the integration of systemic thinking. For example, Framo's approach seeks information about past interactions and perceptions to understand the development of current relationships. Boszormenyi-Nagi gathers information about the past relationships between the child and his or her parents to understand the unconscious needs of parents. Systemic therapists, such as the Milan team, are often interested in tracking the life of the problem from the past into the present, with interventions focused on the client's ability to impact the future (Boscolo, Cecchin, Hoffman, & Penn, 1987).

While the past and present provide background information regarding the context of the program, the future becomes the stage for more flexible options. Herein lies another key concept for an integrated model of change. Regardless of whether data gathering focuses on past or present, the therapeutic direction is always future-oriented; the therapist facilitates hopeful connections between the original problem and future solutions. In later chapters, the reader will be helped to strike a balance between gathering information from the past and present. However, the balance must also include guiding families into "forward thinking" (White, 1986) by gathering data about projected perceptions and behaviors in the future. Positive possibilities may be evoked by such questions as, "What would you imagine your life to be like when you no longer have this problem?" or "What things would you like to be doing when this is no longer a problem?"

The process of data gathering illustrates how the family therapist is required to think about multiple levels of experience and alternate between levels to gather relevant information about the family system that contributes to positive change. Data gathering can be thought of both as an ongoing process that pervades all other stages of the therapeutic process and as an early formalized stage in some cases. In later chapters, skills for data gathering are presented in detail.

As the discussion illustrates, the family therapist must be able to think broadly about families and about how to help them change, whether it is broadly about time or broadly about levels of content and process. This ability to think broadly is also exemplified by the process of hypothesizing.

❄ HYPOTHESIZING

This term, which was used by the Milan team as a formal part of their strategic plan, best describes the individual and collective process by which conclusions are formulated about the data gathered. Hypothesizing comprises the way in which the individuals involved make sense of their experience; in other words, it encompasses what people think about what is going on and also the assumptions that they bring to the situation. As mentioned in Chapter One, specific theories often encourage family therapists to bring certain ideas with them to the therapeutic experience. However, these assumptions may limit their ability to see other possible realities. Just as data gathering can become theory-specific, so can the hypotheses generated by the therapy. Therefore, we want to encourage a style of hypothesizing that is creative and flexible rather than limiting and rigid. Instead of being told what to hypothesize, the beginning family therapist should learn to formulate a hypothesis and then test it through additional data gathering. By asking the right questions—"How do you know?" "What brought you to that conclusion?"—students and trainees can examine and test hypotheses rather than transform their hypotheses into unquestioned truths that may not fit their families' experiences.

Campbell, Draper, and Crutchley (1991) describe this process:

> *The hypothesis is described as a means of organizing the information available to the therapist in order to provide a guide to his or her activity in conducting a systemic interview. It is "neither true nor false," but rather "more or less useful" (Selvini Palazzoli et al., 1980b, p. 3). A hypothesis allows the therapist to search out new information, identify the connecting patterns, and move toward a systemic formulation of the family's behavior. In addition, an interview that is conducted from the basis of a systemic hypothesis allows the therapist to hold on to a view of the family's behavior that is different from the family's simply by being "a difference." The hypothesis, as it guides the interview, will introduce information and structure (or negentropy) into the family system, which tends toward repetitive patterns of behavior and diminishing appreciation of differences. (p. 328)*

The process of hypothesizing is also related to co-creating a definition of the problem. Certain theories generate certain static definitions of problems. However, family members often have their own definition, whether private or public, which has a bearing on how the family responds to therapy. More important than what the therapist thinks is what the family thinks and how the therapist interacts with them around these variant definitions. We submit that the majority of family therapy schools, while specifying certain assumptions about problem formation, become more unified in addressing the interactional process between family therapist and client. Therapist flexibility and the perception of client competencies become woven into the interactional fabric that ultimately determines which definition of the problem becomes shared by therapist and family.

In addition, most schools of family therapy share a basic hypothesis about physical and emotional problems. This hypothesis assumes that some relationship within the family or with some significant other (even a teacher, employer, or neighbor) is possibly part of the problem or, at least, a potential part of the solution. This relational hypothesis leads to the identification of relationship conditions that are important to consider. The following case is an example.

A man in his mid-fifties sought therapy for depression. His wife agreed to accompany him and be helpful. In pursuing a relational hypothesis, the therapist pursued the client's own description of his internal process and the couple's description of how they each responded to his depression. Instead of attempting to convince them that depression is really an interactional problem rather than an individual problem, the therapist chose to acknowledge the internal reality of the man's depression while exploring the couple's attempted solutions and their own interactional process. This discussion eventually led to the identification of perceptual and behavioral sequences that all agreed were problematic. The wife thought of her role as his emotional caregiver. Each time he expressed his despair ("I feel lousy"), she tried to make him feel better ("Cheer up and look on the bright side"). To him, these responses were implicit disagreements with his internal experience. Feeling misunderstood, he became more entrenched in his own position.

As the therapist helped them examine and change this interactional pattern, the man was not robbed of his internal experience and his wife was not blamed for his depression. Instead, they were directed toward a plan that could facilitate the healing process. In this instance, the result was a lifting of the depression as the spouses began to cooperate in a new way. However, had the depression persisted, the couple, equipped with new relational skills, could then pursue additional solutions with their relationship strengthened rather than strained. In this case, the hypotheses of the client were included in an expanded definition of the problem, which grew to include relational factors. Since the couple's hypotheses about the depression had included such things as the man's job change and a strained relationship with his only daughter, these were easily incorporated by becoming the content that their new relational process could address more effectively.

Another relational hypothesis deals with a universal concern for all therapists: what some call resistance. Interpreted as an individual issue, resistance is often described as client rigidity or lack of cooperation. However, a relational hypothesis of resistance suggests an interactional definition that involves the therapist as a participant in the problem. Such a hypothesis helps the beginning family therapist examine his or her own interactional process with the client rather than merely indicting the client alone. Interactional hypotheses can help the practitioner change perceptions and behaviors that may have unwittingly elicited resistant behavior. Like the wife of the depressed man, many family therapists can learn how to be more helpful by examining and changing their part of certain problematic sequences.

❄ SPECIFIC INTERVENTIONS

Specific strategies—behaviors such as questions and directives—should not be thought of as the sole mechanism of change. Our belief is that all the interactions of the therapeutic process discussed in this chapter are important and legitimate interventions in themselves. For example, the family therapist should avoid the temptation to think of the joining process as something that is done before treatment begins. Likewise, examining the referral process is not some preliminary adjunct to therapy but, in some cases, may become the focal point of many sessions to come.

It is helpful to conceptualize the earlier sequences of the process as specific interventions to address specific issues, whereas formalized interventions represent a less strictly defined stage that might take many different creative forms as a logical extension of data gathering and hypothesizing. This process may then be understood as a sequence: Incoming information (data gathering) leads to certain assumptions (hypotheses), which lead to certain actions from the family therapist (interventions) related to the presenting problem. Simple interventions such as questions, directives, and reframing often require minimal data gathering and hypothesizing. Other interventions require more extensive data gathering and could be regarded as more elaborate directives (e.g., experiential exercises, psychoeducation, conflict resolution, communication training, rituals, paradox, and perceptual or behavioral tasks). These specific skills, addressed in later chapters, are only a sampling of the choices that can be made as the clinician gains an understanding of the family's developmental level. We now consider a process that is crucial in determining the developmental level and, ultimately, what is most helpful to the family—evaluation.

❄ Evaluation

This is another process that is informally taking place all the time regardless of whether the family therapist provides the opportunity for family members to formally express themselves. As a process, evaluation can be thought of as each party's response to the larger question of fit: What best fits this client? Implicit and explicit evaluations influence the therapeutic contract to clarify expectations and to develop mutually agreed-upon goals. The beginning family therapist is encouraged to seek explicit feedback from the family to avoid impasses and misunderstandings. Coleman (1985) makes the point that changes in goals that have not been negotiated cooperatively with families can sometimes lead to treatment failures. It is important for the practitioner to learn how to benefit from honest client feedback to make midcourse corrections. Clients' responses to an assigned task can always be an implicit message about whether the task was helpful or relevant to them.

As with many of the other stages of family therapy, this interactional process may occur in microinteractions, as the therapist asks clients, "When I said _____ just now, how did you take it?" Or it can occur as part of a crossroads in the course of therapy, as a therapist says, "We seem to have been discussing _____ the last few sessions. I'm wondering if you think this is helpful or whether we should consider a different direction." Such explicit initiatives toward evaluation respect the clients' role as the consumer, as the ultimate authority on their own lives, and reminds the family therapist that the ultimate evaluator is the clients' perception of helpfulness. While external evaluators such as court systems or schools may sometimes participate in the definition of a problem, the eventual progress made by families in therapy is heavily influenced by the family's evaluation of the therapist's helpfulness. When the beginning practitioner overcomes the fear of being evaluated, he or she discovers that eliciting the family's evaluation is also an intervention that can facilitate change.

These seven interactions, while not strictly occurring in a consistent sequential pattern, nevertheless serve as a guide to help the beginning family therapist anticipate and initiate certain basic interactions that maintain and strengthen the nature of the therapist–client relationship. The first three—referral, joining, and creating a therapeutic contract—can be thought of as broken into smaller parts: data gathering, hypothesizing, intervention, and evaluation. Subsequently, these four processes can also be thought of as a progressive sequence that recurs throughout the middle and later phases of therapy.

We believe that many of these elements are overlooked in traditional literature because specific models often adopt the goal of educating the reader about a theory. In addition, experienced theoreticians and clinicians often become intent on illustrating specific techniques in isolation from the natural ongoing flow of the family therapy experience. Rather than dwelling on the specifics of concepts and theory, this overview of family therapy practice has reviewed key processes that will help the reader through the remaining chapters on specific skill development.

To summarize, the practice of family therapy can be thought of as a series of interactional processes that take place between flexible, competence-based clinicians who employ four basic skills: questions, tracking sequences, reframing, and directives. Using these skills, they proceed through a relational process with individuals and families that targets behavioral and perceptual changes in the clients' personal relationships. Like all relationships, the therapeutic relationship evolves through developmental stages as clinician and family discover new definitions of their problem and corresponding solutions. The family therapist organizes the structure of therapy, joins with each family member, and gathers information that focuses on the family's potential for change. As new information emerges, the therapist develops interventions that match the family's developmental level and the therapist's skill level. As these interactions unfold over time, each side of the transaction—family and therapist—is reviewing and reacting to the process and evaluating the impact and the results of their encounters. The next step is deciding how to integrate and order these elements in a given session with clients.

❄ In-Session Stages of Family Therapy

As the trainee prepares to practice, we think it is helpful to develop a plan that provides a sense of direction. Many models have their own protocols for conducting each session. For example, Todd and Selekman (1991), in their work on adolescent substance abuse, provide a useful model for integrating structural-strategic family therapy with narrative and solution-focused approaches. They recommend starting with the traditional practices of structural-strategic approaches and implementing narrative, solution-focused, or paradoxical modes of practice when impasses occur.

Breunlin, Schwartz, and Mac Kune-Karrer (1992) write about "transcending" the model approach to family therapy. They avoid putting any particular model first. Instead, they provide an inclusive model for integration that weaves collaborative and flexible "presuppositions" with various "metaframeworks" to organize theory. They view family therapy as a set of interactions that involves conversing, hypothesizing, planning, and feedback. In their work, change may happen at the level of action or meaning. They argue for the integration of these elements of change rather than assuming an either/or position.

A comparison of their work and the elements identified here may help readers refine their understanding of the practice of family therapy. In examining basic concepts, differences between these two works tend to center around the order and language of ideas. As illustrated in Table 4.1, similarities with our concepts can be found in some form for every category in the metaframeworks approach. We are not suggesting that there is complete agreement between categories. Each metaframework is developed in a complete chapter and represents a synthesis of many approaches that have influenced Bruenlin et al. However, many of these ideas are compatible with our own. For example, the metaframework of organization uses terms such as *leadership* and

Table 4.1

Metaframeworks	Chapter Two: Integration of Theory
Presuppositions	
Human systems are multileveled.	Macro to micro
Change occurs through collaboration to remove constraints.	
The mind can access multiple realities.	
Power is construed as leadership, balance, and harmony	Family structure
Hypothesizing	
Internal process	Individual experience
Sequences	Family structure Intergenerational relationships Individual experience
Development	Transitions and development Individual experience
Organization	Family structure
Culture	Race and culture
Gender	Gender
Conversing	
Statements	
Questions	
Directives	
Planning	
Relating	
Staging	
Creating events	
Feedback	
Targets for Change	
Action	
Meaning	

Chapter Three: Integration of Practice	Chapter Four: Sequences and Interactions
Knowledge and concepts Perceptions and attitudes	
Therapeutic change Therapeutic relationship Perception of competence	
Therapist flexibility Reframing	
Tracking interactional sequences	Data gathering Specific interventions
	Hypothesizing
	Data gathering Specific interventions
Tracking interactional sequences	Data gathering Specific interventions
Naturalistic change Questions	
Questions Directives	Data gathering Specific interventions
Questions	Data gathering
Questions	Data gathering
Behaviors	
Reframing	
Questions	Data gathering
Directives	
Behaviors	Hypothesizing
Therapeutic relationship	Joining process
	Referral process Therapeutic contract
Questions Directives	Specific interventions
	Evaluation
Behavioral change	
Relational change	
Perceptual change	

influence rather than *hierarchy* and *boundaries*. This is a clear and flexible application related to the concept of structure.

While Breunlin et al. (1992) provide a comprehensive and thorough integration of the concepts of marriage and family therapy, their approach suggests that the circular and evolutionary nature of family therapy practice defies a preconceived order to the process. Although they suggest a "blueprint" for therapy, their guidelines encourage the reader to consider all components, yet to avoid pursuing any one direction too long. Their suggestions seem more suited for intermediate practice and those who have mastered basic elements of the therapeutic process.

The integrative approach we suggest builds on common themes from family process and common elements from practice that we have identified. It is based on our review of family therapy literature and personal experiences with minority and agency-based populations. The order assumes that some interactions occur simultaneously, such as joining and data gathering, because we assume the therapist should always be working on the therapeutic relationship and should always be inquisitive. We also think the process is more manageable if each session is divided into steps or stages. Each step may focus on one element (e.g., joining) or it may contain a combination of elements (e.g., data gathering related to race and culture for the purpose of reframing). The following is our recommendation for ordering the elements that have been discussed thus far. Drawing on the previous discussion about various types of change, we recommend that each session contain the following discussions, in sequence, if possible. This series of discussions should address the tasks of negotiating structure, exploring client experience, addressing relationships, and developing a shared direction.

Negotiate Structure

In an initial interview (see Chapter Six), the professional should take responsibility for exploring what family therapy will be for an individual or family, how it will be organized, and how decisions will be made about the process. In subsequent sessions, discussions about the organization, expectations, and purpose of each meeting should be summarized at the outset to provide an avenue for client or therapist to ask for changes in the structure of the process. For example, if certain members are absent, the impact of this fact must be explored and a decision made as to how the process will proceed in light of this change. These discussions should highlight leadership in the family as it relates to the session. In the event that a crisis has occurred between meetings, this stage could provide an avenue to decide what from the previous meeting is or is not still relevant. Since this is the first stage of each meeting, it can be thought of as a minicontract for that session.

Explore Client Experience

Each session should afford all participants the opportunity to respond to questions about their thoughts, feelings, actions, intentions, and senses. This discussion should elicit interactional sequences and describe the development of each person's perception of the crisis, problem, or issue over time. As therapy proceeds from session to session, systemic themes (e.g., transitions, intergenerational process, gender, etc.) can be chosen as the focus of these explorations (see Chapters Two and Seven). Often, families can say which systemic themes are most relevant to them. Discussions can also include pragmatic reviews of attempted solutions, the identification of behaviors related to success, or the telling of stories that form the basis of a client's worldview. If individuals are seen alone, we recommend that systemic therapists ask about the experience of significant others not present. By including a variety of views in the discussion, the process remains tied to relational factors and maintains a broader view of the interactional context.

Address Relationships

As individuals' experiences form a collective picture of behaviors, perceptions, and relationships, a therapeutic dialogue should develop in which the practitioner tentatively questions or suggests new possibilities or realities based on existing information (see Chapters Two and Eight). Specific interventions from preferred models can be introduced during this stage. If a person is seen individually, interactions should still maintain a focus on relationships, not behaviors or perceptions alone. As clients respond to these suggestions, the clinician should explore whether that particular direction is resonating well with family members or whether additional reflections should be added to the dialogue. When given a choice, we have seen clients respond with their own preference for behavioral or perceptual changes related to their significant relationships. For example, when questioned about whether she preferred a therapy experience in which she was encouraged to make specific behavioral changes to one in which she was able to reflect on various aspects of her situation, one woman chose the reflective mode. The therapist first used questions to reflect on her family's genogram and then suggested the possibility of discovering new patterns. After 4 weeks, the woman reported an incident of spontaneous behavior change at a routine family gathering.

Table 4.2   Integrative Components of Each Session

	Structural	Experiential
Purpose	To organize each session	To understand client experience
Interactional Processes	Referral process (first session) Joining process Data gathering Evaluation Therapeutic contract	Joining process Data gathering Evaluation
Behaviors	Questions Tracking interactional sequences	Questions Tracking interactional sequences
Knowledge and Concepts	Naturalistic change Therapeutic relationship	Naturalistic change Behavioral change Perceptual change
Perceptions and Attitudes	Perception of client competence Therapist flexibility	Perception of client competence Therapist flexibility
Theoretical Themes: Micro to Macro	Family structure Individual experience	Individual experience Transitions and development Intergenerational relationships Race and culture Gender

Develop a Shared Direction

The therapist searches for language, metaphors, themes, or goals that unite family members in forward motion (see Chapter Nine). Once certain interventions are introduced, questions should focus on a "meta"-analysis to determine how each person feels about the process and to discuss any misgivings that arise. These dialogues about direction should provide clients with a summary of the therapist's perceptions of the current session and an opportunity to summarize their perceptions. As a shared understanding develops about the session (metacommunication), goals or suggestions for the next session can be negotiated to address the interests of all members. These decisions should be summarized in the negotiation of structure at the beginning of the next session to allow for a change to be requested by any party in the process.

Relational	Directional
To intervene relationally	To develop a shared purpose
Joining process Data gathering Hypothesizing Specific interventions	Joining process Data gathering Specific interventions Evaluation
Reframing Directives	Reframing Questions Directives
Therapeutic change Relational change	Naturalistic change
Perception of client competence Therapist flexibility	Perception of client competence Therapist flexibility
Family structure Intergenerational relationships Race and culture Gender	Individual experience Transitions and development

These four stages can be referred to as structural, experiential, relational, and directional. They suggest that the family therapist should organize treatment clearly and collaboratively, should explore experience and context from the micro- to the macrolevel, and should pursue behavioral, perceptual, and relational change and work toward a sense of direction that includes the needs of all significant participants. We believe these dimensions provide a map to integrate theory and practice. Table 4.2 illustrates how they coordinate themes and interactions of family therapy process. The family therapy skills covered in the remainder of the book can also be thought of as part of this map. With these four objectives in mind, we now proceed to skill development in each stage.

As we conclude this section devoted to connections between theory and practice, we leave the "parking lot" of training and proceed onto busy streets and highways. (Perhaps we should say that the rubber hits the road!) It is here that countless variations—from new surroundings to road construction—challenge the driver with endless and ongoing surprises. Even the most experienced of drivers knows that the roads of life never stay the same. Thus, adaptability and the application of skills learned over time provide the driver with a way to manage variety. In addition, the activity once referred to as driving a car can now be transformed into many different activities such as going shopping, traveling to Louisville, or racing. Remaining sections of the book provide the driver with skills that apply to a variety of situations and driving conditions. Bon voyage!

Part Two

STRUCTURAL
AND EXPERIENTIAL
SKILLS

Chapter Five

ORGANIZING THE INTAKE PROCESS

REFERRAL INFORMATION

CLINICAL INFORMATION

PREVIOUS THERAPY

FAMILY INFORMATION

SCHEDULING INFORMATION

FORMULATING INITIAL HYPOTHESES

Gathering intake information is crucial to the effectiveness of the initial interview. Wright and Leahey (1984) pay specific attention to the telephone contact preceding the first interview, suggesting that this first contact can have great impact on the course of subsequent contacts. The initial telephone contact has also been an issue of note for other clinicians, many of whom have developed guidelines and strategies for addressing systemic dynamics with the earliest possible contact (Brock & Barnard, 1988; Napier & Whitaker, 1978; Selvini Palazzoli, Boscolo, Cecchin, & Prata, 1978). For family therapists working in agency settings, there may already be an intake process established over which the practitioner has little control. If this is the case, the initial interview may serve as an opportunity to reconcile differences between the process recommended here and that of the practice setting. Another solution to this problem is for the clinician to make an additional telephone contact after the agency intake and before the first session; the family therapist can then provide important direction before the first meeting. For others who have the discretion to structure client contact according to their own preference, this chapter may serve as a step-by-step guide to the beginning stages of family therapy.

Colapinto (1991) further elaborates:

> *Assessment begins with the information gathered during an initial telephone call or by reading an intake sheet. On the basis of simple, concrete information, such as the composition of the family and the ages of its members, as well as more subtle data, such as who makes the initial call and how that person describes the family problems, the therapist generates his or her first impressions about the family's "shape" and some of the possible strengths and weaknesses. These initial hypotheses are invaluable in guiding the first contacts of the therapist with the family, even if they may have to be discarded quickly at that point. (p. 431)*

The intake interview is generally conducted by telephone and includes the following categories of information: (a) referral information, (b) clinical information, (c) previous therapy, (d) family information, and (e) scheduling information. Box 5.1 provides an overview for gathering intake information. After the information is gathered, the family therapist may begin to develop initial hypotheses regarding the nature of the problem.

❄ REFERRAL INFORMATION

It is critical to get full names, addresses, and phone numbers for each member of the family. A distinction should be made between the client of record (per-

BOX 5.1
Steps of the Intake Interview

Referral Information
1. Specify names, addresses, and phone numbers.
2. Identify referral source and the relationship between family and referral source.

Clinical Information
3. Get a brief description of the problem and any recent changes in the family.
4. Ask how the problem is affecting other family members.

Previous Therapy
5. Ask if any family members have been involved in previous therapy.
6. Are there other informal helpers who have positive or negative effects on the family?

Family Information
7. Identify family members and others who are related to the problem.
8. Are there additional extended family members who have strong feelings about the problem?

Scheduling Information
9. Ask for other relevant parties (e.g., spouses, additional children, referral source, extended family, significant friends) to attend the first session.
10. Specify date, time of appointment, and location of facility.

son who makes the call) and other family members (partner or children). This is particularly true in divorced and remarried families where members are living apart. If the family doesn't have a phone, it's important to obtain a phone number of a relative or neighbor who is in regular contact with the family. This information helps identify who else is involved with the family.

Referral sources should also be identified. Family therapists may receive referrals from various sources, including school counselors, psychologists, social workers, previous clients, and family members involved in the problem (self-referral). When a family is referred by an outside agency (e.g., a court or school), they may be suspicious and less willing to attend the initial session. This is particularly true when families are forced to attend therapy by a probation officer or the court (Boyd-Franklin, 1989). If professional referral sources (e.g., social workers or school counselors) make the initial contact, they should be made aware of the family therapist's role and how to make a referral.

If referral sources are aware of overt conflict between their view of the problem and the family's view, they should be encouraged to develop a collaborative understanding with the family before making the referral. If they consider the difference of opinion irreconcilable, referral sources should be encouraged to emphasize the family therapist's independence to minimize client defensiveness. In such cases, the role of the family therapist may involve resolving conflict between the family and the larger system. That role can be carried out effectively only when family therapists establish a stated position of neutrality with respect to the referral source and of support with respect to the family.

When interacting with the referral source, therapists should gather information about the problem and the referral source's attempts to alleviate it. Weber, McKeever, and McDaniel (1985) suggest that it is important to determine what the referring person is requesting (e.g., consultation for self or therapy for the family). The following dialogue illustrates these issues with professional referral sources:

> *Case manager:*   I need your help with a family our agency is involved with. Can I talk to you about them?
>
> *Family therapist:*   Sure. What seems to be the problem?
>
> *Case manager:*   Well, the husband attends our Adult Day Center and has Alzheimer's. I've been trying to get his wife to start planning for his long-term care needs, but she says they're doing fine and she doesn't need anything like that. She's really in denial.
>
> *Family therapist:*   What type of help did you have in mind? Are you looking for a consultation for yourself or therapy for them?
>
> *Case manager:*   I really think they need therapy. We just haven't gotten anywhere with them.
>
> *Family therapist:*   Have you discussed this idea with them?
>
> *Case manager:*   Yes. The wife said she would be willing to talk to you.
>
> *Family therapist:*   Okay. Tell me what you said to her and the reasons you gave for recommending that she come here.
>
> *Case manager:*   I told her that I was concerned about her future with her husband's illness and I thought it would be a good idea if she talked to someone about her options.

Family therapist: How did she respond to this?

Case manager: She said, if I thought it was necessary, she would be willing to come.

Family therapist: Did you mention earlier that you don't think you've gotten anywhere with them?

Case manager: Yes. She just won't look at the future.

Family therapist: Well, I wonder if we could think of this as a difference of opinion between the two of you. You want her to look at the future and she doesn't want to.

Case manager: Well, I suppose you could say that.

Family therapist: If this is the case, she may respond to me in the same way she has been responding to you, unless I'm able to establish a position with her that is independent of yours. Do you think you could raise the issue of this difference between you and explain that I will be a neutral third party?

Case manager: Yes. I can do that. I told her I'd call her back after I talked to you.

Family therapist: Good. Why don't you describe me as someone who is interested in her point of view? Then, you and I should come to an understanding about my role. I've found that I can often help people reach a resolution by increasing their understanding of each other. Would you be open to additional information that might help alleviate your present concerns?

Case manager: Oh, yes. If you can just get her to open up, that would really help.

In this instance, the family therapist should be prepared for the client to be cooperative but not necessarily motivated to pursue the case manager's agenda. However, because the social worker has been prepared for a new agenda—that of increasing their understanding of each other—the family therapist will not be hindered by the previous misunderstandings between referral source and client. Very likely, the goal that the client will be most motivated to pursue is one that enables her to feel more support from the case manager and more freedom to manage her life as she wishes.

When callers are family members, the therapist should determine what role the referral source might have in the definition of the problem. The Milan team recommends that family members who call as the referral source be considered as the client of record. If the family member wants to be excluded from the initial interview, the therapist should refuse to see the family (Selvini Palazzoli, 1985).

With self-referrals, it is recommended that others (referral sources, caregivers) who are related to the problem be asked to attend the initial session to present their view of the problem. However, if the client is uncomfortable with this suggestion, the family therapist can seek a release of information from the family to communicate with the person making the referral. If the referral source does not attend the initial session, the therapist can make permitted contact to (a) understand the source's perception of the problem, (b) clarify what the source wants to happen, and (c) clarify how information should be provided to the referring source (Weber et al., 1985). Likewise, significant others (e.g., friends and relatives) who are concerned with the problem and who can provide support to the family should be encouraged to attend the initial session.

Once information about the problem has been gathered, an agreement should be reached about how treatment information should be shared. Court referrals often require periodic reports summarizing the progress of treatment. School counselors and teachers may want to know how the child is progressing so that they can support these changes. In many cases, families may request a report or evaluation of their progress. If the case is court-ordered, the family must be informed regarding the therapist's responsibility to the court. However, in cases where there is no legal obligation to report, the intake worker should advise the referral source that the family has legal control over what information is shared. The intake worker should make a note of this issue, instructing the therapist to discuss these questions with the family.

❄ CLINICAL INFORMATION

It is important to get a concise statement of the problem. When family members call, they are giving their view of the problem. Often, family members express concern through the use of labels. For instance, they may state feelings of "depression" or "anxiety" or refer to a child as "out of control." While these labels offer a general indication of the problem area, they have different meanings for different people. Therefore, it is important to get concrete examples for each label. For instance, "out of control" may mean that the child "doesn't come home on time."

Likewise, the intake person should ask how the problem is affecting other family members. For example, if a mother calls and reports that her teenage son is "out of control," it is important to determine how his behavior is affecting her or, if she is married, her relationship with her husband. She may report that she and her husband "disagree about how to handle this problem" or she may report that her husband is the only one who can handle him. Finally, it is important to summarize the referring family member's view of the problem ("So you see the problem as your son being 'out of control,' that he won't come home when you tell him, and that you and your husband don't agree about how to handle him").

A brief dialogue illustrates how intake information can be gathered from the referral person:

> *Intake worker:*   Can you give me a brief description of the problem?
>
> *Referral person:*   My husband and I are not getting along.
>
> *Intake worker:*   Can you tell me what is going on that makes you feel that way?
>
> *Referral person:*   We never go out. We just don't seem to have anything in common since Laura, our daughter, left for college.

It's important to note that the intake worker questioned the referral person immediately following her description of the problem. Therapists should train intake workers to get a quick and concise description of the problem.

It is also helpful to obtain information about previous marriages, divorce dates, recent deaths, illnesses, and any other significant changes that have occurred in the family system. This information may be useful in formulating hypotheses, particularly if a marriage has followed soon after a divorce or there have been other significant changes in rapid succession.

❄ PREVIOUS THERAPY

Assessing previous therapy helps determine what works and what doesn't work. Noting prior therapy on the intake sheet alerts the therapist to ask about those experiences. This information helps the therapist determine how the family viewed the previous therapy. If a family left therapy because the therapist wanted to focus on the marriage rather than the child, the therapist knows not to focus on the marriage (i.e., not to make the same mistakes as previous therapists). In addition, if any family members are currently in therapy, the therapist can ask the family to sign a release so that information and services may be coordinated.

After determining the effects of previous therapy, family therapists should ask about others who may have offered help or shared opinions about the problem in the past—friends, neighbors, clergy, or extended family members. What suggestions have they made? How does the family feel about these informal helpers? If such parties have significant influences with the family, it may be wise to ask about the possibility of their inclusion in the first session.

❄ FAMILY INFORMATION

Family information includes names of the client of record and partner or spouse, birth dates, level of education, and place of employment or school. Blank lines are also included for the children. It is critical to determine who is living in the home as well as those who are related to the problem. This information helps determine who will attend the first session. All family members who live in the household should be asked to attend this session. If the contact person is unwilling to bring the whole family to the initial session, then treatment options may vary. Therapists could meet with family members who are most concerned about the problem, or they may insist that all family members must attend therapy. However, when significant others are excluded from the process, family therapists must ask questions during the assessment process to bring to light information about the missing parties' points of view and how much influence they have on other family members. Then, as understanding increases about each person's position in the system, the therapist should look for opportunities to address the exclusion of key family members and negotiate their subsequent inclusion. Such strategies are addressed in Chapter Six.

❄ SCHEDULING INFORMATION

It is helpful to know scheduling requirements (times available to be seen) and who will be attending the first session. Intake workers should be instructed to encourage all family members living in the home to attend the first session.

Once this information is gathered, an appointment date should be set for the family. The date, time, and location of counseling should be provided. Families should be instructed when to arrive and be given all relevant information about the intake procedure and fees. The family should also be made aware of the cancellation policy if there is one.

Often, family members making the appointment may be hesitant to invite others to the first session. They may report that their spouse's work schedule prohibits attendance or that they are reluctant to impose on extended family members not living in the home. As mentioned previously, some may also sense an adversarial relationship with the referral source and refuse to include that person. In these instances, family therapists should prioritize the various parties who could be included. All family members living in the household are the highest priority; next are influential extended family; and last are referral sources. If the client of record has objections to all three possibilities, household members should become the primary focus. When the client is a single adult living alone, it is often best to proceed with the initial interview individually. During this time, the clinician can determine who the significant others are and how others might be successfully included (see Chapter Six).

The following intake dialogue illustrates how the interviewer might address the reluctance to include other members of the household:

Intake worker: Is your husband willing to attend the first session with you?

Wife: Well, I don't know. He told me that he is perfectly happy and that it's my problem.

Intake worker: What do you think about his assessment?

Wife: He's probably right. He usually is.

Intake worker: So, what do you think would happen if you asked him to come?

Wife: I don't think he would come.

Intake worker: Have you ever been afraid that he would become violent with you?

Wife: Oh, no! He would never do anything like that. He's just stubborn.

Intake worker: Let's think about some other issues for a moment. Even if he agreed to come, can you think of some ways that you might be more uncomfortable if he was included?

Wife: Well, I guess I would probably clam up. I don't like to make him mad, and every time I bring up how I feel, he gets mad.

Intake worker: So you're afraid that things would go just like they do at home?

Wife: Yes.

Intake worker: I see. You may be right. I'm wondering if you might be able to tolerate that possibility to get the very best help.

Wife: What do you mean?

Intake worker: Our family therapists generally find their greatest success when they are able to hear all sides of the question. Even if your husband thinks the problem is yours, it would help the therapist to understand your husband's point of view. That way, since you plan on staying married, she could give you the kind of direction that would be good for you and your relationship. Sometimes, therapists give suggestions that seem good for the person, but that turn out to threaten their marriage in some way.

Wife: But I don't know how to make him come in.

Intake worker: Would it be possible for you to simply quote me? You could tell him, "The intake worker at the agency says your opinion is important to the process to help me with my feelings. He knows you're not seeking any help right now, but he'd like to know if you would at-tend a session and give your opinion about what you think my problem is. He says it's customary for the therapist to meet the person's spouse before proceeding with individual work. Would you be willing to at-tend the first session with me?"

Wife: Okay. I'll try. What if he still won't come?

Intake worker: Let us know what happens and we'll ask your as-signed therapist to contact you for further direction.

In this dialogue, the intake worker explores the reluctance from the hus-band's and the wife's points of view. Although the wife was focused more on her husband's reluctance, her own unspoken reluctance may be a significant factor as well. Without trying to change the husband's mind (something the wife may do repetitively), the intake worker suggests a rationale that meets her overall goal (help) without escalating the conflict between them. If the in-take process reveals the presence of violence in the relationship or the wife's intention to follow through with divorce, the initial interview may be conducted individually, unless the therapist has advanced training in how to engage violent men in therapy (Jenkins, 1991).

❄ FORMULATING INITIAL HYPOTHESES

The information gathered from the initial telephone contact helps the therapist formulate initial hypotheses by assessing whether the family's evolving structure (organization) is appropriate for their particular developmental stage. For example, a young couple seeks therapy, each complaining that the other places their career above their marriage. The following hypotheses are all possible views of the problem:

1. They have not learned to negotiate closeness or distance in their relationship—a major developmental task of the beginning family.
2. They did not successfully clarify beliefs, roles, and expectations—a developmental task of courtship and mate selection.
3. Over time, there has been some structural change in their relationship that they cannot understand or resolve.
4. Their communication and problem-solving styles have not brought about successful conflict resolution (more of the same or the solution becomes the problem).

The therapist can pursue each of these hypotheses until concrete information eliminates or verifies them. In addition, the system can be assessed as to whether interactional change (the way they behave) or cognitive change (the way they think) will be the focus of the therapist's interventions.

In addition, hypotheses about the nature of the problem can be generated:

1. Is the problem situational, transitional, or chronic?
2. Does the family need help in solving a specific problem ("We're fighting constantly") or in tolerating an uncomfortable adjustment in their life ("We just filed for bankruptcy and both of us must work longer hours to catch up")?

Hanna (1997) has noted that *situational* problems are new conflicts with no preexisting history. *Transitional* problems are related to normative life stages in families that have had successes in earlier stages, but have been unable to complete a current stage's adaptation in a normative period of time. *Chronic* problems are those that can be traced to difficulties that may have started as situational many years ago, persisted through a transitional time period, and now have such an extensive history that they have become an organizing influence on additional emerging problems. By placing the problem in its developmental context, the clinician can begin to hypothesize about what therapeutic posture will be most helpful to the family. In general, we have found that the more chronic the problem, the more indirect the solution. The differences between direct and indirect interventions are discussed in Chapter Nine. By approaching the initial session with an array of questions to be answered, the family therapist can be directive in providing a structure for the interview, while remaining tentative enough to allow the uniqueness of the family to emerge.

Box 5.2 is a sample intake interview form. Box 5.3 presents sample case material on the intake form. From the information in Box 5.3, the following hypotheses can be generated prior to the initial session:

1. A rapid remarriage may have left no time for the new marital subsystem to successfully organize parenting responsibilities or for the biological parents to resolve custody and visitation issues.
2. There may be divorce-adjustment and grief issues lingering for Robert and his mother.
3. There may be conflict between Jerry and Robert.
4. There may be some historical interactions between Robert and his mother that have become an ongoing pattern.

While there are additional possibilities, these serve as examples of developmental, structural, and interactional hypotheses that family therapists can use to begin their exploration of the family. These hypotheses provide a sense of direction until other information is available. Once the initial interview occurs, these hypotheses may be eliminated or expanded with additional information. For example, in the first session, the therapist may discover that Jerry works many evenings, leaving little opportunity for conflict with Robert. However, when he is home, Robert seems to respond more obediently to Jerry than to his mother. This information may eliminate Hypothesis 3 and strengthen Hypothesis 1, 2, or 4.

Whereas the family therapist gathers much factual information from the intake interview, the initial interview, which we consider next, is an opportunity for more personal and involved interactions between therapist and family.

BOX 5.2
Intake Form

Date _____

Referral information

Client of record   Last _____   First _____   Mid. _____

Partner/Spouse   Last _____   First _____   Mid. _____

Street _____   City _____   State ___   Zip _____

Phone #s: Home _____   Work _____

Other _____   Phone _____

Referral source: Org. _____   Name _____

Phone _____   Status _____

Clinical information

Problem description _____

_____

_____

_____

Previous relationships: Client of record _____   Dates _____

Partner/Spouse _____   Dates _____

Current marriage date: _____

Previous therapy

Name	Org.	Address	Dates
_____	_____	_____	_____
_____	_____	_____	_____
_____	_____	_____	_____

Family information

First name	Last name	Birth date	Ed.	Employ/School
_____	_____	_____	_____	_____
_____	_____	_____	_____	_____
_____	_____	_____	_____	_____
_____	_____	_____	_____	_____

Scheduling information

Appointment date _____   Time _____   Therapist _____

BOX 5.3
Completed Intake Form

Date 5/13/95

Referral information

Client of record   Last Russell   First Barbara   Mid. S.

Partner/Spouse   Last Russell   First Jerry   Mid. L.

Street 2553 Hawthorne Ave.   City Batesville   State IN   Zip 47006

Phone #s: Home 451-8484   Work 276-3533

Other _____   Phone _____

Referral source: Org. Hawthorne Elem.   Name school counselor

Phone _____   Status inactive case

Clinical information

Problem description Mrs. Russell stated that her son, Robert, is failing the 4th grade. He also resists rules at home. This started after her remarriage last year. She thinks Robert is depressed about being away from his biological father who moved out of state last year.

Previous relationships: Client of record widowed   Dates spouse died 3 yrs ago

Partner/Spouse divorced   Dates married 1980, div. 1991

Current marriage date: October 1991

Previous therapy

Name	Org.	Address	Dates
Mrs. Russell	The Family Ctr.	1337 W. Main St.	May, 1990
			2–3 sessions

Family information

First name	Last name	Birth date	Ed.	Employ/School
Barbara	Russell	9-1-43	H.S.	Sec., Ford Motors
Jerry	Russell	10-5-40	H.S.	Sales, Lincoln Ins.
Robert	Starks	10-10-82	4th gr.	Hawthorne

Scheduling information

Appointment date 5-20-95   Time 4 pm   Therapist Jim Austin

Chapter Six

THE INITIAL INTERVIEW: PROVIDING STRUCTURE

JOINING
Methods of Joining
Identifying Family Strengths

EXPLORING THE REFERRAL PROCESS

DECIDING WHOM TO INVOLVE

DEFINING THE PROBLEM
Assessing Clients' Definitions of the Problem
Tracking Interactional Sequences
Enacting the Interactional Sequence

SETTING GOALS

DEVELOPING THERAPEUTIC CONTRACTS
Describing the Therapeutic Process
Finalizing the Contract

SUMMARY

QUESTIONS THAT BEGINNING CLINICIANS OFTEN ASK
1. How Should I Handle the Issue of Alcohol If I Suspect It Is a Part of the Problem?
2. How Should I Deal With a Suicide Threat?
3. What Should I Do If I Discover Family Violence?
4. How Should I Handle Family Secrets?

A review of family therapy literature reveals that several approaches share some elements of the initial interview. Breunlin (1985) noted a beginning phase of family therapy in which the therapist organizes the referral system, convenes the family, begins the helping relationship, assesses the family, and develops a definition of the problem. Haley (1976) described the initial interview in four stages: social, problem, interactional, and goal setting. According to Segal and Bavelas (1983), the goal of the initial interview is to gather specific behavioral information regarding the nature of the complaint and the client's attempted solutions; this resembles Haley's interactional stage. The general pattern for many schools of thought involves the evolution of the therapeutic system where family and therapist come together in an exchange of information to determine the who, what, where, when, and how of family therapy. The key elements discussed here include joining, exploring the referral process, deciding whom to involve, defining the problem, setting goals, and developing therapeutic contracts.

❄ JOINING

The process of joining begins with the first family contact and continues as the foundation for effective family therapy. Rather than an event, it is more a process of understanding and building rapport with each family member. While some family members may be more central than others, an understanding of all members is often necessary if family therapists are to succeed. General psychotherapy models share the goals of empathy and positive regard for clients; however, family therapy integrates these goals with systemic thinking. The result is a type of systemic empathy in which the clinician identifies and describes the unique roles and dilemmas experienced by each family member.

Methods of Joining

The methods therapists use to join a family are often just beyond their conscious awareness and appear to be much like those in ordinary human relationships. The past few decades of pop culture have produced several expressions to describe the phenomenon: "On the same wavelength," "in the same grove," and "on the same track" refer to joining. Each family has a unique blend of characteristics that serves as interpersonal cues to family identity. Additionally, each family has a complex structure that provides rules for its interactions among members and with the outside world. Family therapists place a high priority on being attentive and responsive to family members.

If therapists are to be effective in this context, they must connect with the family. Joining is both an attitude and a skill. To connect with the family, the therapist must convey acceptance of family members and respect for their way of seeing and doing things. It is critical to validate each family member and acknowledge his or her experience and actions. The therapist must let family members know that they are understood and their views are important. Family members must be encouraged to express their feelings and views and to understand that these feelings are normal. The therapist can join with family members in the following ways:

1. Greet each member of the family by name.
2. Make friendly contact with each member. The therapist should ask each member what he or she does, where they live, to share information about the children, and so on.
3. Respect the family hierarchy. The therapist must begin with the parents when asking each member about his or her view of the problem.
4. Acknowledge each member's experience, position, and actions ("So, Ms. Brown, you think your son ran away because he was angry with you").
5. Normalize experiences, views, and actions. ("It is common for people in your situation to feel the way you do").
6. Validate positive things you can say about a family member whenever possible. ("Ms. Jones, I know you have tried your best to help your son. It shows how much you care about him.") Reinforcing or validating a family member often confirms that individual and helps other members view the problem differently.

In some cases, the therapist may join with the family by connecting with one of its members. This process is called *selective joining* (Colapinto, 1991). The therapist may often choose to affiliate with the most peripheral member in the family or, in some cases, make special efforts (mimesis of language and tone of voice) to get closer to the family member who will most likely bring the family to therapy.

There may be occasions when the therapist is unable to join with a family. It may be difficult to join with a family in which members have values different from the therapist's (e.g., parents who abuse their children) or in which members have hostile or detached personalities. While these feelings are understandable, therapists must find some way to engage the family if they are to be effective in altering the situation. Milton Erickson developed a process called *utilization* to address this issue (Erickson & Rossi, 1979). He learned to use, rather than challenge, a person's way of relating. For example, he would think of hostility as honesty and encouraged the client to use it in solving the problem. He would reframe a detached personality as cautious or careful and search for a context in which this behavior would be advantageous. Family members must feel that the therapist is supportive and understands them before they change how they interact with each other.

One trend in family therapy facilitates the joining process by helping the therapist identify family strengths in spite of the severity of the problem (Karpel, 1986; Zeig & Lankton, 1988).

Identifying Family Strengths

A good relationship with the family focuses not only on problems but also on family strengths. Knowledge of family strengths helps the therapist understand how families cope with problems and how they promote growth and development. Assessing a family as potentially healthy—rather than adopting a deficit (problem) model—gives the family hope that they can solve their own problems. While this may seem obvious to most clinicians, it is frequently overlooked when family therapists become more intent on solving the family's problem than on developing a good relationship with them.

Focusing on the family's strengths and resources contributes to the development of self-confidence, inspires hope, and enhances growth within the family. Each family has unique strengths that may be buried or forgotten. The therapist must explore and probe to discover these strengths. Family members must be encouraged to discuss how they have coped with problems.

The following guidelines will help beginning clinicians join with the family by identifying their strengths:

1. *Emphasize positive statements reported by family members* (e.g., "My mother listens to me when I have a problem"). It is also important to observe behaviors that reflect sensitivity, appreciation, or cooperation between family members.
2. *Encourage family members to share their stories about themselves.* Pay particular attention to aspects of their stories that reveal how the family has coped successfully with problems.
3. *Note family interactions that reflect strength and competence* (e.g., "I like the way you help your daughter find her own answers to the problem"). Underscoring positive family interactions helps the interviewer identify other strengths and competencies.

4. *Emphasize times that family members enjoy together.* What are they doing? What makes it enjoyable? These questions offer opportunities to discuss strengths and capabilities.

5. *Reframe problems or negative statements in a more positive way* (e.g., "Your anger shows how much you care about him"). Reframing consists of changing the conceptual or emotional viewpoint so as to change the meaning of the problem without changing the facts. The situation doesn't change, but the interpretation does.

6. *Emphasize what families do well.* All families have areas of strength (e.g., patience, skills, and coping behavior). By asking questions, the therapist can learn how families utilize these strengths to solve problems (e.g., "What works best with your child?" "Tell me about the times you were able to get him to _____ . What did you do?" "How were you able to get him to _____ ?" "What does that say about your ability to get him to do that in the future?").

If the family therapist thinks of joining as the primary task of the initial interview, then it is possible to see each stage of the interview as an opportunity to join with family members and develop rapport. Each of the following sections represents specific content to be covered, generally through the systematic use of questions. As the interview progresses, the clinician may develop a rhythm that follows this general pattern:

1. Therapist asks questions.
2. Family responds with verbal and nonverbal messages.
3. Therapist responds to family by identifying strengths, reframing problems, validating feelings, or asking more questions.

❄ EXPLORING THE REFERRAL PROCESS

The referral process often includes interactions within the family and between the family and other systems. Understanding these interactions can help the clinician answer the following questions:

1. Which relationship should be the central focus?
2. Which parties are most relevant to a successful outcome?
3. Who is the most motivated participant in the therapy process? Who is most reluctant?

These questions, which can be answered indirectly through conversation with the family, direct the family therapist toward an exploration of the referral process. When individuals are being interviewed alone, it is important to assess whether their motivation for counseling is internal or whether they have been sent by family or friends who want them "fixed." The therapist can inquire directly:

1. Whose idea was it to seek outside help?
2. Who agrees or disagrees with the idea of seeking outside help?
3. How did you know to come here?

When it is discovered that an outside party has suggested counseling, it is likely that the definition of the problem will have to focus initially on the relationship between those being interviewed and the referral source. This might be the family versus another system or the individual versus family, friends, or employer. Thus, if a family has sought therapy because the school is concerned about Johnny's behavior, the therapist must decide how much the family agrees or disagrees with the school's perception of Johnny. If a husband has come alone for counseling because his wife has given him an ultimatum, the therapist must determine who has defined the problem and whether the husband agrees or disagrees with that point of view. He may want to save his marriage, but he may be unable to fully represent his wife's point of view. The intricate politics that have led to her exclusion from the session must also be investigated: Does she have her own therapist and feel that he should take his turn? Has she already privately decided on divorce and identified the therapist as someone her husband can turn to when she "lowers the boom"? Does she think he is totally to blame for the problem in marriage? Has he been violent and has she had to separate to capture some degree of control over her life? Detailed questions about the referral process often help the family therapist expand the definition of the problem. When it is not feasible for the referring person to be included in sessions (e.g., as in the case of court workers and abused or abusing spouses), the problem can still be defined as an issue between the client(s) and the outside party.

If intake information has noted previous experiences in therapy, these should also be explored as part of the client's problem-solving history. Work with other therapists may be related to this current request for help. However, even if previous therapy seems unrelated, the current therapist should always explore the effects of these other experiences on family members by asking:

1. What was your experience like with Dr. _____ ?
2. Was there anything uncomfortable about your work with him?

3. What things do you remember as being helpful?
4. Why didn't you return to him for help with this problem?

These questions often facilitate the joining process with families by revealing how other types of help have had an influence. Do clients think their current therapist will be just like the last one? Are there certain things that make them drop out of therapy? Can the current therapist discover what fits for this family by listening to their descriptions of past therapy? This information is often crucial to future successes with any client who has had previous helpers. In fact, the same questions can often be asked about informal helpers (friends, family, co-workers) with equally fruitful results. Sometimes informal helpers become unrecognized influences on the course of therapy unless they are identified during such a discussion.

This focus on the referral process often provides a macroview of diverse relationships that may have some bearing on the problem. As this larger context is taken into account, the clinician should then pursue more specific questions regarding the potential structure of subsequent therapy sessions.

❄ DECIDING WHOM TO INVOLVE

Certain questions provide the family therapist with the information necessary to determine the structure of the therapy process. Are significant people absent from the session? If so, their absence can be addressed by exploring the client's expectations for service and whether including others conflicts with the family's perception of help:

1. How did you decide who would participate in today's session?
2. Maybe you are more comfortable without _____ here. Are there some reasons why you prefer to leave them out?
3. What do you think might happen if _____ were invited?
4. If I became insistent about inviting them, would it be so uncomfortable that you might consider dropping out of counseling?

The answers to these questions help the family therapist determine whether to insist on others' attendance. Certainly, there are many situations in which a person's own framework for help would be violated and such an insistence would be inappropriate. Conversely, there are times when a family therapist considers the attendance of others to be essential to a positive therapeutic outcome. To resolve this dilemma successfully, the family therapist should conduct a self-evaluation on these issues:

1. Have I elicited and acknowledged fears the client has about inviting others to join us?
2. Have I illustrated to the client how I can orchestrate a constructive outcome when others are included?
3. Do I know enough about these other people, and do I have the skills necessary to set goals that guarantee the outcome of such a meeting?
4. Am I ignoring messages (verbal or nonverbal) from the client about what is essential to them?
5. Am I operating out of a model that narrows my perception of how I can be helpful?
6. Does the client have important information to which I should defer rather than insisting on a certain structure?

The answers to these questions can help the practitioner weigh priorities and skills. In some cases, clients can be shown how inclusion of others is helpful. Of particular value is the work of a research project in which family therapists helped drug abusers involve their family of origin in therapy (Van Deusen, Stanton, Scott, Todd, & Mowatt, 1982). Sometimes the invited people become motivated clients in their own right if the therapist helps them personalize what they may gain from the process. At other times, they may come and provide helpful information without agreeing to further involvement. Still others may come and be successfully enlisted as consultants as long as the family therapist refrains from overt or covert attempts to turn them into clients. However, if clients are still opposed to inviting others after they have explained their reluctance and they have been given reassuring explanations, it is imperative that the therapist accept the clients' position.

Meanwhile, the family therapist can take this as important information that can invoke the influence of the larger system without actually including the additional parties. A subsequent discussion can be conducted about why it is best to meet alone so that the family therapist gathers important information about specific sensitivities in significant relationships. Identifying these specific obstacles can lead the clinician to an understanding of a client's personal reality. Accepting this reality enables the therapist to begin the joining process successfully. Some family therapy is conducted with only one person present in the room. This can be done effectively when these macrodynamics are incorporated into the content of therapy.

However, as therapy proceeds with an individual or a family group, it is also important to develop greater specificity about the problem. Therefore, if the client context, agency context, or therapist skill level does not permit the inclusion of others, the beginning practitioner can focus on systemic characteristics through a careful definition of the problem that includes interactional, familial, and organizational (structural) dynamics.

❄ DEFINING THE PROBLEM

The definition of the problem ultimately governs the goals and process of family therapy. Historically, the various schools of family therapy have adopted problem definitions such as "undifferentiated ego mass" or "diffuse boundaries," which are outgrowths of specific theoretical concepts. While they might be seen as problems through the eyes of a specific theoretician, rarely are these definitions written in lay terms consistent with a client's language and experience. Such discrepancies have become stumbling blocks for beginning practitioners. Suppose that a family comes in seeking help for a chemically dependent member. If the family therapist suggests that the problem is really a family problem, the family is likely to leave the session thinking to themselves, "But we still think the problem is *his* drinking!"

Such instances underscore the importance of developing a problem definition that includes diverse opinions. If an individual has come to the session alone, the definition of the problem might evolve from questions not only about the individual's opinion but also about his or her significant others' opinions. If a couple or family has come for family therapy, the definition might incorporate each person's opposing view of the problem. For example, if a husband says the problem is too little sex and his wife says the problem is too little communication, the family therapist might suggest that the problem is the couple's inability to meet each other's needs. The newly formulated problem definition must include the diversity expressed by the client(s).

Ultimately, this stage must evolve from an exploration of clients' definitions of the problem toward a more systemic and interactional perspective. This can be accomplished through questions that focus initially on family members' opinions and then move toward the tracking of interactional sequences.

Assessing Clients' Definitions of the Problem

To begin a dialogue about the problem with a family or individual, the family therapist might ask the following questions:

1. What brings you here?
2. What would be helpful for us to discuss?

3. Who first noticed the problem and how long ago was this?
4. What led you (or another person) to conclude that this was a problem?
5. Who else agrees or disagrees that this is the problem?
6. Who else (inside or outside the family) has an opinion about the problem?
7. Have you or anyone else thought of any other possibilities regarding what the problem might be?
8. Are there times when the problem isn't occurring? What is going on at those times?
9. What are the differences between times when the problem does and doesn't occur?
10. What will happen if things don't change?

It is important to accept the family members' description of the problem without criticism or premature advice. It is also essential to validate the importance of each member's contribution ("That's a very good point. You seem to have thought a lot about this issue."). If family members interrupt each other, remind them that each will have an opportunity to express his or her views.

As these questions are pursued, the client information that begins to emerge will guide the therapist in two possible directions. If outside parties have heavily influenced the definition of the problem and the referral process, the therapist should remain curious and ask specific questions regarding how those other parties are involved. Such information can lead to a hypothesis that defines the problem within that specific relationship. If the problem has become defined within the microenvironment of those attending the session, the therapist should help each family member reduce the size of the problem.

In either case, family therapists must be prepared to ask questions that bring about greater specificity. Clients often express global concerns through the use of labels (depressed, angry, nervous, etc.). While labels offer a general indication of the problem area, they often mean different things to different people. For example, a family member may say she is unhappy, which really means "I don't want to go to school." A therapist might use the following to help each family member clarify the problem:

1. What do you mean by _____ ?
2. Give me some examples of _____ .
3. Describe a situation when you _____ .

4. How does this affect you now?
5. How does _____ affect you?
6. Tell me the last time _____ happened.

The goal is to help each family member be specific and concrete so that the problem defined becomes more solvable.

Often, a family member presents several problems. In such cases, clinicians need to clarify the problem by providing questions that prioritize the person's concerns:

1. What needs to be changed now?
2. So the first change we need to make is _____ .
3. What might happen if _____ doesn't change?
4. What do you think would happen if _____ occurred?

The therapist also wants to focus on times when the problem is not occurring:

1. When are you able to handle the problem?
2. What are you doing differently in these situations?
3. What seems to be different when you are able to manage?

Understanding when they are able to manage the problem helps family members get in touch with their strengths and resources. As the family members share their views, therapists can use this information to further clarify the interactional sequences that surround significant family experiences.

Tracking Interactional Sequences

The approaches used in tracking a family's communication are similar to relationship techniques derived from client-centered therapy (Rogers, 1961). The therapist's open-ended questions, ability to reflect content and feelings, and attentive demeanor help establish a supportive relationship with the family. More complex techniques of tracking center on the therapist's efforts to "listen with a third ear." The therapist responds to thoughts and feelings that family members may be unable to acknowledge. When family members begin to talk, they usually describe the content of the problem. For example, a parent might say that a child "won't come home" or "won't do what I tell him." While therapists may listen to what family members say about each other (content), they are mainly concerned about the process—how family members interact with each other. Do family members talk for each other? The therapist who focuses only on the content is not able to assess the interactional pattern that contributes to the problem. Colapinto (1991) states:

> Following the content and the process of the family interaction, like the needle of a record player follows a groove, is the basic structural procedure to collect information on the family map. As the therapist listens to and encourages the contributions of family members, observes their mutual dances, and asks for clarifications and expansions, he or she begins to draft first answers to structural questions: Whether family members can converse without being interrupted, whether they tend to interact in age appropriate ways, how they organize each other's behaviors, how they deal with or avoid conflict, what alliances they tend to form. (pp. 431–432)

In some instances, the therapist may use metaphors to represent patterns of communication. The therapeutic use of metaphor helps reframe a family's reality by simply tracking the family's communication from the content to the process level. Minuchin (Minuchin & Fishman, 1981) is a master of such tracking skills, using metaphors for family process as diverse as, "You're wired to one another," "You're his alarm clock," or "You're her memory bank." Often, he will derive a metaphor from a family member's occupation. With an electrician (content), he might say, "You are wired to each other" (process); with a mechanic, "You need a tune-up." If there is a point of family pride, as with a family whose policy is "never a late payment," he might say, "You are indebted to each other." When illustrating a family rule, as with a family that has a strong work ethic, he might say, "Playtime should never be done slipshod!" Tracking is a form of accommodation because it is effective only when therapists are able to tune themselves in to the family language rather than imposing their own.

When a family member begins to describe a problem, the therapist must explore with whom this problem exists and how the sequence unfolds. The following dialogue illustrates how this may be accomplished:

Mother: He won't listen to me.

Therapist: Who won't listen to you?

Mother: My son, Eric.

Therapist: What does he do to indicate that he doesn't listen?

Mother: He just sits silently and watches TV when I tell him to do something.

Therapist: And what do you do when he does that?

Mother: Sometimes I go in and make him listen to me.

Therapist: How do you do that?

Mother: I go in and shut off the TV to get his attention.

Therapist: And then what happens?

Mother: He usually throws a tantrum.

Therapist: So what happens next? How does your husband get involved?

What is important here is that the therapist is thinking about the pattern of interactions that surrounds the problem. By assessing this pattern of interactions, the therapist begins to decide who needs to speak to whom in resolving the problem. The therapist might assess such patterns of interaction by asking:

1. When do you first notice the problem? What is going on? Who is talking to whom? Who notices first?
2. Where does the problem take place? Where is he or she when this happens?
3. What next? What does he or she do then? What does he or she say then?
4. How do others get involved in the problem? What does your husband (your wife) do when you say that to your son? How does your mother get involved?
5. So what happens after he leaves the house? How long is he gone? What happens when he returns? Who agrees or disagrees with you that this is a problem?
6. Has it always been this way? When was it different? What else was different then?

The family's interactional description of the problem tells us who should be talking to whom about it. For example, can a mother and stepfather discuss the problem in the presence of their child? Rather than reporting about the problem, the family shows how they respond, thus verifying the interactional sequence before and after the problem. The therapist probes the family by asking:

1. How have you (e.g., mother and son) tried to handle the problem?
2. When you're arguing with your son, what does your husband do?
3. Is that normally the way you talk to each other?

When the therapist asks specific family members to discuss the problem, the hierarchy and family structure often begin to emerge. For example, a grandparent may be responsible for a child and complain about the mother's irresponsibility. If the therapist asks the mother to take responsibility for the child in the interview and the grandparent interferes, then the interactional sequence around the presenting problem (the process) becomes clear: While the grandparent complains that the mother is irresponsible, she interferes when the mother takes responsibility.

A typical sequence of communication that may occur with this type of organization is:

1. Grandmother is responsible for the child while complaining of mother's irresponsibility.
2. Mother withdraws and grandmother continues to be responsible for the child.
3. The child misbehaves.
4. Grandmother is angry with mother because she should not have to discipline the child.
5. Mother moves in to take care of the child.
6. Grandmother criticizes mother for not being competent and moves in to rescue the child from mother.
7. Mother withdraws, allowing grandmother to be responsible for the child.
8. The child continues to misbehave.

Another common interactional sequence involves one parent who is overinvolved with the child while the other parent remains peripheral. The typical sequence of interactions that often occurs with this type of organization is:

1. Mother is overinvolved with the child.
2. The child acts up, expressing symptomatic behaviors.
3. Mother calls in father to assist.
4. Father deals with the problem ineffectively.

5. Mother criticizes father for not dealing with the problem appropriately.
6. Father withdraws.
7. Mother and child continue to be overinvolved until they reach another impasse.

This interactional sequence consists of an overinvolved parent–child dyad (a cross-generational coalition) and an underinvolved or peripheral parent. The child's misbehavior thus serves to trigger an interactional sequence between the parents.

Enacting the Interactional Sequence

In some cases, the therapist needs to decentralize his or her participation and direct the family members to enact rather than describe the problem sequence. Here the therapist is creating a context for functional and dysfunctional interaction. The therapist might ask the family to "discuss the problem with each other" or to "continue last night's argument." The therapist must be specific, such as, "Tell your son what he must do to gain your trust." After the directive has been given, the therapist should pull his or her chair back, observe how family members resolve conflict, and attempt to get information to the following questions:

1. How is the message delivered?
2. Does the family member talk firmly?
3. Does he or she make eye contact?
4. How does the other family member respond?
5. Does he or she get angry?
6. Does he or she acknowledge the other family member's point of view? How?
7. Are any of the children involved in the discussion?
8. When do they get involved?
9. How do they get involved?
10. Does the therapist get involved in the interaction? When? How?
11. When do members change the subject?
12. How does the interactional sequence end?

The answers to these questions help the therapist assess the interactional sequence. Focusing on these sequences begins to transform the definition of the problem from an individual attribute (e.g., "He's depressed") into an interactional definition ("When he's depressed, we don't agree on the solution"). Special attention should be given to repetitive behavioral sequences that occur around the problem. As these sequences and the relevant family members become identified, family therapists can integrate this information with referral information in deciding whom to involve in therapy. As the definition of the problem becomes more interactional in nature, therapists begin to develop a therapeutic plan—that is, an understanding of whom to invite to participate in subsequent sessions.

❄ SETTING GOALS

The goals pursued in family therapy should develop from information gathered about how the family defines the problem, what made them seek help, and who the primary participants will be. While many schools of family therapy have goals that are theory-specific, an integrated set of goals usually involves behavior change, perceptual change, or a combination of the two (O'Hanlon, 1991). Ultimately, negotiated goals must address the client's definition of the problem. Additionally, the initial interview should produce a problem definition that is clearly stated in behavioral or perceptual terms. When this does not occur, the clinician needs more sessions to evolve a clear and concrete problem definition. In the interim, therapist and client must agree on some preliminary process goals such as exploration, clarification, and experimentation.

These goals are aimed at developing a more specific definition of the problem. For example, if an individual states the goal as, "I want to stop hating my father" or "I want to have a better relationship with men," the therapist may pursue present-oriented interactional information only to discover in later sessions the existence of childhood sexual abuse. Therefore, if the problem definition is still vague at the end of the initial interview, family therapists are encouraged to negotiate a process goal to maintain a sense of direction with the client. For example:

> *Mary Ann, it sounds like there are many factors that enter into your desire to "stop hating" your father, and I want to make sure I fully understand your relationship with him before we develop more specific goals. You've been very helpful today and I'm wondering if we could take another session to explore all of your feelings about this issue. If you decide to return, I would like*

to continue clarifying this situation until we are able to develop specific problem-solving strategies for you to try.

In this way, the therapist helps the client anticipate a two-step process of problem resolution: clarification of context and development of strategies.

When a family or couple is interviewed, the process is similar. Families are usually so intent on getting results that they become oblivious to their own process. This is why certain situations benefit from a shift to process goals. Such goals can be explained to the family as a first step toward eventual problem resolution, to be followed by a second step in which strategies for change are developed. In the first step, focusing on the perspective of the family, the therapist can ask questions that begin to associate specific behaviors and perceptions with the description of the problem. This microinformation can then be used to develop specific goals and strategies for change in the intervention phase of therapy. The family therapist might negotiate such a two-step agreement by stating:

It sounds to me like you have an idea about what the problem is but are struggling with how to go about resolving it. In the past, I've found it useful to help people develop a very specific understanding of the behavior, thoughts, and feelings that they would like to change. After that, it's much easier to help them develop solutions. If you decide to return, I would want some time to explore more details about the problem [perceptual change], so that all of us can come to some agreement about what should change. After that, if you're satisfied with the direction we're heading, we can pursue a specific plan of action [behavioral change].

If clients already have a clear set of behavioral goals when they enter family therapy, the negotiated goals may be determined by whether the practitioner has a clear sense of direction at the end of the first session. This sense of direction is usually related to the therapist's skills and the model of change adopted. Breunlin (1985) notes that structural-strategic family therapists are comfortable intervening on the basis of a partial assessment of family functioning, whereas therapists using other models prefer a more thorough assessment before developing interventions. We believe that both methods are of value. Thus, in the initial interview, if a beginning family therapist is ready to interrupt certain interactional sequences and assign tasks, he or she may negotiate a behavioral goal such as experimentation. That signals an emphasis on a quick strategic turnaround rather than a longer developmental process such as clarification or exploration.

Because the type of goal is tied to a certain sense of timing as the practitioner moves through the stages of family therapy, process goals also become closely tied to the type of working contract that the family and therapist develop.

�֎ DEVELOPING THERAPEUTIC CONTRACTS

Contracting is a form of structured bargaining that specifies clearly what is expected. In its most basic form, the contract for family therapy services is an explicit understanding between the therapist and family members about the specifics of the treatment process.

Contracts help families to be good consumers of services. Personal services are most effective when families have the opportunity to take responsibility for the terms under which the services are rendered. Does the family prefer a long or short assessment period? What are the pros and cons of each? Do they want insight or only results? What constitutes informed consent when a person or family sees a family therapist? These questions are quite unorthodox compared to current norms of practice; however, even in court-ordered cases, service delivery can be administered more cooperatively if the practitioner reviews the setting and determines what elements of the process can be presented to family members as choices. For example, a violent husband who has been ordered into treatment as part of a deferred-prosecution agreement may not have a choice about the frequency or duration of sessions, but there may be some element of the content or process that he can influence, such as the topics to be discussed (violence, patterns, relationships), the role of the therapist (director, guide, consultant), and goals (behavioral change, perceptual change, or both).

When a contract is negotiated between therapist and client, it is largely a commitment by both parties to participate in an initial treatment plan. One type of contract might be a request to include certain people as sources of information during the assessment process, with the expectation that a different type of contract will be agreed on for treatment. Another type of contract could define the role of the therapist as a consultant rather than a referee in the case of a highly emotional couple. Still another contract with an individual seeking help for depression might formalize the client's choice regarding which topic to pursue: family-of-origin influences that bear on the client's depression or strategies for day-to-day coping with the depression. To account for the essential elements of a therapeutic contract, the clinician should review these questions:

1. Do I know what the client's initial expectations are for the therapy process?
2. Have I provided a rationale explaining why the process may depart from his or her expectations?
3. Does the client have an understanding of what specifically will occur from session to session and how these activities will address his or her presenting problem?
4. Have I explained the process goals of family therapy (assessment, exploration, experimentation, etc.) and the role of each family member?
5. Have I enlisted each member in the process and addressed their objections or questions?

Developing a contract is a process of sifting information related to the definition of the problem, the decision to seek therapy, the likely participants, and their expectations for treatment. As this sifting takes place, the nature of the therapeutic process begins to evolve from the important elements that surface. The result is a contract that specifies the role of the therapist, each family member's role, intermediate and long-range goals, and an initial plan for achieving the goals. Although these initial roles, goals, and plans may be changed many times throughout the therapeutic process, grappling with them in a systematic way during the initial interview helps the family therapist begin the process in an organized manner. As the therapeutic contract evolves, the therapist should help the family anticipate the experience by describing the process.

Describing the Therapeutic Process

Once therapists have begun to develop a contract, they should start orienting the family or individual to the process of therapy—that is, the staff involved and the specific techniques employed to pursue the goals. It is important at the outset to provide at least a minimal structure of the therapeutic process. Just as a travel agent might provide an itinerary for a family vacation, the therapist might provide the following overview of the therapeutic process:

> *If you decide to see me, we'll talk about things that concern you [your family] and discuss what you want to do about them. Maybe we can pool our ideas and come up with some things you can try. I usually spend a few sessions learning everything I can about what works best for you. After that, we*

start to develop a plan of action. If you try something and it doesn't work, we'll talk about it and figure out what else might help.

The description of the therapeutic process varies depending on the family's previous experience in therapy. Families who have not been to therapy or who are uncertain of what to expect require more specificity. On the other hand, with families who have had previous therapeutic contact, it is important to explore their expectations for service. After hearing about the family's previous experiences with counseling, family therapists may need to describe the current process to clarify how it may be the same or different from that of other practitioners.

One of the questions clients may ask is whether the therapist will reveal what is said in the session to others (e.g., parents, a probation officer, a social worker). Before the question arises, family therapists should say that what is discussed is held confidential except under certain conditions. A promise without this qualification can prove frustrating. There are cases where it is in the clients' best interests that the information be shared. There are also laws in many states that mandate reporting under certain circumstances. If clients find their statements have not been confidential when the therapist promised total confidentiality, the trust is damaged and the therapist loses effectiveness. Consequently, these qualifications should be included. For example, the therapist may say:

> *I will try to keep what we talk about between the four of us, but if one of you said you were planning to do something that would be harmful to you or someone else, I probably would tell someone else and try to keep anyone from getting hurt. I promise that I'll let you know if I'm going to tell anyone what we've talked about. And sometimes, if I think it would be helpful for someone to know something you've told me, I may ask if it's okay for me to mention it. For example, if you told me you were having trouble in school, I might ask you if you minded my discussing it with your teachers. It is also important for you to know that the law requires that I disclose information in certain cases. These include . . .*

Questions concerning the therapist's role or the therapeutic relationship may come up throughout the therapy sessions and should be answered as they arise. What's crucial in explaining the therapeutic process is to relieve initial anxieties that clients may have, give them some expectations about what is likely to happen when they come, and help them feel at ease in the therapeutic situation.

Finalizing the Contract

A practitioner's setting may influence whether a therapeutic contract is written or verbal. Fees, liability, releases of information, and other legal aspects of therapy are usually written to become legally binding. In some instances, clients are provided with statements regarding their rights to obtain records or to file grievances. In addition to these considerations, the following checklist is provided to help beginning practitioners achieve a satisfactory understanding with families about the process of therapy:

1. Who will attend? (referral source, extended family, others)
2. What will each person's role be? (consultant, client, provider of information)
3. What are the goals? (assessment then treatment, further exploration to define the problem, specific behavioral changes)
4. When will sessions be held? (frequency or pace)
5. How will sessions be conducted? (in-session directives, circular or systematic questioning, out-of-session tasks, genograms, specific interventions, psychoeducation)
6. When will the terms of this contract be renegotiated?
7. What resources, space, time, and help are needed?
8. Who else needs to be made aware of the contract?
9. Are there any barriers or costs to the contract?

It is empowering for clients to know that the therapist expects to renegotiate and evaluate the process on the basis of the client's personal experience. Too often, therapists develop expectations that clients will blindly participate in the process without holding the therapist accountable for his or her part of the contract. When no-shows occur in clinical settings, it is an indication that the terms of the contract had not been mutually agreed on. Many consumers are more compliant when they are in crisis, only to find later that they need to renegotiate but are too intimidated to do so. Dropping out of therapy becomes the most expedient option.

Beginning practitioners sometimes try to maintain client commitment in indirect ways such as persuasion or lectures about why clients should return for treatment. At other times, therapists may expect clients to continue attending and paying for sessions in spite of lingering reservations. These situations may be avoided by thoroughly exploring and validating the concerns and reservations that clients express in the first session. By assuming a one-down position, the clinician is able to empower the client to feel a sense of entitlement when it comes to dictating the terms of therapy. The clinician always has the right to refuse to see a client, and the client must be allowed the same right when services do not seem helpful.

❄ SUMMARY

Box 6.1 summarizes the key questions from each portion of the initial interview. In some instances, the time allotted for an initial interview may not allow the therapist to cover each section adequately. In such cases, the therapist may want to explain the initial stage of therapy as one of exploration leading to an initial treatment contract. Then, the second session can be used to address remaining topics before an initial plan is proposed. In other cases, the therapist can propose a contract that allows for an assessment period with recommendations from the clinician. At the end of this assessment period (from one to four sessions), the family can decide whether they would like to continue.

As beginning practitioners prepare for the first session, they may review Box 6.1 and the intake information in Chapter Five to decide what aspects of the outline they should emphasize. If initial hypotheses have been formed, they can determine which aspects of the initial interview best address these hypotheses. As the interview proceeds, the outline can serve as a guide for the practitioner to know when to move on to the next section.

In addition to this outline, there are questions that beginning family therapists often ask as they approach their early clinical experiences. These questions represent common clinical situations that may have a significant impact on the course of therapy. The following section provides some initial guidelines to help beginners address such issues.

❄ QUESTIONS THAT BEGINNING CLINICIANS OFTEN ASK

1. How Should I Handle the Issue of Alcohol If I Suspect It Is a Part of the Problem?

When family members identify alcohol as part of the presenting problem, this issue must be addressed if therapy is to be successful. The therapist must assess the function of alcohol and its relationship to the problem in the family. Is the family concerned that one of its members is abusing alcohol? How has the family dealt with this problem? How are family members affected by the alcohol abuse? Do those affected family members have a plan for addressing the

BOX 6.1
The Initial Interview

I. Joining
   A. What common ground can I share with the family?
   B. What family strengths can I identify and validate?
   C. How can I address issues of race, gender, culture?

II. Exploring the Referral Process
   A. Whose idea was it to seek help?
   B. How do you feel about the idea of getting help?
   C. How did you know to come here?

III. Deciding Whom to Involve
   A. How did you decide who would come to today's session?
   B. What would happen if other people were invited?

IV. Defining the Problem
   A. Clients' definition
      1. What brings you here?
      2. Who first noticed the problem and how long ago?
      3. How was this conclusion reached?
      4. Who agrees/disagrees with these opinions?
   B. Tracking interactional sequences
      1. When you first noticed the problem, what was happening?
      2. Who says what to whom?
      3. What happens next?
      4. How do others get involved?
      5. What does each person do or say?

V. Setting Goals
   A. Exploration (creative discovery or cognitive change)
   B. Clarification (reframing or cognitive change)
   C. Experimentation (behavioral change)

VI. Developing Therapeutic Contracts
   A. Address client expectations
      1. What are you hoping a therapist can do to help?
      2. What did you think would happen in counseling?
   B. Negotiate the role of the therapist (related to process goals)
   C. Provide a rationale for the goals and roles
   D. Explore each person's motivation/commitment to the process
      1. Is there anything that doesn't fit for anyone?
      2. What would have to happen for the process to be more beneficial?
   E. Address issues of informed consent (confidentiality, etc.)

issue? Treadway (1989) suggests that, if the therapist and family are thera-peutically joined, they may raise issues of chemical abuse. He emphasizes the importance of remaining allied (joined) with the substance abuser and re-maining neutral about the chemical-dependence problem. The beginning therapist should understand that discussion of the alcohol use provokes resis-tance on the part of the client unless those two objectives have been achieved.

Phrases such as "problem drinking" or "alcohol use" are preferred to "al-coholic." Treadway also suggests that the therapist and client develop a controlled-drinking contract (e.g., time-limited abstinence). If clients are un-able to comply with this plan, they should be referred to Alcoholics Anony-mous (AA) and a chemical-dependence assessment. If other family members object to this type of plan, the clinician can use their objections as an opportu-nity to intervene with the family and begin encouraging the new patterns of thought and behavior necessary for successful recovery.

When the therapist suspects alcohol is contributing to the problem but family members do not identify it as part of the problem, the issue should be considered as a preliminary hypothesis that must be explored and validated before focusing treatment in that direction. Tracking interactional sequences and exploring the referral process can elicit information about the evolution of the presenting problem. As this is done, the practitioner can assess alcohol use by asking if any member was using alcohol or drugs before, during, or after the sequences described. Steinglass, Bennett, Wolin, and Reiss (1987) en-courage clinicians to make a distinction between families who have become organized with an alcoholic identity and those who happen to have an alco-holic member. Their research sheds much light on various types of alcoholic families, suggesting that the stereotype of a dysfunctional family does not rep-resent the diverse levels of competence and strength that may exist among families affected by alcohol.

2. How Should I Deal With a Suicide Threat?

A suicide threat brings with it tremendous responsibility. The first step in deal-ing with a suicide threat is to understand the extent of the client's thinking. Do such clients have a well-thought-out plan for conducting the suicide? What keeps them from completing this plan? What effects does the suicide threat have on the family? What message is the client trying to send by expressing this threat? Is the suicide threat linked to other losses in the family? Is the client at-tempting to help another family member avoid a painful transition? Beginning therapists may be tempted to offer the person advice or argue against suicide. At the beginning of a conversation about suicide, it is important to explore and ask the preceding questions with concerned curiosity. If the therapist takes too strong a position, the determined client may decide to go underground and withhold information to maintain personal control. If the therapist remains concerned and exploratory at the outset, the client is more likely to share fully regarding the extent of his or her progression toward an actual attempt.

Once therapists have listened to and explored the client's experience, they may proceed toward an intervention strategy. If the danger of suicide presents itself during an individual session (due to previous attempts or the presence of a specific plan), therapists should discuss a no-suicide contract that will stay in force until a family or network intervention can be organized. Family members and significant others should be notified immediately. The family and others (e.g., referral person, agency personnel, or physicians) should be convened to build a coalition to cooperate around therapeutic goals. One group of family therapists developed an in-home crisis intervention strategy that avoided hospitalization in 42 of 50 cases (Pittman, DeYoung, Flomenhaft, Kaplan, & Langsley, 1966). Madanes (1981) provides guidelines for addressing suicidal adolescents, and Scalise (1992) reports the successful structuring of a family suicide watch in the case of a suicidal adolescent. In the case of suicidal adults, the family therapist should engage spouses, significant others, or extended family members in discussions regarding any significant life-cycle transitions or changes in family roles that might assist in understanding how the suicide threat may be a response to some unrecognized problem (Pittman et al., 1966). Efforts should be made to involve the network in treatment. Making sure that all the members of the therapeutic system (family, friends, caseworkers, etc.) commit to the goals and the successful completion of treatment is a critical feature of this therapy (Landau-Stanton & Stanton, 1985).

3. What Should I Do If I Discover Family Violence?

Increased awareness of family violence has drawn the attention of family therapists to their responsibilities in this area. The therapist must be aware of behaviors that indicate physical abuse. For example, a mother may appear depressed although seeking help for her children rather than herself. Families often feel shame that makes it difficult for members to discuss the abuse. Most therapists are legally bound to report violence to the appropriate agency (e.g., adult protective services) if they suspect it. It is important to inform clients properly of this legal responsibility early in the initial interview so that, if abuse or violence becomes apparent, clients do not feel betrayed by the therapist.

As the issue of reporting is addressed with clients, family therapists should explain the procedure as it is carried out in the given community. In some communities, if clients are already voluntarily seeking therapy, the consequences of reporting may be minimal, with little disruption to the family or their therapy. However, in other cases, there may be more formal involvement with the legal system. In view of this diversity, beginning practitioners should thoroughly investigate local procedures under a variety of circumstances to be as accurate as possible in explaining the process to families. In addition, it is important for practitioners to understand the legal definition of abuse in their community to avoid unnecessary reports.

In all cases, it is best to maintain a position of partnership with all family members, with special emphasis on maintaining an empathic bond with the abuser. The process of reporting can then be an opportunity to join with the family by highlighting the courage it takes to discuss the violence and by suggesting that many people are never able to muster the courage to do so (Jenkins, 1991). By emphasizing what courage has already been shown, the therapist can lay a positive foundation for the reporting process.

In some cases, therapists are able to persuade clients to personally make the call in the office as a manifestation of their commitment to improving the relationship. By speaking directly with authorities, clients are able to take greater control over their lives, and correspondingly, they often feel empowered and respected. They receive information directly from social services and do not have to be dependent on the therapist for interpreting the process. Families who remain reluctant to participate in reporting may be helped by encouraging an anonymous telephone call for information, followed by the actual report. If danger is not imminent, it may also be possible to delay the report until the clinician and family can agree on how the report will be made. In these cases, however, the issue should not be confused; the question is not whether a report will be made, but only how the report will be made—who will call, what will be said, and so on.

In defining the problem, the therapist must view the violence as the problem rather than as a symptom of something else. While other dynamics such as gender socialization, communication patterns, or faulty belief systems may encourage violence, family therapists must remain firm in defining the initial problem as violence with the hope of creating a safe foundation for examining the related dynamics. However, without addressing the safety issues first, a climate for further growth cannot occur.

4. How Should I Handle Family Secrets?

Family secrets usually become an issue in two ways. First, there are times when family members or referral sources want to disclose information about other people to the therapist (thereby forming a covert coalition). Second, there are times when family members disclose information about others in individual sessions that they are unwilling to discuss in the presence of those involved.

Such revelations need not be disruptive if the therapist takes a few precautions. One is to decide how such information may affect the therapist's relationship with other family members. For example, Keith and Whitaker (1985) give an account of a young practitioner who received a telephone call between sessions about a family member's alcoholism. He decided to share the information with the family. Subsequent sessions were preempted by a suicide attempt on the part of the identified patient. Keith and Whitaker suggest that families have their own wisdom about how much information they can tolerate. In this case, they argue, the clinician violated the family's threshold for emotionally charged information. These professionals suggest that it may be unnecessary to reveal secret information if the therapist abides by the family's intuitive judgment on such issues. They make the assumption that there is no such thing as a secret in families because members know at some covert level and have merely agreed not to address it openly.

The Milan team has chosen to avoid receiving disclosures altogether (Selvini Palazzoli & Prata, 1982). Instead, they maintain a strict rule that, if the discloser must share the information, it is not kept confidential and he or she must be willing to be exposed as the source of the information. In receiving between-session phone calls, they begin by stating that anything disclosed must be discussed in the next session. Then, callers have the opportunity to decide how much to say. If family members are unwilling to change their rules of communication, the Milan team is unwilling to become part of a covert coalition. With this approach, maintaining the neutral position of the therapist (process) takes priority over gaining additional information (content).

These examples illustrate issues of context and therapist bias. However, in cases where individuals share personal information that is difficult to share in conjoint sessions, family therapists must make decisions about structure that depend on the stage of the therapeutic process. Since we are discussing the initial interview, the therapist should take into account whether a client's spouse will eventually be engaged and how the therapist will delay the potential alignment with the client until both parties are present. When individuals come in without other family members, the order of the initial interview presented here is designed to help the therapist stay away from detailed and intimate content until the structure of the individual's significant relationships can be identified. In addition, it is helpful if the therapist explains to the client that the order of the initial interview leaves the most detailed information for last to obtain a general picture of the client's relational world. Then, if an individual is willing to invite a partner, the therapist can suggest that the details of problem definition be saved for the next session. In later stages of the therapeutic process, clients may request individual sessions in which they begin to disclose information on a different level from that shared in conjoint sessions. The therapist must assess family and couple dynamics to determine how these disclosures should be handled given the current goals of the therapeutic process.

When the information disclosed concerns abuse or safety issues in the current relationship, therapists must assess whether their relationship with the abuser is strong enough to confront the abuse directly without escalating danger for the spouse. In the worst case, more individual sessions with the victim might be required to develop an initial safety plan. Sheinberg (1992) has addressed treatment impasses at the disclosure of incest by integrating constructionism and feminism into strategies that respect all sides of three major dilemmas: social control versus therapy, pride versus shame, and loyalty versus protection. Her work makes an important contribution to addressing secrets of this nature.

If the information disclosed is important but not related to physical or sexual safety, it is best for the therapist to go slowly, taking the time to understand the complex issues of secrecy, privacy, and confidentiality. In particular, family therapists should consult a collection edited by Imber-Black (1993), makes a detailed study of the topic. In this work, she encourages clinicians to understand their own biases about the sharing of information and to grapple with the complexities that make many unique situations call for careful understanding by the professional. For example, people who are HIV positive must develop strategies for maintaining their privacy that minimize potential discrimination. Some choose never to disclose their diagnosis to certain family members. Others choose to deal with their shock and depression before disclosing to their children. This delay enables them to be more available to the needs of those children as they adjust and cope to new circumstances. Understanding the dilemmas that accompany each circumstance is an important goal during the initial stages of treatment.

Chapter Seven

THE ASSESSMENT: EXPLORING CLIENT EXPERIENCE

GENOGRAMS

CIRCULAR QUESTIONING: IN RELATIONSHIP TO WHAT?

TRACKING INTERACTIONAL SEQUENCES: FACTS VERSUS ASSUMPTIONS

TRACKING LONGITUDINAL SEQUENCES: NARRATIVES ABOUT CHANGES OVER TIME
Developing a Rationale for the Time Line
Creating a Sense of Movement
Summarizing Details

THE WILSONS

In family therapy, the assessment process can be thought of in several ways. First, whatever information the therapist seeks should be related to intervention—to what will eventually bring about change. Second, gathering information is, in itself, a type of intervention that can often bring about change. Third, information seeking should complement the joining process by communicating interest, concern, creativity, and a desire to fully understand the experience of each family member. To this end, it is important to take into account how the assessment process might be impacting clients.

As a starting point, the assessment process should involve an exploration of client experience. Gaining a sense of "systemic empathy" for each participant is an important goal. This sense of empathy must capture the complexity of each person's perspective, the relationships that have influenced their perspective, the dilemmas that may have evolved from these relationships, the unique order of events as they emerged in the family drama, and each person's stated goal or reason for participating in the session.

The primary sources of information for most family assessments are therapist observation of self and the system, family members' responses to therapist directives, and family members' answers to therapist questions. In this chapter, we review specific methods that can be used to conduct an assessment and to organize the information obtained. Then, we illustrate how these suggestions can be incorporated into the initial stages of family therapy.

Historically, the field of family therapy has not focused on any one procedure for conducting assessments. Bowen (1978) popularized the use of genograms for collecting family-of-origin information. Structural and strategic therapists engage in tracking interactional sequences as a way of learning about common relational patterns (Minuchin, 1974). Social constructionists inquire about the evolution of family issues over time as told in stories that the family relates (Boscolo, Cecchin, Hoffman, & Penn, 1987; Sluzki, 1992; White & Epston, 1991). Since most family therapists use similar methods, we review each of these procedures and illustrate how they may be systematically employed to gather micro- and macroassessment data.

❋ GENOGRAMS

In the early days of family therapy, Bowen began to diagram a person's family of origin by means of a three-generation family tree that came to be known as the genogram. This diagram starts at the bottom with the identified patient's generation, including siblings, and moves up through the generations to each parent's family of origin, including parents and siblings. As the field progressed, numerous practitioners from a variety of orientations have adapted the genogram to their use. As McGoldrick and Gerson (1985) note:

> *In family therapy, genogram applications range from multi-generational mapping of the family emotional system using a Bowen framework, to systemic hypothesizing for Milan-style paradoxical interventions, to developing "projective" hypotheses about the workings of the unconscious from genogram interviews, to simply depicting the cast of characters in the family. (p. 4)*

In addition, Kuehl (1995) has used the genogram to concentrate on solution-focused material such as exceptions that manifest the breaking of an undesirable pattern across generations (e.g., "You seem to have decided not to repeat your grandfather's mistakes. How did that happen?"). He has also used genograms to normalize current behavior by depathologizing it in the context of generational influences (e.g., "It's understandable that you are coping in this way, given the family challenges surrounding you"). Hardy and Laszloffy (1995) use the genogram to explore influences of the therapist's culture. Such influences as race, class, and gender are explored to highlight "pride/shame" issues that may impede a balanced therapeutic posture.

The genogram is a diagram of three or four generations of a family. Figure 7.1 describes examples of common notations used to construct one. It includes family members (and their relationships to one another), ages, dates of marriage, death, divorce, and adoption, and places of residence. Women are symbolized by circles and men by squares. Horizontal lines are used for couples and dates. Marriages are noted by solid lines; common-law unions are noted by dotted lines. Vertical lines extending down from couple lines connect parents and children. For further instructions on the conventions of genograms, consult McGoldrick and Gerson (1985) or Carter and McGoldrick (1989a). In Figure 7.1 we see that the client has experienced untimely deaths of males and has assumed child-rearing responsibilities for an entire network.

In Figure 7.2, we can see that the husband is 51 and the wife is 45, and they were married in 1970. They have three children—two daughters, 18 and 17, and a son, 15. The two-generation family can be expanded to include the grandparents on each side of the family. The double slash in the line joining the paternal grandparents indicates they were divorced in 1968; the grandfather remarried in 1969 to a woman whose daughter is currently 49. The grandfather and his wife live in Louisville, Kentucky. The paternal grandmother remarried in 1972 and currently lives in Monticello, Indiana. The maternal grandparents were married in 1947. The maternal grandfather died in 1980 at the age of 53 and the maternal grandmother currently lives in Indianapolis.

Figure 7.1

Figure 7.2

Whenever possible, year of birth, death, marriage, and separation helps to track sequences. Box 7.1 provides a summary of suggested questions that can provide the family therapist with information at both micro- and macrolevels of family functioning.

We suggest that genograms be constructed with the family as a type of public note taking that can help the family begin visualizing their own system. Since a family therapy model seeks to expand the area of focus regarding the presenting problem, a genogram is helpful in expanding the interpersonal area of focus from individual to family and from family to extended family. As the family therapist becomes aware of certain relationships that are important to the client of record, relevant areas of discussion can be determined through the construction of a genogram, and potential sources of family support are usually identified. In family sessions, the genogram helps family members consider where the presenting problem fits into the larger context of their three-generation heritage. In individual sessions, the family therapist learns to understand clients through a knowledge and understanding of their families. When the practitioner wants to know "where a client is coming from," the genogram becomes a vehicle for such an understanding in a most literal way because most clients come from a family with a tradition and a history.

To make successful use of a genogram, the family therapist must be able to articulate a rationale for its construction that is meaningful and reassuring to the client. In cases where the presenting problem may seem unrelated to family or extended family, practitioners can explain that a diagram of the family helps them understand significant relationships that might be a resource in

BOX 7.1
Questions and Guidelines for Genograms

Roman numeral entries are questions to clients. Alphabetical entries are directions to the therapist.

 I. How is your family different from other families you know?
 A. Begin writing brief words on the genogram that represent the responses to this question.
 B. Use public note taking as a form of acknowledging each person's comments.

 II. How are Mom and Dad different from each other?
 A. List adjectives near the corresponding person on the genogram.
 B. When negative labels are given, try to reframe in a neutral, positive, or empathic way.
 C. Use these questions as an opportunity to tease, joke, and set people at ease.
 D. Many people will be privately fearing judgment, criticism, and psychological analysis; therefore, the less "therapeutic" the environment, the better.

 III. How is _____ (each child) different from everyone else in the family?
 A. List adjectives near the name of each person.
 B. As the interview continues, take notes and diagram any information that will help in answering the general assessment questions of this section.

 IV. Who is most like Dad? Who is most like Mom? What makes you say that?

 V. How does your family express affection?
 A. Ask how they communicate positive feelings to one another.
 B. Ask how they know when a given family member is feeling positive toward them.

 VI. Who gets the most angry? How do you know when _____ is mad?
 A. Reframe anger as pain or feeling overwhelmed.
 B. Ask who else gets angry besides _____ . Ask what they get angry about.
 C. Whenever the family characterizes any member as being an extreme in any way, follow up the comment with, "Who is the next most _____ ?"

 VII. Who runs the family? Who gets the last word?
 A. Give each member a chance to respond.

SOURCE: Adapted from Hiebert (1980).

addressing the presenting problem. The therapist begins by posing the question, "What people are most helpful to you when this problem is bothering you?" As family members respond, the therapist can ask permission to diagram the relationship of these important people. In these instances, the genogram may be sketchy, noting minimal information in a short amount of time. However, if the questions elicit important information, the family therapist can ask if this line of questioning seems to be a useful direction for understanding clients' experience. Nonverbal behavior of family members often suggests whether they are engaged in the process.

Other rationales can be provided based on the particular direction of the therapist. The following are examples of certain approaches and the rationales that can be used by the therapist for constructing genograms:

Problem-solving approach: "By mapping your family, I can explore the ways you have solved other problems and see what types of solutions are most comfortable for you."

Solution-oriented approach: "When I draw a family tree, I look for ways that other people in your family have solved similar problems. This may give us some new ideas." (Kuehl, 1995)

Cultural or family-of-origin approach: "It sounds like part of your difficulty is related to a clash between two worlds, the world of _____ and the world of _____ . I'd like to diagram these influences and see how we can begin to change these problems."

With African American families or others who may be anticipating judgmental views from the therapist, a genogram should be constructed only after a period of joining has occurred so that the family is reassured that the genogram will not invite criticism of diverse extended family structures. With these families, it is best to preface the genogram with an explanation, such as:

In order to help you, it's important for me to understand something about the significant people in your life and what they mean to you. It's my usual practice to diagram family and personal relationships so that I can get the big picture of a person's life. I think African American families often have unique strengths because of the variety of relationships that exist and be-cause they often have endured much hardship together. Would you be will-ing to let me get acquainted with the members of your family by putting them on a diagram?

In cases where clients were adopted or transferred through many foster placements, the genogram can be adapted with dotted lines, arrows, or spe-cific symbols to depict the multiple settings and relationships that have be-come the norm for their development. However, even with early disruptions, some clients may still have a desire to know and understand their family roots. Thus, the main objective of a genogram may be either to chart biological pat-terns of behavior and relatedness or to discover and diagram the nature of any interpersonal patterns that shaped the development of family members, in-cluding thoughts, behaviors, and values that were imbedded in significant re-lationships. In either case, the end result is a visual representation of important relationships in which similarities and differences are identified. These patterns are used to target attitudes or behaviors that may be involved in perpetuating the presenting problem. Often, such details are elicited through the use of circular questions.

❋ Circular Questioning: In Relationship to What?

Although the Milan team was the first to speak of circular questions, family therapists from a wide range of models now use the term generically in refer-ring to questions that make "connections among actions, beliefs, and relation-ships of individuals within the system" (Campbell, Draper, & Crutchley, 1991, p. 346). Box 7.1 offers examples of circular questions that seek out per-ceptions of difference in family life. Systemic therapists find that circular ques-tions elicit a broad range of information about family dynamics, including individual roles that make family members unique; marital patterns of power, communication, and intimacy; and coalitions among subsystems within the family. This "information about differences," as Bateson (1972) once labeled it, becomes the family therapist's foundation for understanding the family as a social system. As this understanding evolves, hypotheses and interventions are formulated.

The important focus for the family therapist is to gather information that compares one piece of information about perceptions, roles, and relation-ships with another (information about differences). As clients make state-ments, the therapist should be processing the information according to relationships, contrasts, and comparisons. The following sample dialogue illustrates this point:

Mother: Becky is driving me crazy! I can't go on this way!

Therapist: (seeking a comparison) I can see this is very upsetting for you. Is there anyone else who is upset by Becky's behavior?

Mother: Yes. My mother is very concerned.

Therapist: (seeking a relationship) How does she become affected by Becky? Tell me about their relationship.

Mother: She tends Becky every day after school while I'm at work. By the time I pick Becky up, she's at the end of her rope.

Therapist: So, something happens between the two of them that leaves your mother upset. (seeking a contrast) Was there a time in the past when things were different?

Mother: Not recently. We've had trouble with her for a long time.

Therapist: (still seeking a contrast in time) What about in the *distant* past? How far back in time do we have to go to find a time when things were different?

Mother: Oh, my! (thinking) I guess when she was tiny—2 or 3 years old—she was so cute and she loved her grandma. I guess things changed when she started school.

Therapist: How were the three of you getting along then?

Each piece of information about relationships, comparisons, and contrasts could be explored more fully in a real interview. The point here is to use therapeutic conversations to develop a broad view of those who have some relationship to the problem, an understanding of differences and similarities related to the problem, and a preliminary hypothesis about how the problem developed.

Fleuridas, Nelson, and Rosenthal (1986) provide guidelines for teaching circular questions at each stage of the therapeutic process:

> *This form of questioning serves as an efficient process for soliciting information from each member of the family regarding their experience of: (a) the family's presenting concern; (b) sequences of interactions, usually related to the problem; and (c) differences in their relationships over time. This*

provides the family and the therapist with a systemic frame of the problem, thereby enabling the therapist to generate hypotheses and design interventions (or additional questions) which interrupt dysfunctional cycles of interrelating and which challenge symptom-supporting myths or beliefs (cf. Minuchin & Fishman, 1981; Papp, 1983; Selvini Palazzoli et al., 1978, 1980b). (p. 114)

In addition, circular questions may compare people across generations ("Who is most/least like the identified patient?"), developmental time periods ("Has it always been this way? When did things change? What was it like before?"), and meanings ("Who agrees/disagrees that this is the problem?"); explore differences in perceptions of relationships ("Who is closer to Mom, your brother or your sister?") or differences of degree ("On a scale of one to ten, how were you able to solve problems this week?"); focus on before and after distinctions ("Did she get angry before you told her or after you told her?"); and pose hypothetical possibilities ("How would things be different if you spent more time together?") (Boscolo et al., 1987). These questions help track family members as they evolve through different experiences, developing beliefs and attitudes about family life as they go.

In Box 7.1, the circular questions used with genograms focus on contrasts in the interviewee's perceptions of family relationships, roles, and emotional climate. The first question, "How is your family different from other families you know?" gives respondents an opportunity to give information about the interface between this family and the outside world. If certain obvious differences exist (e.g., a child with Down syndrome, racially different, religiously different), the therapist may make the question more specific to elicit the most useful information. For example, having a child with Down syndrome gives a family different experiences and a different identity from other families. However, all families with such a child do not seek family therapy, and many cope with their sense of difference in creative and insightful ways. If a family answers with the obvious difference first, it may also be important to ask, "Compared to other families affected by Down syndrome, how is your family different?" or "Compared to other Amish families you know, how is your family different?" These questions elicit clues about the client's sense of difference at personal, familial, and cultural levels. They often generate interesting information that acquaints the family therapist with themes and unique factors relevant to treatment planning.

The other questions in Box 7.1 follow a similar logic, proceeding to smaller and more intimate levels of observation. As these questions of difference outline family members' unique perceptual blueprint, the therapist can develop an exploration of how these perceptions and beliefs impact behavior. This can be explored on both micro- and macrolevels by using questions that focus on sequences of immediate interaction and on sequences of important changes through time.

❄ TRACKING INTERACTIONAL SEQUENCES: FACTS VERSUS ASSUMPTIONS

As an assessment proceeds, the family therapist may discover certain relationships at the microlevel that seem to have ultimate importance in the client's mind. For example, in the previous dialogue with the mother of Becky, the therapist may ask this mother which relationship (i.e., Mother–Becky, Grandmother–Becky, Mother–Grandmother) seems most relevant to the problem at hand. When these relationships are discussed, the therapist must gain a description of facts, not merely assumptions (O'Hanlon & Weiner-Davis, 1989). This can be done by tracking interactional sequences that occurred during important moments in the relationship:

> *Therapist:* How would you describe your relationship with your father?
>
> *Mother:* I'd say it's strained.
>
> *Therapist:* (draws a line on the genogram between father–daughter and writes "strained") How is it strained?
>
> *Mother:* Oh, it goes way back. He always tries to make me feel guilty. I can never do anything right.
>
> *Therapist:* (writes "guilty" on the genogram next to daughter) When you say he always tries to make you feel guilty, what does he do or say that gives you that impression?
>
> *Mother:* Well, when we talk on the phone, he'll say something like, "I sure would like to see you more often," implying that I don't visit him enough. Then, if I do come to visit, he complains that I haven't stayed long enough.
>
> *Therapist:* (writes "wants to see her" on the genogram next to father) So, when you're on the phone with him and he says he wants to see you more often, what do you say back?
>
> *Mother:* I try to explain to him that I'm busy and can't just pick up any ol' time to travel all that way.

Therapist: And then what does he say?

Mother: He usually starts to lecture me about how families ought to be close.

Therapist: And then what do you say?

Mother: I don't say anything. I just let him go on and on.

Therapist: So you clam up.

Mother: Yeah.

Therapist: And you're probably thinking to yourself—what?

Mother: Here we go again!

Therapist: Okay. So this is a familiar pattern with the two of you.

Mother: Oh, yes!

Therapist: Well, let's backtrack for a minute. When he first says he'd like to see you, what is going on right before that part of the conversation? Anything in particular?

Mother: Mmm. Usually just talk about what he's doing and what I'm doing.

Therapist: So in the earlier part of the discussion, you're talking and interacting with him, telling him about yourself, and then it changes when he makes his statements.

Mother: Yes. It usually starts out okay and then goes downhill.

In this discussion, the client is making an assumption about her father's intention based on what he says to her. The therapist does not challenge her assumption at this point, but merely seeks to illuminate the facts—in this case, what her father actually says to her. Then, as the facts become known, they are put in sequence with her responses, and the entire sequence is placed in the larger context of their conversation and how it evolved over time. In the same interaction, the therapist could also follow up on the client's statement that her father complains when she comes to visit. The word "complain" could be written on the genogram and explored in the same way because it connotes a negative intent on the part of the father. By gaining microinformation about what is actually said and what happens before and after the father's statement, the facts and assumptions begin to separate.

As the facts are described, the clinician can start to identify patterns of thinking and assumptions that may be hindering the development of a new pattern. The daughter believes that her father wants her to feel guilty. If the therapist has developed a supportive relationship, it might be appropriate to begin challenging her assumption during this phase of an assessment (e.g., "Is it possible that your father is trying to send you a different message besides wanting you to feel guilty?"). On the other hand, the client may have more concrete evidence through other experiences with her father that his intent is that of inducing guilt. In this case, behavior patterns can be challenged as attempted solutions that have become unsuccessful ("When you clam up, does this solution give you the result that you want?"). In any event, the decision to intervene must be based on the presenting problem and whether the client perceives the intervention as relevant to stated goals. If the presenting problem was a child-focused problem, genogram discussions and the tracking of interactional sequences may provide information to help the clinician develop a broad understanding of the client's relational patterns, but interventions should be related to the problem (e.g., "Do you ever find that your son tries to make you feel guilty like your father does? How does he do that?"). Then, as similarities and differences are identified, the client's responses can be indicators of whether she is ready to consider alternative views.

If the presenting problem was directly related to the father–daughter relationship, the therapist may still want to complete the genogram, learning about the nature of other family relationships and tracking other important sequences before deciding on a treatment strategy. Sometimes, clients respond to the genogram with their own ideas about what is the best way to address the problem or who in their three-generation system could be most helpful with the problem. At other times, more developmental information may be needed to put a presenting problem into the context of family process over time. This may be done by tracking longitudinal sequences.

❄ TRACKING LONGITUDINAL SEQUENCES: NARRATIVES ABOUT CHANGES OVER TIME

In gathering information about developmental progress across different stages of family life, it is often helpful to diagram a horizontal time line that illustrates the family's story during significant time periods or provides a chart of their life at the macrolevel of observation. Hiebert, Gillespie, and Stahmann (1993) use a time line for marital and premarital counseling as a means of tracking the interpersonal "dance" of each couple and identifying the developmental roots of their presenting problem. Stanton (1992) uses a time line to discover clues as to what might have triggered the family's problem. Hanna

(1997) uses a time line to dissect the accumulation of stresses over time that have brought a family to the point of crisis. All these applications adopt the premise that the identification of developmental patterns of interaction is an important step in developing hypotheses that are born out of client experience and that address nodal events related to key patterns. We believe these events and patterns may give rise to significant thoughts and beliefs that continue beyond the event and lead to subsequent difficulties. As these difficulties unfold, they may appear unrelated to previous events. However, we often discover that they are bound in relevance by certain patterns that originated with a prior nodal event. To change the patterns, it is often empathic and helpful to discover how they originated.

Other family therapists also emphasize assessments with a historical element. Hargrave and Anderson (1992) conduct life reviews based on questioning to validate an older person's life history, but without the use of a visual chart. Fleuridas et al. (1986) provide examples of time-oriented circular questions exploring changes and transitions in the past that may be affecting the present. In these cases, the focus on historical information helps family members reflect on significant experiences that may stimulate their own natural abilities to heal or change.

The advantages of using a visual time line are similar to those of using a genogram. Because families often feel stuck in a problem when they enter family therapy, a chronological account of important transitions can restore an element of movement and flow to the family's self-perception. If a genogram has already been constructed, it is a logical transition to take information already recorded there and begin putting the significant events in sequence. The in-session process thus transforms awareness from the family as a system to the family as a larger story that extends beyond the presenting problem. Marriages, births, deaths, illnesses, job changes, graduations, and other significant events often cluster at certain points in a family's life story. These clusters may be developmental times at which certain themes in the family developed. By tracking the sequences of these events through time, the therapist is able to broaden the family's perception of how they came to be stuck and to summarize important information in a graphic manner. Consider the following example:

> *Randy and Betty were rebuilding their relationship after Randy served a jail sentence for drug trafficking. They had both been married previously and met while Randy was in recovery from substance abuse. A review of their early relationship revealed his sobriety and exemplary recovery as an important attraction for Betty. She was attending Al-Anon after having been mar-*

ried first to an emotionally distant, autocratic man and second to an alcoholic. Randy was attracted to Betty because of her strength and determination. They dated for over a year. However, the month before their wedding, Randy began using prescription drugs again. Betty was unaware of his relapse until their wedding day when he offered her drugs on the way to their honeymoon. She was devastated.

Figure 7.3 is a time line of Randy and Betty's early relationship. As it was constructed, the therapist highlighted strengths of the couple (spiritual talks, flexibility), tracked interactional sequences, and explored each person's evolving perceptions of the other during courtship. As the relationship progressed beyond engagement toward marriage, the therapist began asking the couple about whether they thought anything should have been different.

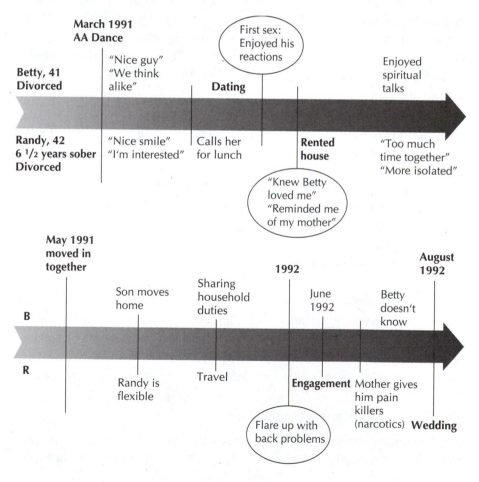

Figure 7.3

Randy acknowledged that they became isolated. Betty reported not knowing about the pain medication.

As the time line brought the therapist and family up to the present day, it provided the clinician with an opportunity to reflect on this couple's courage and endurance as important qualities needed to overcome obstacles in the future. Since a time line shows progression over time, it becomes an unspoken voice for the inevitability of change. These narratives about strengths and resilience in the face of adversity are important outcomes that therapists should pursue when constructing time lines. In this case, the therapist could empathize with Betty and Randy's pain, highlight their strengths, and puzzle with them about how to address the problems they identified.

In addition, dissecting microprocesses in the family provides developmental information that is important to the change process. White (1990) suggests a process of deconstruction in which a client's core belief (e.g., "I'm no good." "She's lazy." "We can't go on together.") is addressed through careful and detailed questioning of how that belief developed. Questions might follow this sequence:

1. When you say _____ , I'm wondering how you came to that conclusion?
2. Who are the people that have influenced your thinking on this?
3. What experiences have led you to think in this way?
4. Would you be interested in comparing your point of view with others?
5. If you were to consider a different point of view, would there be a backlash from important people?
6. How would you cope with such a backlash?

Each question might evolve into a lengthy conversation. People and experiences can be noted on a time line. Future projections about coping can be noted beyond the present point of time. In this way, perceptions, behavior, and relationships are identified as part of the problem. These elements are dissected to develop opportunities for relational change as part of the solution.

Developing a Rationale for the Time Line

Clinicians must provide a rationale and description for the time line that emphasizes their neutral point of view and their desire to understand how the family came to be in its present position. The following sample rationale could be used in an initial interview to develop the contract:

> *Listening to your account of the problem that brings you here, I have been impressed by your sincere desire to solve it. In spite of your best efforts, things have not changed, and you seem to be stuck. When people try as hard as you have to solve a problem, but to no avail, there is usually something missing in their understanding of what the problem is. I can usually help people solve this puzzle by reviewing the experiences they have been through together, each person's point of view, and how they have come to this point. By looking at the big picture of their life, we are able to discover some new direction that proves successful. I would like to propose a few sessions in which you give me the chance to review important experiences with you. Then, we can see what solutions will best fit for you in view of your unique experience.*

As with genograms, other rationales can be presented based on the therapist's chosen perspective, whether problem solving, solution-focused, or cultural. If a person is deconstructing a client's beliefs, a time line may become a natural extension of noting important experiences. In such cases, a rationale may only need to explain a reason for extending the time line into other conversations. The most important task is learning how to relate this process to the presenting problem in a meaningful way. Chapter Six suggests possible strategies for setting goals and developing therapeutic contracts. These may also be helpful in developing a rationale for genograms and time lines. When the initial goal is clarification or exploration, these assessment procedures provide a time-limited sense of direction. When the goal is experimentation, these tools are used to gather ideas about previous successes and behavioral sequences.

Creating a Sense of Movement

For the beginning practitioner, creating a sense of movement along the continuum is the primary goal. Therefore, it is important to develop a different rhythm for each family or individual that captures the uniqueness of their movement through time; in some cases, lengthy discussions occur at some points along the time line and only superficial coverage is necessary at other points. However, the clinician must make sure that certain emotional points in time do not derail the discussion before it reaches the present; otherwise, the sense of movement may not be achieved. As significant events are explored but left unresolved, the therapist can develop a list of themes and experiences that family members identify as most influential. After the time line is complete, the identified issues can be explored more fully using questions that seem most relevant from Chapter Two. This list of issues noted by clients forms the foundation of a treatment plan.

One of the advantages of using a time line is that it helps the family therapist keep a sense of direction during stages of exploration when emotional issues may be raised before a therapeutic direction has been explicitly defined. It becomes understood, through constructing the time line, that both therapist and family are moving forward, from past toward future. The time line allows an emotional issue to be explored in its original context as a point along a continuum rather than as an end in itself. In this way, microinformation through deconstruction generates empathy; macroinformation through mapping nodal events generates perspective.

Summarizing Details

Boxes 2.2 and 2.3 in Chapter Two give examples of questions in developmental interviewing that elicit microinformation, but it is not necessary to write details or complete sentences on a time line. Key words, themes, or events with the month and year are adequate. Too many details clutter the family's visual perception of their movement over time and leave them feeling just as overwhelmed. Therefore, if the clinician helps a couple have a lengthy discussion about a misunderstanding that occurred 15 years earlier when their first child was born, it is enough to note the event together with important reframings, questions, or alternative views that emerge from the discussion.

Hanna (1997, p. 112) uses the following questions to assess the relationship between events, behaviors, and perceptions. This information can be summarized on a time line:

1. What was the first (or next) significant event you shared as a family?
2. When this happened, how did each of you react? What was the sequence of these reactions?
3. After it ended, what conclusions did you draw about yourself and others?

For couples and families, the usual starting point for a time line is when the couple first meets, with progression from left to right through courtship to the birth of each child and so on. For individuals, the usual starting point is at birth, unless the presenting problem is child-oriented or work-related, in which case the time line may start at some significant marker in the sequence of a person's life—college graduation, divorce or marriage, or some other important change. To illustrate how the time line can be used with genograms and circular questions, the following case study provides an integration of the assessment process.

❄ THE WILSONS

The Wilsons were a white, middle-class family who sought family therapy after their son, Bob, 15, was caught smoking at school twice and was subsequently dropped from the basketball squad at school. Bob's parents were John, 42, and Kristin, 39. He also had a sister, Sue, 14, who attended the first session. John was a hospital social worker and Kristin was a nurse. They had been married for 19 years. Both were raised in small rural communities. They met and married while attending college. Figure 7.4 shows a genogram of the Wilsons. It summarizes information gathered in the initial sessions of family therapy with all members present. Figure 7.5 is a time line of the Wilson's family story, noting transitions that have affected the family. Family members reminisced over happier times in the past. They were able to compare earlier stages with current circumstances.

Figure 7.4

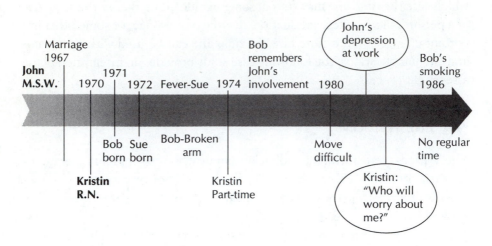

Figure 7.5

FIRST SESSION

Intake and Initial Interview

Joining process: *Therapist uses this information to identify with their particular life-cycle stage.*

During the initial intake, the family therapist asked both parents about themselves, their place of work, and their level of education. The children were asked for their ages, dates of birth, and year in school.

Defining the problem: *Everyone is asked to comment, but the therapist notices that Kristin is the most verbal and Bob is the least verbal during this stage of the process.*

After some initial small talk, the therapist asked, "What brings you here?" The family responded with various accounts of Bob's recent problems at school and how each family member felt about the recent progression of events. He was caught smoking at school twice, was suspended for 3 days, and was dropped from the basketball team after playing in the first two games. John and Kristin expressed their concern and stated that they wished Bob would "open up."

Tracking interactional sequences:
How did you find out about Bob's smoking?
What did you do when you found out?
Bob, what did you do when your mother confronted you?
Sue, where were you and what were you doing while all this was going on?
John, how did you find out and what did you do?

Precipitating events: *Attention is shifted away from the topic of "What did Bob do?" (present-oriented) to the topic of "What has been happening to Bob?" (recent past). This shift diminishes his shame and provides a developmental perspective on how problems evolve from a sequence of events.*

With the focus on present events, the therapist investigated interactional patterns of the family as the problem developed. Information came forth about Bob's tendency to withdraw, John's tendency to lecture, Kristin's tendency to interrogate, and Sue's tendency to stay busy when there is conflict.

Since Bob appeared reserved and uncomfortable during this part of the discussion, the therapist decided to engage him in conversation that might be less threatening. "It seems unusual for a guy of 15 to already be starting on the basketball team. How were you able to do this?" At this point, Bob opened up and told the story of how the coaches noticed his unusual height and coordination while he was still in middle school. Anxious to have him play, they began to encourage him to try out for the team the summer before he started high school. He began attending practices and easily made the team. However, as the season approached, he began to feel bad, although he couldn't explain why. His parents also stated that they did not understand why he would be feeling bad when things seemed to be going so well. However, they believed that he had negative feelings about himself and quoted him as saying, "Things don't matter. I wish I could fry my brains out."

Goals: *All members are able to agree on the same goals. This is acknowledged by the therapist as a strength.*

The therapist asked what the family would like to see happen. The parents stated their goals for therapy as wanting Bob to feel better about himself and wanting to improve communication and intimacy in the family. Bob and Sue both agreed that these would be good goals.

Contract: *Since the family's goals are abstract (intimacy and communication) at this point rather than concrete behavior goals, the therapist suggests an interim process goal of exploration, which will produce more concrete goals to work on during the intervention stage.*

At this point, the family therapist responded to the family's story by describing the assessment process and clarifying expectations for change: "It sounds as if all of you care about each other and want to solve the puzzle of how to help Bob. It also sounds as if no one is certain about what the real problem might be. In view of this, one possible direction is to take a couple of sessions to explore the problem in greater detail. Once we have a definition of the problem that we all feel comfortable with, our efforts at developing solutions will be more effective and we can move on to developing a plan of action. How does that sound as a starting place?" The family agreed to a plan for three assessment sessions, after which subsequent sessions would be devoted to developing a plan for helping Bob.

Data-gathering phase (genogram):
The family is invited to shift their attention away from the immediate problem in the present to a discussion about general family relationships and extended family influences.

With time left in the first interview, the therapist explained that it would be helpful to understand the family relationships most important to them as a group and how grandparents may have solved similar problems. Drawing a genogram with John and Kristin's marriage as the central relationship, the therapist proceeded to sketch a skeleton genogram that included Bob and Sue as the youngest generation and both sides of the extended family. Listing only the names, ages, deaths, and hometowns of the parents, the therapist had time afterward to ask circular questions regarding individual differences in the nuclear family and how the parents would describe their experience in their own families of origin (see Figure 7.4).

How are family members different from each other?

John is quiet; Kristin is more expressive, suggesting a possible complementary marital relationship. She stated, "We have a hard time expressing gut feelings." Bob watches a lot of TV and stays home more. Sue is immersed in school activities and homework.

What was each parent's experience in his or her family of origin?

Kristin expressed regret that her own family did not care more about her and told the story from her younger years of how her family, hardworking farmers, never came to see her perform when she was a cheerleader.

John described his family as very controlling of him and recounted an important experience: his decision to finally assert himself with his parents and change majors in college. As Kristin and John shared their experience, Bob expressed surprise at his father's account of standing up to the grandparents. Bob and Sue described their grandparents on both sides as "old-fashioned." John also explained how he had been a "98-pound weakling " as a youth and therefore couldn't understand why Bob was not enjoying his enviable athletic ability; John would have given anything to have had Bob's height and strength. At this point, Bob was silent, eyes looking at the floor.

At the end of the session, the family therapist thanked them for their openness in sharing information about their family and indicated that the next session would be an opportunity to explore the development of their family and what events might be related to Bob's current feelings.

SECOND SESSION

Tracking longitudinal sequences (Figure 7.5)

In this session, the family therapist constructed a time line of the family's life together over the 19 years since John and Kristin married. The rationale was that Bob's difficulties could possibly be related to various changes—recent or past—that may have affected him in ways no one was aware of. Thus, it would help the therapist if the family could describe the various transitions they had been through together.

What does the family consider to be the major changes that they have experienced together in the areas of personal development, job experience, and family roles?

The time line on the Wilson family began with their marriage in 1967 and continued to the time of their family therapy experience in 1986. When they married, John had recently graduated with a master's degree in social work (MSW). Kristin graduated with her nursing degree in 1970; Bob was born in 1971; Sue in 1972. Kristin reminisced about Bob's early accomplishments and how she enjoyed his first steps of independence and progress. The parents reported success as a beginning young family: They were happy with each other, John's work, and their young children.

From 1972 to 1974, there was some stress in the family. Sue developed a serious fever as a baby, Bob broke his arm when he fell off his bicycle, and Kristin began to work part-time so they could buy their first home. The family weathered these challenges through hard work and sacrifice.

The horizontal time line is divided into major time periods and labeled as the family discusses each stage (e.g., 1980: move). Short descriptions note important issues as the chart moves from left to right, from past to present (see words in bold). Family members may be included by placing parents' experience above the line (e.g., Dad: depression) with children's experience below the line (e.g., Bob: verbally abused). As the time line progresses toward present-day concerns, the therapist uses the visual diagram to stimulate a reflection and reconceptualization of the problem as developmental-interactional in nature.

In **1980,** John got a better job offer, and they contemplated a major **relocation.** Soon, they were reestablishing themselves in a new city, with new jobs and a new school for the children. From this time forward, life proved more difficult. John's job required many more hours, and he was assigned patients with terminal illnesses. In addition, the salary increase he was promised after 3 months was put on hold because of the financial instability of the hospital. He became depressed and sought individual counseling for his **depression.** After 2 years, rumors were prevalent about possible mergers, layoffs, and terminations because of the hospital's continued financial difficulties. John reported that his main way of coping was to tell himself that things would get better if he could only **work harder** and get a promotion. He found himself trying harder, but with **no results.**

In the meantime, Kristin was hired at a different hospital and was assigned to a critical care ward. She worked with patients whose conditions were listed as serious or critical. Bob remembered his mother talking about her work and how anxious she felt about the stresses there, but he was completely unaware of his father's depression. Sue also indicated that she was unaware of her father's depression.

Kristin reported that John talked a great deal to her about his depression, to the point that she remarked, "I wish someone would **worry about me** once in a while." In the last 4 years, the children had become more involved in school activities: Bob played hockey and basketball in middle school and Sue developed her hobbies and musical abilities. The parents stated that time spent with the children during this stage was usually after dinner and on some weekends when Kristin was not working.

John and Kristin also said that their time together was usually when the children were busy or early in the morning. It had been years since they had scheduled any **regular time** for themselves.

What were the main differences between various life-cycle stages for this family?

Asked how their past had been different, all the family members agreed that the period before 1980 had been much happier for everyone. Bob was very active in this discussion, reminiscing that his **dad** had been **more involved** with the family during those days. He also defended John in some surprising ways, given the fact that he had a great aversion to his father's lectures. The family agreed that Kristin was more involved with the children during the

The therapist notes nonverbal cues as to the impact of the assessment process on the family: Bob becomes more verbal and involved.

week, and John was home on the weekends but uninvolved with the children while Kristin worked.

The therapist uses the assessment process to identify and emphasize family strengths, while externalizing the problem away from Bob: Life got hard. Patients at the hospital were struggling with life-and-death issues, and everyone at home began to feel the effects of each parent's stress. Assessment begins to overlap with intervention.

The therapist ended the session by commenting extensively on the life-cycle transitions, reflecting back for this family a picture of themselves that included many successes, their closeness and caring as a family, the unexpected stresses after 1980, and the unintended consequences of these stresses as John's depression and Kristin's anxiety began to shape family interactions.

THIRD SESSION

A return to the presenting problem, with an exploration of cultural issues, interaction patterns, family structure, and the meaning of the symptom

The therapist began with a discussion about Bob's smoking and how he had taken up the practice. It emerged that he had started during the summer that the coaches began recruiting him for the team. When asked about the summer practices, Bob related experiences in which he felt **verbally abused** by the coaches and thought about quitting. When asked what he thought might have happened if he had quit, Bob said he knew his dad would have been disappointed. John indicated that he had no idea that Bob was feeling this way.

Cultural issues, family values: How do the parents feel about smoking in general?

The parents were emphatically against Bob's smoking. John had smoked earlier in his life and quit for health reasons. The family was very religious and had firm values about living a temperate life. This was an area where John had frequently lectured Bob, and there had been many attempts to get Bob to stop smoking.

Family interaction and structure: *How did the family handle other issues?*

By this time, Bob was much more comfortable discussing his relationship with his parents directly. He complained about how his mother "nagged and interrogated" him about his schoolwork when he came home. He would retreat and go to his room or become distance by "vegging in front of the TV."

Transforming assessment to intervention through reframing

By the end of the third session, the therapist moved further into formal interventions by beginning to make implicit family process more explicit: "It seems that there are some things going on in the family that have been invisible until now. One is the fact that Bob was struggling and feeling overwhelmed by the coaches, but no one in the family knew. Another is that John has been depressed at work, but only Kristin knew, and she has become overwhelmed by his depression and the stress of her work. Even though Dad envies Bob's size and ability, I wonder if Bob is really more like Dad on the inside, sensitive and caring, which makes it harder to tolerate his competitive relationship with the coaches. At the risk of being called a quitter at school and disappointing Dad at home, maybe getting caught smoking was the best way for him to change the direction of his life. By the same token, it sounds like Kristin has needed more support than she has been able to get in the family, and she has dealt with her struggle by trying to get Bob to do things that would be more helpful to her. When we meet next time, I would like to get your reactions to these ideas and see if you're ready to develop a plan of action for meeting your goals."

The formal assessment for which the family had contracted concluded with the third session. As the process unfolded, it became an opportunity for the family to shift their focus from the immediate intensity of the presenting problem to a more reflective focus on their life together. In addition, the therapist was able to continue the joining process, to identify strengths, and to experiment with reframing to determine the clients' cognitive flexibility. The degree to which they were open to the reframing became information used in developing a treatment plan. Would direct or indirect interventions be more useful with this family? Would perceptual change, behavioral change, or both be needed for this family to achieve their goals?

To adopt a pragmatic approach, the beginning clinician must understand something about how different hypotheses relate to the change process. In the case of the Wilsons, the therapist made the following tentative hypotheses:

Gender-Related

1. Bob may have felt trapped into playing basketball by the expectations of the coaches and his father. His lack of self-esteem may be related to interactions with other males and resulting feelings of inadequacy.

2. Bob's mother may also have expectations of him that he perceives as overwhelming.

3. Since Kristin stated, "I wish someone would worry about me once in a while," she may be a catalyst for change in the area of gender patterns if her feelings are a manifestation of disempowerment in her marriage.

Culture-Related

4. The Wilsons both come from rural, religious backgrounds. Conformity to parental authority is expected. Bob may be breaking with tradition and feeling the effects of parental disapproval; however, both parents seem firm about adherence to family traditions.

5. Both parents have jobs in the helping professions. They believe in the values of respect, empathy, and promoting self-esteem within their family. These values may become catalysts for change in their relationship with Bob.

Intergenerational

6. Bob's grandparents have not been resources for this family. Both parents report a lack of closeness with their families of origin. Lingering conflict over their own disengagement may make it difficult for them to be comfortable with Bob's individuation.

7. John's adolescent image of himself as a 98-pound weakling may prevent him from empathizing with his son and may thus contribute to Bob's discouragement. The pain that John still experiences over his inadequacies as a youth may become a catalyst for resolving personal beliefs that complicate his relationship with Bob.

8. There are cross-generational similarities in the temperament of Kristin and Sue, John and Bob. Perhaps Bob's low self-esteem is related to John's style of coping.

Transitions

9. The family successfully completed early stages of development but experienced overwhelming discomfort after 1980 as a result of job stress that precipitated a change in lifestyle and a significant sense of disengagement among all members. Bob's low self-esteem may be a consequence of parental stress which leaves them no energy to address the tasks of families with adolescents and prevents the family from grieving their losses since 1980.

Family Structure

10. There may be a complementarity in the marital and parental subsystem that leaves Kristin overfunctioning for John and Bob but underfunctioning for herself. Her sense of overresponsibility for Bob may be the force behind her "interrogations" of Bob that leave him feeling criticized and suffocated. John's underinvolvement may leave Bob feeling abandoned.
11. The interaction pattern that surrounds Bob's depression usually runs as follows: Bob comes home from school. Mother becomes involved by questioning Bob's homework. Bob retreats. Father becomes involved by lecturing. Bob retreats. Sue returns from school activities, and the family focuses on her accomplishments.

Individual Development

12. Bob is different from his father athletically, but similar to John in temperament. His aversion to the subculture of male competition could be looked on as a strength and as a way in which he is loyal to his father's humanitarian values.
13. Bob's intent is to please his father. However, he feels abused by coaching strategies, embarrassed with his friends, and misunderstood within his family. Seen in this context, his actions (smoking and withdrawal) could be regarded as resources in that they served to help him out of his dilemmas at school with the coaches and at home with his mother and father.

Since some of the hypotheses were related to resources for change and some were not, it is appropriate to ask which of these hypotheses fit best with the family's goals. The presenting problem was the fact that Bob was caught smoking and suspended from the basketball team. The parents stated that they wished Bob would open up and discuss his problems. Because of the parents' background (i.e., their expectation of conformity to parental authority) and disengagement from their family of origin, the therapist might hypothesize that they do not have a model for encouraging Bob to open up. This may be exacerbated by the pain that the father still carries from his adolescence. Acting on this hypothesis, the therapist might explore the parents' family of origin to understand how the past gets played out in the present. What current belief systems and new frames of meaning from the culture and family of origin can the therapist find to assist the Wilsons in resolving the problem? On the other hand, the therapist may also hypothesize that unrealistic gender expectations are contributing to the problem. This might lead the therapist to emphasize Kristin's desire to get help as a strength or to explore alternative ways in which Bob can meet his masculine needs or his mother's expectations.

The therapist may also view Bob's problem as a metaphor for the parents' job stress and may wish to explore some alternative ways to cope with that stress. Or the therapist may hypothesize that the problem is structural and that, if Kristin curbed her impulse to be helpful, Bob could learn to be more responsible; or it may be that Mr. and Mrs. Wilson need to work together and help Bob become more responsible. The therapist must also consider individual strengths such as Bob's loyalty to his father and internal resources when choosing an intervention.

Knowing the parents' stated goals for therapy—wanting Bob to feel better about himself and wanting to improve communication and intimacy in the family—the therapist may review the list of hypotheses and see which ones might relate to their stated goal. Hypotheses 3, 5, 7, 12, and 13 all recognize potential resources and strengths that might lead to change. Since intimacy and communication are often blocked by problematic interactional sequences, the therapist used Hypotheses 3, 5, and 6 to motivate the family to accept some tasks that would indirectly address Hypotheses 10 and 11. By appealing to the parents' strengths and good intentions, the therapist made an assignment for Kristin to quit asking Bob about his homework at any time during a 2-week experiment. In the meantime, Bob could decide in the next 2 weeks what he would initiate and talk about on his own regarding his progress in school. The parents were asked to find one night a week that was exclusively reserved for themselves and to set aside time in which Kristin was given a chance to vent her feelings and John would be willing to do more listening to her.

In addition, the therapist decided to address Hypotheses 12 and 13 directly by reframing Bob's behavior, his reason for smoking, the dilemma he had found himself in, and the strength that he had been exhibiting. After 2 weeks, the family reported Bob's depression was lifting, and he and Kristin had no conflicted encounters about homework. He had successfully initiated conversation on his own about school progress, and Kristin was relieved and satisfied with this. The family desired to continue with the current experiment and were also asked to add another dimension to their plan: John was asked to find some time to talk with Bob about how John felt as a young man when he began smoking. He was to share his memory of his feelings toward parents, peers, and others at the time he started smoking. Then he was to share his feelings and thoughts when, as an older man, he decided to quit smoking on his own. The parents agreed to maintain their plan and asked if they could attend the next session alone. During this session (the sixth), they reported continuing improvement in their relationship with Bob and used the time to discuss their own relationship—the imbalance and disempowerment that Kristin had been feeling and ways that they as a couple could restructure their lives for improved satisfaction.

We think that all family therapy models share certain assessment procedures that make them effective in facilitating change. They each gather certain information about the family in the form of stories and nodal events that families relate to the therapist. Regardless of whether the therapist's theme is life cycle, intergenerational relationships, or nuclear family structure, the therapist takes the family's story and begins to evolve an alternative story. Thus, it is possible that any assessment from any model of family therapy is a plausible foundation for the remainder of the change process.

In the case of the Wilsons, the next three sessions involved the development of the plan and its follow-up. The family reported success in accomplishing their goals; there were no further school problems with Bob. Treatment involved six sessions in all. An analysis of how change actually occurred in this case must take into consideration the impact of the structured assessment process and the in-session interventions embedded in the questions and dialogue that took place during the genogram and through tracking their longitudinal sequences. Also included in the change process were the tasks and assignments that helped the family modify their behavior between sessions. The assessment was an opportunity for the family to tell their story and have an audience in the form of the therapist, who could reflect back their story with only slight modifications (e.g., through reframing). The intervention stage was an opportunity for behavior change to start and, if successful, stabilize during the last weeks of the treatment period.

The process evolved through several stages, each with its own sense of mystery as to what the family would bring to it. With experience, the practitioner can develop a sense of timing and rhythm in being able to move comfortably from one stage to the next. After narratives provide the therapist with a sense of understanding for each person's predicament and the family's movement through time, the salient issues can be organized and addressed as relational issues. The next chapter provides direction on various methods used to facilitate relational changes. By this stage in the therapeutic process, the therapist has focused on how interpersonal dynamics relate to the problem by eliciting descriptions of client experience. These descriptions are the basis by which participants begin to see that all problems have behavioral, perceptual, and relational components. In family therapy, relationships are sometimes the background of a problem and sometimes the foreground. We have noted that as clients have their experience known and understood, they become more open to a change in the story or in relevant relationships as they have known them. Their understanding of the problem evolves into one where they can see that certain relational aspects need to change. To help them, the therapist can devote a group of sessions to a number of pragmatic processes that encourage relational change.

Part Three

RELATIONAL
AND DIRECTIONAL
SKILLS

Chapter Eight

FACILITATING RELATIONAL CHANGE

MANAGING IN-SESSION PROCESS
Focusing
Increasing Intensity
Boundary Marking
Unbalancing
Making the Covert Overt

RECONSTRUCTING BELIEF SYSTEMS
Identifying Current Belief Systems
Reframing the Meaning of Symptoms
Stressing Complementarity
Emphasizing Strengths
Using Metaphors
Introducing Paradox

EXPLORING NEW BEHAVIORS
Generating Alternative Solutions
Finding Exceptions As Solutions
Resolving Conflict
Coaching Communication
Assigning Tasks
Developing Rituals

ADDRESSING CLIENT RESISTANCE

Family therapists must be facilitators of relational change. Such a process can take many forms since, most often, the clinician chooses, adapts, and combines interventions from various schools of thought. The result, however, should be a strategy for a specific family in a specific culture at a specific stage in their life. While there are a variety of strategies available, the following are the major categories of therapist behaviors and processes which represent interventions that target behavioral change, perceptual change, and relational change: (a) managing in-session process, (b) reconstructing belief systems, (c) exploring new behaviors, and (d) addressing client resistance.

❄ MANAGING IN-SESSION PROCESS

All families evolve interactional patterns that vary in their degree of flexibility and permeability. Some family patterns may be too rigid (inflexible) and therefore make it difficult for family members to adjust to new situations. The permeability of a family pattern or subsystem pattern refers to the amount of access that family members have across boundary lines (e.g., children's access to parents). Some families' patterns are too permeable and allow too much access (or interference by other family members or society). In that case, the therapist must block such patterns to permit new, more functional patterns to evolve.

As the therapist begins to accommodate to the family system, he or she observes behavioral or transactional clues to areas of possible dysfunction. The therapist may then want to focus on these areas and formulate hypotheses for testing. For example, to explore parental interactions, the therapist might focus on the behavior of one of the children, who is interrupting the parents' conversation. Accordingly, the therapist suggests that the parents "get the child to behave" so that the discussion can continue. If the child continues to interrupt the parental interaction, the therapist intervenes with a variety of techniques (Minuchin & Fishman, 1981). The therapist may wish to focus on a particular topic, build intensity by lengthening the time of interaction, or limit participation to specific members as a way of boundary marking. Other conditions might require the therapist to unbalance the system or to make the covert overt to alter family interactional patterns. Each of these options is considered in turn.

Focusing

Focus refers to the therapist's selection of an area to explore from the vast quantity of information presented by the family. Initially, the therapist focuses on the content of family communication—what the family is saying—but soon the focus shifts to the process—how the family members interact with each other. For example, parents may report that their child is "out of control." Without disregarding this content, the therapist is concerned primarily with observing how family members interact with each other: Do family members speak for each other? When the child begins to speak, does Mom or Dad interrupt? Do parents argue about how to solve the problem? Focusing on the process helps the family function better as a system.

The following techniques are helpful in focusing:

1. *Look for areas of content that might illustrate how family members typically interact with each other.* Some problems are too small or too large; that is, some problems are of such little concern or so severe that family members are unwilling to discuss them. It is sometimes important to look for recurring themes such as, "Mom doesn't trust me" or "Dad has to make the decision." These areas often say the most about the family's interaction pattern.

2. *Avoid jumping from one area of content to another.* Beginning therapists often make the mistake of searching for the area that resolves the family's problem. Consequently, they move from area to area and never focus on what the family gives them to understand the family's process.

3. *Ask permission before focusing on a specific area.* By asking the family's permission, the therapist ensures that the family has control over the content and gains useful clues to the family's interaction pattern.

As an illustration of focusing, consider the case of a family who comes to therapy because their daughter is so "disagreeable." The mother and father present themselves as perfectly happy and compatible, except for their daughter's behavior. Early in the session, the therapist begins to notice that each parent's description of how he or she responds to their daughter's unpleasantness appears to displease the other parent. Their expression of disagreement is a detail that does not fit with the content level of their report. The therapist slowly expands the conversation about how they disagree. As the session unfolds, the therapist develops a hypothesis: This family doesn't know how to express disagreement. By focusing the therapy on this theme, the therapist could work to change the family structure by reframing their beliefs about disagreements—that is, by persuading them that family disagreements are normal and even beneficial.

Increasing Intensity

Intensity is a term used to describe the degree to which an emotion is being felt in the session. Family systems have coping styles that evolve to reduce anxiety by absorbing or deflecting outside intrusions. These protective mechanisms become dysfunctional only when the system's boundaries are so impenetrable that information necessary for change is deflected or when the family's boundaries are so permeable that individual boundaries must compensate for the lack of system security. Either way, some families have a low threshold for experiencing anxiety and attempt to modify the therapist's message by fitting it into their preestablished response patterns.

It is important to emphasize that transmission of a message to the family by the therapist does not mean that the family is ready to act on the message. They may have heard the message and responded to it in a positive manner but failed to make any changes. Therapists, therefore, should cultivate a personal style that accommodates intensity by widening their range of potential responses beyond those that are deemed appropriate by cultural norms. Drama, timing, and intensity are not part of daily discourse, and a family therapist must be comfortable with the tension such behaviors can create.

Techniques for building intensity include (Minuchin & Fishman, 1981):

1. *Use a simple repetition of the message*   Simple repetition creates intensity because the therapist focuses on one theme, resisting the family's attempts to avoid the message. The therapist may continue to repeat the question or highlight the same message in a variety of ways until he or she gets the desired response. The therapist may also create intensity by repeating messages that appear to be different yet focus on a single direction for change.

2. *Encourage continuation of the interaction beyond the family's comfort limit*   This pushes the family past the regulatory threshold that usually warns members they are entering an area of discomfort. In some cases, the extension elicits the necessary conflict or yields access to normally unavailable family resources (e.g., warmth and tenderness). In either case, the family breaks out of its predictable path and experiences new patterns of relating.

3. *Avoid accepting the family's expectation of how the therapist should relate to them*   For example, the therapist may insist that all family members attend the session even though some family members insist they cannot come, or in some cases, the therapist may appear confused when the family requests an expert opinion.

4. *Manipulate the physical space of the therapy session*   By moving closer to a family member or moving two members closer to each other, the therapist is able to take advantage of the emotional response inherent in a change in personal boundaries. Because family members grow up learning the comfortable distance to maintain with other members, closer proximity creates momentary tension. If the tension is similar to the therapeutic message, the therapist is able to increase intensity.

To illustrate how a therapist might utilize these techniques, consider a parent with a teenager who doesn't get to school on time. The therapist might repeat the message by (a) letting the child wake himself and (b) letting him walk to school if he misses the bus. These messages are different, but both send the message that the parent needs to encourage the teenager's responsibility. The therapist might encourage the mother and child to move closer together when they discuss the issue, thereby violating the normal comfort zone. The therapist continues to keep the parent and teenager on the problem despite their attempts to avoid the issue.

Boundary Marking

Boundary marking comprises a series of operations with the common goal of changing the family's structural boundaries. As the therapist begins to accommodate to the family system, he or she observes behavioral and transactional clues that aid in identifying the existing boundary structure of the family. Interruptions by family members are blocked so that transactions can be completed. In some cases, individuals or subsystems (parents or children) might participate in a separate session with the therapist to strengthen this behavior. For example, a therapist may meet with an adolescent boy to help him understand his mother's concerns and discuss some ways he can respond to these concerns. Likewise, the therapist may meet with the mother to help her recognize the son's needs for autonomy. Once individual sessions are completed, a conjoint session could be held to discuss these issues.

The therapist can mark boundaries in the following ways:

1. *Rearrange the seating.* The therapist can rearrange the seating to allow family members to carry out their functions. If a child is sitting between her parents, the therapist might move her further away so that the parents can discuss their issues without interruption.
2. *Reframe the problem.* When therapists reframe or reinterpret a family's view, they are reconstructing reality. Families often get locked

into problems because they see the problem from only one perspective. A discussion of how to reframe the problem is included in the next section.

3. *Block interaction patterns.* The therapist can block inappropriate interactions by (a) moving closer to the family member, (b) raising a hand to stop the interaction, and (c) giving a directive. Staying in close proximity to family members permits the family therapist to disrupt an interaction by physical contact (a touch of the hand).

For example, a family consisting of a single mother, 20-year-old twin daughters, and a 15-year-old daughter who had been truant from school was referred to a family service agency. In the initial session, the therapist turned to the 15-year-old and inquired whether she had trouble waking up in the morning. At this point, the twins began to complain how difficult it was to wake her and how they had to use extreme measures to pull her out of bed. Assuming a weak parental and sibling subsystem, the therapist changed the seating arrangement by putting the mother and the 15-year-old next to each other, with one twin next to the 15-year-old and the other next to the therapist. He suggested that the twins were taking over the mother's job and neglecting their responsibilities. When the therapist focused on the mother's expectations for her 15-year-old daughter, she was interrupted by the twin. At that point, the therapist raised his hand to block the twin and reframed the interruption as a need to avoid her own responsibilities by helping the mother.

Unbalancing

In family therapy, unbalancing comprises those operations by which the therapist attempts to tip the balance of power within a subsystem or between subsystems. Specifically, the therapist uses unbalancing techniques purposefully to align or affiliate with a particular family member who is in a position of low power. By asking for help, the family grants power (or influence) to the therapist, who then uses that power therapeutically. The only time that this power may not exist is when the family is externally commanded to therapy, as by a court referral.

The family members often grant power under the assumption that the power will be exercised equally or that they personally will not feel its weight—that is, only the "sick" member will be asked to change. On the contrary, in therapy, the therapist's power is often used to support one family member at the expense of the others in an attempt to alter the family structure, thus creating new alternatives that allow for greater complexity and flexibility in the family system.

The therapist can unbalance the family system in the following ways:

1. *Align with a family member who has less power.* The therapist aligns with a family member not because he or she necessarily agrees with that member's position but because he or she wants to lend power to a family member to modify the structure. The therapist might say, "I can see why you would feel that way" or "She needs to be convinced of your position."

2. *Refuse to recognize a family member.* This technique is extremely powerful because it challenges the excluded family member's need to belong. A disengaged, oppositional, or controlling member of the family may begin to fight the therapist for a way back into the family. Because therapists control the interaction, they can influence how a family member comes back in; that is, the price of admission may be participation or tolerance or whatever facilitates an improved system.

An example of unbalancing can be found in the case of the single mother, twin daughters, and 15-year-old "troublemaker." The therapist used his power to unbalance the inappropriate parental subsystem. He empowered the mother to fire the twins from their parental role, even though the action and resulting loss of role placed temporary stress on the twins. He also did not let up on the pressure when the twins tried to reinvolve themselves. The family therapist is able to maneuver in this manner because the treatment plan focuses on the whole family system or organism and not on its individual members.

When the therapist sides with a family member—saying, in effect, "I agree with you. They need to be convinced of your position."—it is important to note that the content of the interaction matters less than the structural issues; that is, the therapist aligns with a family member simply as a means of modifying the family structure. For instance, the therapist may align with a depressed wife in her complaints about her husband's work habits not because the therapist also objects to the work habits, but because the therapist hopes to unbalance the marital subsystem.

Making the Covert Overt

Families seeking help are often characterized by vague communication and unclear role expectations. When a problem arises, the family often adheres to the same old rules and customs. Satir (1972) describes dysfunctional families as closed systems "in which every participatory member must be very cautious about what he or she says" (p. 185). Honest self-expression is discouraged and considered deviant by these families. Such families often reach an impasse during a life-cycle transition. When passing through this transition, interactions become more rigid and symptomatic behavior may develop. If therapists are to be effective with these families, they must make the covert messages overt.

Satir (1972) suggests several ways to encourage honest and open communication:

1. *Ask family members to speak in the first person singular and take the "I position"* When a family member uses referents such as "we" or "they" (e.g., "We don't like to go to Father's house"), the therapist should ask the family member to speak for himself or herself ("Tell me what you want to do"). "I" statements are a good indication of whether family members are taking responsibility for themselves. The therapist can often encourage the family member to take an "I position" by first saying, "I feel . . ." and then allowing the family member to complete the sentence with his or her own feelings (e.g., "I feel unhappy"). Family members who are able to state their own feelings are taking responsibility for themselves.

2. *Ask family members to level with each other* When family members level with each other, their tone of voice matches their words and bodily expression. The therapist can get family members to level with each other by asking them to be specific ("Be specific and tell him what you want him to do").

3. *Help family members sculpt the structure of the family* Family sculpture may be used throughout the therapeutic process to increase family members' awareness of perception and thereby alter family relationships. To implement this technique, the therapist positions each family member in a composite living sculpture as other members see him or her. Satir (1972) also asks family members to express feelings through exaggerated facial expressions such as extreme smiling or frowning at each other. Family members may also be encouraged to express the way things are or the way they would like them to be. In some cases, family members may be asked to role-play their feelings.

These techniques help the therapist raise the family's self-awareness to a new level. When clients are helped to address issues that they normally observe but do not discuss, they begin to "metacommunicate" (Watzlawick, Beavin, & Jackson, 1967)—to communicate about their own interpersonal process. As this occurs, individual family members begin to accept the reality that each family problem involves more than their own singular points of view.

As practitioners attend to in-session process through directive structural interventions, families are helped to develop more order in their interactions and a clearer understanding in their communication. They begin to develop more self-control (e.g., to refrain from interrupting others), and parents begin to see effective leadership modeled by the therapist. These interventions address the microprocess of the family on a behavioral level; the therapist may also assess the need to address the microprocess on a perceptual level. This entails addressing the language and beliefs that the family incorporates into their understanding of the problem.

❄ RECONSTRUCTING BELIEF SYSTEMS

The influence of social constructionists on traditional structural-strategic models of family therapy has prompted an increased interest in how beliefs, values, myths, and perceptions restrain family members from choosing alternative behaviors and solutions (Bateson, 1972; Selvini Palazzoli, Boscolo, Cecchin, & Prata, 1978; White, 1986). Selekman and Todd (1991) noted the limitations of their structural-strategic approach with a certain subgroup of adolescent substance abusers. Generally, when there had been multigenerational drug abuse or past treatment failures, they found indirect interventions to be more effective. Interventions that address perceptions and beliefs are generally more indirect than structural interventions. In this section, we review a few basic interventions that help the beginning practitioner address problematic aspects of the family's belief system and language patterns. The strategic use of language affords a new understanding of family problems.

Identifying Current Belief Systems

Several family therapy models have emphasized the importance of belief systems in contributing to the problems that families bring to therapy (Brown & Christensen, 1986). Indeed, self-defeating thoughts typically lead to feelings of self-pity, anger, and blame. None of these reactions are constructive. Rather, they lead a person to feel that things should not be as they are because he or she doesn't like them that way, or they make the person feel inadequate or incapable. In either case, the anxiety, depression, or feelings of inadequacy prevent family members from behaving in a constructive fashion to change the situation. Different family members process cognitions or beliefs in different ways. For example, suppose that a person walks across the room, trips over someone's foot, and falls to the floor. One person's first reaction may be extreme anger. Another person may feel little or no anger. The different reactions are due to different belief systems. The first person probably thought something like, "That rude, inconsiderate clod! He has the nerve to trip me! I know he did that purposely." On the other hand, the second person may have thought, "Oops, I'd better start watching where I'm going. He didn't mean to trip me. It was an accident." The therapist should be sensitive to these differences and respond accordingly.

The family members' belief systems are often at the core of the problem. Snider (1992) discusses this issue as follows:

> *Some clients present themselves with a symptom such as depression or anxiety. After evaluation, it becomes clear that their agenda is to change someone else's behavior to get them into therapy. I saw one woman who presented symptoms of depression. After reviewing her situation, it became clear that she thought her husband should be in therapy. Her presumption was that if he changed then she would not have any problems. . . . Sometimes people seek therapy because they are alone and lonely. I saw an elderly widow whose children lived in other parts of the country. She had had a successful experience in therapy many years earlier. She presented symptoms around a difficulty in relationship with her children. After discussion, she acknowledged that there was nothing wrong with her relationship to them except the distance between them. She needed to talk and felt that this would be an appropriate entree. Her fantasy was that I would help her find a way to get her children to move back to the same city. (p. 145)*

Understanding the family members' belief systems helps the therapist to understand the underlying problems and formulate goals for change. In identifying current belief systems, the therapist should explore the presence of constructive and nonconstructive beliefs related to the problem.

The therapist can identify current belief systems in the following ways:

1. *Identify beliefs that contribute to the problem.* Helpful questions include: "What do you think when _____ is going on?" "What makes it better?" "What makes it worse?" "What goes through your mind during this time?"

2. *Ask family members to complete incomplete sentences.* Such sentences might begin: "I think . . . "; "I believe . . . "; "I should . . . ";

"My husband thinks I want . . . "; "When my wife comes in the door, I think . . . "

3. *Identify family members' self-talk.* Everyone engages in some kind of internal dialogue. This dialogue or self-talk expresses the family members' belief system. The therapist can identify self-talk through the following questions: "What do you say to yourself at this time?" "When she uses that tone of voice, what do you tell yourself?" "What are you telling yourself before this happens?"

By identifying current beliefs and thoughts that contribute to the problem, the therapist can identify thought patterns that must change before constructive action can be taken to correct the problem.

Reframing the Meaning of Symptoms

Reframing—sometimes known as relabeling—refers to a change or modification in the family members' thoughts or views of the problem. When therapists reframe a family's view, they are suggesting a change in the family's definition of the problem. Reframing often shifts the focus off the identified patient or scapegoat and onto the family system in which each family member is an interdependent part (Watzlawick, Weakland, & Fisch, 1974). Thus, reframing alters the way the family thinks about the problem.

In reframing, the therapist must first alter the family's view of reality. By using the technique of focusing, the therapist takes bits and pieces of what the family supplies and provides information that forms a new perspective. The therapist attempts to create a therapeutic reality from a family reality. For example, a family may describe their son as "defiant" or "hard to control," whereas the therapist may view the son as "independent" or "discriminative." By voicing these alternative descriptions, the therapist helps the family see their son in another way. Such a reconstruction is only possible, however, if the family has a worldview that includes such a possibility. For example, the therapist may reframe a child's tantrums or uncontrollable behavior as a signal that the parents have taught their child how to express independence, but this may be ineffective if it is too far from family or societal norms.

The therapist can also accomplish reframing by taking the symptom and giving it universal qualities. For example, a child who is having difficulty following rules may be redefined as "having difficulty growing up." If a therapist is working with a family whose religious culture emphasizes a dominant patriarchal order, the therapist might challenge the image of a distant, emotionally controlled father by saying, "Surely you realize that it is only the courageous patriarch who is able to show tenderness to his family." By drawing on universal symbols, the therapist is able to pair a dysfunctional family belief with a universal belief that offers a new frame or view of the problem.

In addition to these strategies, the therapist can also reframe the meaning of the symptom in the following ways:

1. Relabel problem behaviors to give them more positive meanings Giving new labels often provides family members with a new way of thinking about the problem so that it can be resolved. For example, therapists can relabel "jealousy" as "caring" and "anger" as "desiring attention."

2. Relabel deficits as strengths All behavior can be viewed positively and negatively depending on the person's perspective. For example, a child who has trouble getting things done may be viewed as a "thinker" or a "perfectionist" depending on the circumstances. Family members are more likely to accept a reframe if their strengths are emphasized.

3. Reframe the context of the problem Reframing the context of the problem permits the family to decide with whom a given problem behavior is appropriate (Cormier & Cormier, 1991). Every behavior has costs and benefits. Thus, when a wife complains that her husband leaves during their arguments, the therapist might help the couple identify those situations (contexts) where leaving is useful (e.g., when there is a threat of violence).

4. Give homework to reinforce new beliefs Cormier and Cormier (1991) believe that homework helps family members practice aspects of the problem that go undetected. For example, a husband and wife might be required to observe those times when the husband attempts to walk away from a situation. What was going on? What was each thinking at the time? What happened afterward? The therapist can then discuss this information to help the family discover new beliefs and perceptions of the problem.

Reframing helps family members get unstuck from rigid thought patterns that contribute to the problem. A new view or perspective helps the family look for alternative solutions to their dilemma.

Stressing Complementarity

The therapist often finds it useful to help family members understand that they are interconnected in ways that make one member's actions complementary to another's. For example, a therapist might underline a couple's complementarity by congratulating the wife for the husband's change in behavior. The therapist in this case is teaching the couple that they do affect each other and that they have the potential to do so constructively. This intervention also allows the husband to reconnect with his wife by encouraging him to praise her for helping him express his feelings. Complementarity also helps the family understand their relationship over time. During an assessment, if family members begin to describe each other as opposites in some way, the therapist should note these as potential examples of complementarity. Some common examples occurring in most families are shy versus outgoing, dominant versus submissive, stable versus unstable, and emotional versus rational. While these labels may need to be reframed for the family, the dynamic of complementarity can still be addressed.

Jorge Colapinto (1991) describes the process of complementarity as follows:

> *Family rules develop primarily through a process of correlated differentiation: The behaviors of any two family members mutually accommodate in such a way that one develops selective aspects of himself or herself, while the other develops a complementary trait. Typical examples are the harsh and soft parents, the active and passive spouses, the left brain and the right brain siblings. When all the members of the family are considered, the resulting image is like a jigsaw puzzle, where the irregular borders of the various pieces fit—complement—each other. Carrying the metaphor further, the salient borders of each piece represent the traits expected from each member (harshness, passivity, left brain) while the concave sections represent traits not expected. In well-functioning families, complementarity takes the form of effective teamwork. (pp. 422–423)*

Complementary relationships become a problem when they fail to provide flexibility for individual members. Traditional fixed male and female roles often have costs that lead to problems. A father who insists on making all the decisions may take away the mother's executive role when she is home with the children. At the same time, the father may feel overly responsible, which doesn't permit him to enjoy or play with the children. When these patterns become fixed, families experience problems in moving through developmental transitions.

The therapist can emphasize complementary roles in the following ways:

1. *Ask a family member to relate his or her behavior to what another family member is doing.* For example, a husband who describes himself as

"jealous" may be asked what he is noticing about his wife when he begins to feel jealous ("What things do you see or hear her doing when you begin to feel jealous?").

2. *Congratulate a family member for another member's accomplishments.* For example, a wife may be congratulated for helping her husband express his feelings. Here it is important to look for small changes in a family member's behavior that contribute to another family member's behavior (e.g., a smile that another family member notices and reacts to).

Complementarity broadens the family's perceptual framework by emphasizing the interpersonal nature of the problem. Thus, rather than focusing on a problem residing within the individual (e.g., jealousy), the therapist focuses on current interactions that contribute to the problem (e.g., the husband's behavior). Moreover, the therapist can emphasize complementarity to punctuate interactions that alleviate the symptomatic behavior (e.g., the therapist congratulates the husband for the wife's change in behavior). The therapist is thus teaching them that they do affect each other, and they have the potential to do so constructively.

Emphasizing Strengths

The exploration of strength in the family is not limited to any one therapeutic maneuver. This core technique of family therapy is based on the assumption that, under the right conditions, the family has within itself the necessary ingredients for development. Such optimistic assumptions form part of a strategy to create a therapeutic reality. Whether finding and emphasizing competence in the identified patient or creating intensity by implying that a couple can work their conflict out if they just continue arguing, the therapist communicates an optimism based on the family's own unique strengths.

The therapist can emphasize strengths in several ways:

1. *Emphasize things that families do well*   Family members rarely identify their strengths. Instead, they "demonstrate and describe strengths and capabilities by way of example" (as in, "When my wife has to be at the hospital with Johnny, we all pitch in to do whatever needs to get done around the house") (Dunst, Trivette, & Deal, 1988, p. 73). The therapist should underscore these behaviors ("You obviously know how to pull together to help each other") and their implications for resolving their problem. White (1986) believes that if the therapist focuses on exceptions to the problem, clients are able to see aspects of themselves that reflect a new view or story of themselves.

2. Ask family members to talk about ways they coped successfully with other problems   Learning how family members have coped successfully with other problems helps them to be more aware of their strengths when confronting current problems (e.g., "How did you handle this in the past?" or "How were you able to overcome this problem?").

3. Ask family members to describe their daily schedule   Asking family members to talk about a typical day (as in, "Tell me what happens when you all are home for dinner") helps the therapist learn how the family deals with difficult tasks. Moreover, describing daily routines often provides information about resources (e.g., enjoyment) and how the family handles their daily needs (Dunst et al., 1988).

The ability to identify strengths can be a major asset in empowering families to resolve their problems. O'Hanlon and Weiner-Davis (1989) believe that therapeutic approaches based on strengths and possibilities create self-fulfilling prophecies; that is, when therapists and families are optimistic, positive changes are likely to occur.

Using Metaphors

A metaphor is a word or phrase that represents another condition by analogy. Metaphors can be used to characterize family relationships or a condition, such as a symptom. In using metaphorical tasks, the therapist chooses an activity (e.g., writing bad checks) that resembles the problem (say, a daughter's overinvolvement with her mother). The activity must be one that family members can discuss and in which they can produce change. The therapist typically assigns tasks—such as having a heated discussion and obtaining separate checking accounts—that will produce a change in the desired area—for instance, increasing autonomy (Haley, 1976). If the mother and daughter are able to accomplish the task (i.e., get separate checking accounts and pay their own bills), they will be more likely to accomplish separation around the more difficult issues later on.

There are six steps to designing of appropriate metaphors (Cormier & Cormier, 1991):

1. *Examine the nature of the family member's problem.* The symptom may often be a metaphorical label for conceptualizing the problem. A metaphorical message usually contains an explicit element (e.g., "I have a headache") as well as an implicit element (e.g., "I want more attention" or "I am unhappy"). The therapist must identify the problem or theme and develop a metaphor that parallels it.

2. *Choose a representative "character" for the metaphor (e.g., an animal, personal symptom, or inanimate object).* It is helpful if the therapist has a character to use in developing the metaphor ("So, when you come in the door, you are like a bull in a china shop").

3. *Select words in the metaphor that match the family member's visual, auditory, and kinesthetic frame of reference.* For example, the second author recently suggested to an electrician and his wife that their marriage needed to be "rewired." Similar metaphors could be used with a mechanic ("Your marriage needs a tune-up") or a doctor ("You need a new prescription").

4. *Develop an interactional process in the metaphor to match the interactional process in the problem.* The cycle of interaction in the metaphor should parallel the pattern of interaction around the problem. For example, the family's interactions about the child's problem will be similar to their pattern regarding the mother's problem when one is a metaphor for the other.

5. *Expand or embellish the character to promote behavioral change.* For example, a therapist may knock on the table as if it was a door as a metaphor for a new marriage.

6. *Develop a story that includes an element of mystery.* For example, the therapist may tell a story of a person who miraculously overcame a disease and went through a transformation that brought a new meaning to her life.

In some cases, the therapist gives a directive metaphorically without making explicit what he or she wants the family to do. Family members are often more willing to follow this kind of directive because they aren't really aware that they have received one. When therapists give a metaphorical directive, they are encouraging family members to behave in a way that resembles how they want them to behave in the symptom areas, such as assigning a couple to have a gourmet meal as a metaphor for a better sex life (Haley, 1976).

Introducing Paradox

In the early stages of family therapy history, the use of paradox generated much controversy. Hanna (1995) suggests that the paradox associated with strategic models of family therapy often had elements that could be perceived as manipulation and dishonesty. Such strategies were considered by some to be disrespectful of clients. However, as the field progressed, paradox has become a way of understanding the change process with all of its complexities. For example, Weeks (1991) suggests that much of psychotherapy in general has the following paradoxical elements:

1. The therapist takes charge by placing the client in charge.
2. The therapist maintains a positive view of symptoms through accepting and understanding the client.
3. Change is not directly attributed to the therapist but to the interaction with clients, inviting them to attribute the change to themselves.
4. Clients are encouraged to "work through" a problem, not flee from it. They are asked to move toward the symptom and examine it. "Don't change quickly and be who you are."
5. Responsibility for change is put back on the client, either directly or indirectly.
6. What was once uncontrollable eventually becomes controllable.

Contemporary family therapists make use of paradox as an element that encourages perceptual changes in subtle ways. For example, the Purdue Brief Family Therapy model encouraged families to "go slow" with the change process. The therapist explains that there can be "side effects" to the change process and sometimes it is helpful to approach change cautiously to properly prepare for any of its negative effects (Lewis, Piercy, Sprenkle, & Trepper, 1991). The deconstruction process of White (1990) also follows this direction (see Chapter Seven). The person is invited to explore the backlash that might occur in significant relationships if change occurs. The process then turns to an exploration of how one might cope with change rather than continuing to focus on the change itself.

These recent applications of paradox suggest that change sometimes happens in indirect or "slow" ways because there are, in fact, some disadvantages to change. Our rule of thumb is, "When some things get better, other things might get worse." We have watched many clients become animated and engaged in a discussion of the possible disadvantages of change. These disadvantages, such as a change in the way people view a person, the uncertainty of one's self-perception, or even depression (e.g., in the case of substance abuse recovery), constitute real dilemmas that should be taken seriously as a precursor to the actual change. When family therapists encourage discussion of these legitimate dilemmas, such a paradoxical direction can be seen as a deeper form of respect and empathy for the client's unique drama (Hanna, 1995). These discussions also help change beliefs about the problem for both therapist and client.

An example of the respectful use of paradox came during work with a 28-year-old woman who was obese. She wanted to lose weight and had tried for many years, but to no avail. A genogram and time line were effective in explaining how her weight problem emerged shortly after her parents' divorce and how conflict with her mother began to center on her pattern of overeating at that time. However, when the family therapist began asking about the disadvantages of losing weight, more specific information came forth about how her friends might consider her a threat in vying for certain men and how the messages her weight was sending to each parent might be silenced. At this point, the therapist helped her compensate for these projected effects of change by developing strategies to maintain a secure circle of friends and by communicating more directly with her parents about her needs. She began to see that her weight problem was a relational problem, not merely a problem of "willpower."

Exploring New Behaviors

Generating Alternative Solutions

Generating alternative solutions is central to the problem-solving process; the goal is to identify as many potential solutions as possible. This process is based on the following three assumptions: (a) There are a number of potentially effective ways to handle a problem; (b) families are often aware of some alternative ways to alter a problem; and (c) generating solutions increases the likelihood of selecting a manageable solution to the problem. Families are more likely to implement a solution if they suggest it. When the family generates alternative solutions, it helps them take greater ownership of the solution and work collaboratively with the therapist.

In generating alternative solutions, the therapist uses a brainstorming procedure. There are three basic rules for good brainstorming: (a) If the therapist or family member suggests an alternative solution (e.g., "Maybe I need to set a time aside for homework"), each party refrains from critiquing the other; (b) the therapist and family can take an idea and improve on it; and (c) both parties should attempt to generate as many solutions as possible. The more solutions generated, the more likely it is that an effective solution will be found.

The therapist can generate alternative solutions in the following ways:

1. *Explore possible solutions to the problem.* The therapist might say, "Let's think of some ways you could handle this situation" or "What are some things you could do now to handle this problem?"

2. *Encourage family members to improve on another member's idea.* The therapist might say, "What do you think about John's suggestion? Do you have anything you want to add to it?"

3. *Ask family members how two or more ideas can be combined to form a better idea.* In some cases, two suggestions can readily be combined into a better idea ("So, Mary, you want to wait to talk about the problem after dinner and, John, you want to be relaxed. What might be a good time and place to talk this issue over?").

Finding Exceptions As Solutions

In a solution-focused model of family therapy, symptoms are viewed as problems in accomplishing some specific everyday tasks that are a normal part of the family's life. The therapist assumes that the family has made numerous unsuccessful attempts at solving the problem. Therefore, the therapist is very interested in what solutions have been tried and why family members believe they did not work. The family therapist works collaboratively with the family to find solutions that reduce the severity of the problem. This model recognizes the therapist's role in assisting a family to build on what is working. The model does not see problems as signs of failure, but rather as an inevitable part of family development. The relationship between the therapist and the family becomes less hierarchical and moves closer to a collaborative problem-solving relationship.

Solution-focused therapists believe that therapeutic relationships are weakened by discussions of problems and deficits. Families often become defensive when discussing the problem. This is particularly true of families who have had a previous history with community agencies. Solution-focused therapists work at normalizing problems to provide hope for the family. This does not mean that therapists should normalize violent or destructive behavior; rather, they should acknowledge it as a problem and explore when attempts to change it were successful and unsuccessful.

The therapist often encounters families when they are discouraged. In this state, it is difficult for them to see any solutions to the problem. Family members may say, "I can't trust him!" or "He never does what I ask him to do." Solution-focused therapists help family members identify any exceptions to their interactional pattern. Looking for instances when someone didn't lie, didn't create a problem, or was different from before gives each family member an opportunity to understand what made that exception possible. The assumption is that if there are times when they are problem-free, they can learn how to achieve those circumstances again.

For example, in the case of a couple who always argues over money, the therapist might ask if there are any times in which they find themselves discussing their finances without an argument. The couple may agree that there must have been a time when they did not argue about how money should be spent. The therapist then helps the couple identify how they behaved differently when they avoided conflict. They might also describe what the other can do to reduce the conflict in those moments. These are considered actions that trigger the problematic cycle. Armed with this knowledge about their individual and interactional patterns, the couple can experiment with new behaviors that might help them get such interactions under control.

Resolving Conflict

Skills in conflict resolution and problem solving comprise a set of well-developed strategies for dealing with disagreements when they arise (Stuart, 1980). Problem solving and conflict resolution have proven effective in treating marital conflict (Jacobson & Margolin, 1979). The process has two distinct phases: problem definition and problem resolution. In the problem-definition phase, the critical issue or problem—for example, "You don't care about me"—is defined in operational terms. An operational definition of the problem is much more likely to lead to an effective response.

The problem-resolution phase emphasizes behavior change rather than insight. It is best to choose a solution that can be implemented by the family with a minimum of help. Solutions should be kept simple, since complex plans often fail because the costs (in time and energy) outweigh the benefits (say, parenting skills).

There are several things a therapist can do to help families choose the best solution:

1. Choose a solution that is acceptable to family members   Once the family has generated alternative solutions, the therapist can help the family select one of them. Family members have the option of striking out any that are unacceptable. The remaining solutions can be subjected to a cost-benefit analysis for all family members. The best solution is then selected from the most promising alternatives. Note that the best solution will produce an outcome that requires some accommodation from all family members.

2. *Decide how the solution will be implemented*   How will the solution be put into practice, and who will work with the family to carry it out? Because specificity and consistency are essential to success here, it is often helpful to prepare a written plan or contract listing procedures, where the plan is to be implemented, conditions, resources (both personal and material), and the amount of time that it will be in effect. The plan ensures that the family and therapist follow the agreed-upon steps and do not change their practices midway through the program. It also reminds the family of the resources they will need. The following questions can be used to develop a written plan:

What is the chosen solution?

What are the steps to carry out the solution?

Who will work with the family to help them carry out the plan?

When will the plan begin and end?

Who else should be involved in this plan?

When do we meet again?

3. *Evaluate the proposed solution*   How will each family member carry out their agreed-upon responsibilities? Are responsibilities or tasks being carried out according to the specifications in the contract? These questions can best be answered through data such as self-reports, collateral reports from social workers or teachers, and so on. Once information is collected, the therapist should hold a meeting with the family to discuss progress toward the goals adopted.

4. *Renegotiate the contract if necessary*   The evaluation may suggest that the contract should be renegotiated. Do the results meet the desired level of satisfaction for the family? If not, are more cost-effective solutions available to reach the goals? What has the family learned from the attempted solution that can help them find a better way to resolve their problem? What adjustments (changes in behavior) must be made to reach the desired goals? In some cases, the family's level of satisfaction may not increase as the goals are attained. Here the therapist should help family members decide whether negotiated agreements—what they will talk to each other about and under what conditions—will be more satisfying over time or whether the family should set new goals.

Coaching Communication

Regardless of the therapist's orientation, coaching communication is a core component of therapeutic change strategies. Coaching communication is effective for couples (Rappaport, 1976), parents and adolescents (Crando & Ginsberg, 1976), and divorced parents (e.g., Brown, Brown, & Portes, 1991). Related programs often last from 3 to 15 weeks and contain the following core components.

Modeling   The first step in helping a couple communicate more effectively is to demonstrate, or model, the appropriate communication skill; that is, the family therapist shows each spouse what the response looks like or how it sounds. Therapists themselves model behavior throughout the treatment process. Modeling has been effective in teaching information-seeking behavior (Krumboltz, Varenhorst, & Thoresen, 1967), reducing feelings of alienation (Warner & Hansen, 1970), and improving attitudes toward drug abuse (Warner, Swisher, & Horan, 1973).

Another common practice is to provide live or symbolic models (e.g., on audiotapes or videotapes) who show, in sequential steps, the specific behaviors necessary to solve the problem (Hosford & de Visser, 1974). Taped or filmed models have been used successfully (Hansen, Pound, & Warner, 1976). The models only demonstrate the desired behaviors; there is no opportunity for interaction between the models and the spouses. However, the taped models may help stimulate discussion, which is important to prevent rote imitation by the spouses. If new behaviors are to be effective, spouses need to learn a variety of responses for a particular problem situation.

The therapist may also wish to develop models for each of several sessions. For example, the therapist could develop tapes that teach each spouse to (a) listen, (b) express a compliment, (c) express appreciation, (d) ask for help, (e) give feedback, and (f) express affection (Goldstein, 1973). Each skill could be modeled and practiced during a session if the spouses' skill level allows. Each modeling sequence could thus represent a closer approximation of the final behavior.

Effective modeling includes the following procedures:

1. *Model a clear delineation of the desired behavior*   The behavior must be identified clearly so that family members know precisely what the therapist is actually modeling. If the modeling sequence is too vague, there is little likelihood that any learning will take place. For example, rather than trying to model "awareness" to a family member, the therapist should operationalize this by identifying and labeling emotions. To teach relationship skills, the therapist might break the relationship down into "expressing" and "responding." These areas might be broken down further into subskills such as responding to anger, affection, and so on. It is always beneficial to operationalize the skill to be learned; that is, the skill should be such that it can be seen and heard. After operationalizing the skill, the therapist explains what the model (in this case, the therapist) will be saying or doing and tells family members what they should look for. For example, if a family member is having difficulty asking for help, the therapist might say, "John, I need you to _____ when I'm feeling down."

2. *Model behaviors that hold the family members' attention*   Familiar and relevant experiences are more likely to hold attention and facilitate learning. In addition, models are generally most effective when they are the same sex as a family member and similar in appearance, age, and so on. Because of this, the therapist may want the family to identify personal resources (friends) who could serve as models. If the family member is having difficulty entering a social situation, a friend who is accepted in that situation and who is similar to the family member might be asked to model or demonstrate how to get involved. The therapist might say, "I would like you to show Mary what to do when she wants to have a conversation with others." A model who verbalizes his or her own uncertainty (as in, "I'm not sure, but here is one way to try it") and offers subsequent problem-solving or coping strategies can be helpful in eliciting the family members' attention. Another useful technique is to emphasize those behaviors to be modeled. The therapist might ask the model to speak more loudly during the relevant responses or to repeat a key passage ("Would you repeat that, please"). Tone of voice and mannerisms can also be used to gain the family members' attention.

3. *Ask family members to discuss what they have observed*   Unless family members are able to understand and retain the essential characteristics of the model's behavior, the intervention is of no avail. When the modeled behavior is particularly abstract, retention may be facilitated if either the model or therapist discusses the important features of the model's performance. For example, a model demonstrating how to express affection to a family member could discuss different ways to show affection. The therapist could evaluate the family members' understanding by asking them to summarize the main features or general rules of the model's performance.

4. *Reinforce the modeled behavior*   The therapist must provide incentives that encourage family members to perform the modeled behavior. When modeled behavior is not reinforced, imitation does not occur; the likelihood that imitative behavior does occur increases with the probability of receiving reinforcement. To reinforce the modeled behavior, the therapist might respond to the model's statements with positive comments ("That's an interesting point" or "That's a thoughtful idea"). By observing that the model is reinforced for expressing an opinion or solving a problem, the family members learn the most effective response in that situation.

Instruction   Once the family has attended to and understood the model's behavior, the therapist should provide instructions before the family begins practicing the new behavior. The therapist can focus attention on the relevant and essential aspects of the model's performance. The instructions may be spoken or written by the therapist or provided in the form of an audiotape or videotape. The therapist might say, "Watch how I show appreciation to your husband," and then model the appropriate behavior, adding, "Now I want you to show appreciation for something your husband has done recently."

Instructions can be provided in the following ways:

1. *Prompt specific behaviors for members to try*   The therapist is now essentially serving as a coach who prompts specific behavior for the family to try. Instructions generally may be positive (do this) or negative (don't do that). The therapist gives numerous specific examples. Instructing a wife to give feedback to her husband, the therapist might say, "Look directly at your husband and tell him how it makes you feel when he doesn't call to say he won't be home. Don't just accuse him of being inconsiderate."

2. *Help family members decide when to give feedback to each other*   The therapist might discuss when to give feedback—for example, "when you have time to sit down" or "when you are not so angry"—since family members may know what to say but not when to say it. By going over the demonstration, the therapist can pinpoint behaviors by the model (therapist, friend) and discuss why such behaviors can serve as a cue to a family member to perform a specific behavior.

Practice   Having received instructions on what to say and do, the family is ready to practice the behavior; practice is an essential part of the learning process because people learn by doing. Family members role play new relationships or problem-solving behaviors. If either spouse shows resistance to this idea, the therapist can provide examples of the usefulness of practice. The crucial point is that each family member must feel that he or she is not just learning a role that is artificial and unusable. Consequently, the role playing situations should be as realistic as possible and should include verbal responses with which each family member feels comfortable.

The following are important guidelines:

1. *Prepare the family member for practice*   The family must accept the idea that practice is an appropriate way to develop new coping or problem-solving behaviors. If the family shows some resistance to this idea, the therapist can provide examples where practice has proven useful. Experience, drills, rehearsal, recitation, homework, and exercises all involve practice. The therapist might say, "Maybe we could practice expressing appreciation to your son. I'll role play your son, and we'll see how it goes. If you have trouble thinking of something to say, I'll help you."

2. *Start with a situation that the family can perform with little difficulty*   Practice is more successful when the initial situation is familiar to the family. For example, in a parent–adolescent conflict, the therapist might ask both parties to start by "talking about something that happened at school today." If they are unable to do this, the therapist might ask them to engage in less threatening activities such as sitting next to each other. Regardless of the activity, the therapist should begin with a nonthreatening situation.

3. *Break the behavior down into small steps*   These steps should range in complexity from simple (e.g., giving a compliment) to the complete new behavior (e.g., asking for help). In this case, the social interaction varies according to the level of difficulty.

4. *Prompt family members when they can't think of what to say or do*   The therapist can provide a sentence that fits within the context of the interaction (e.g., "It's important to me to know how you feel"). It is essential that the prompt occur only when the family member pauses or hesitates (generally for about 5 seconds). In addition, the therapist can use hand signals to raise or lower the family member's voice or to signal to come closer. Prompts should be faded as family members become able to practice the behavior unaided. At this point, the therapist should praise the family members for expressing the desired behavior in their own words.

Feedback   When family members have practiced the skills, each must receive feedback on their performance. Such feedback provides an incentive for improvement. Information received about poor performance can be potentially as helpful as knowledge regarding positive performance.

The following guidelines are important in providing feedback:

1. *Solicit the family's ideas about feedback prior to practice*   The therapist might say, "I'll observe you and try to give you some helpful hints." When a family member denies or disagrees with feedback from the therapist ("That's not the way it sounded to me") or attempts to justify a response ("The reason I said that was . . . "), then feedback was probably not solicited or agreed on prior to practice.

2. *Describe rather than evaluate the family members' behaviors*   For example, the therapist might replay a videotape of what a family member said and comment, "Here you say 'My mother thinks I should . . .' Do you remember we agreed you would say, 'I think I should . . . '?" The therapist's feedback statements should avoid blame. Statements such as, "That just doesn't sound right" or "I don't know why you can't do that" fail to provide helpful information.

3. *Reinforce a family member's response and at the same time prompt similar responses*   For example, the therapist might say, "That's a good question to get him to talk to you. Sometimes, however, your husband may not want to talk about his job. Can you think of some other questions you could ask him?" By prompting additional questions, the therapist not only helps reinforce the spouse's use of questions in a practice session but also facilitates its generalization to other situations and people.

The therapist should provide opportunities for the family to practice their skills at home and should supply guidelines or work sheets to facilitate such practice. Therapy is more effective when family members are able to practice skills successfully in everyday interactions.

Assigning Tasks

Tasks attempt to change the sequence of interaction in the family. They may help a family become more organized, establish operational boundaries, set rules, or establish family goals (Madanes, 1981). Tasks might include (a) advice, (b) explanations or suggestions, or (c) directives to change the interactional sequence in the family (Papp, 1980). For example, in the case of a family with a mother and daughter who are overinvolved and a father who is peripheral, the therapist might give the following explanation to the mother: "Your daughter needs to treat you with respect. She will be able to do that when you have your husband's support. Right now, he gets called on as the bad guy when you aren't able to deal with her. This is a critical time when your daughter needs to spend more time with her father." Unfortunately, advice may not be successful because family members often know what to do but don't know how to do it.

In many cases, the therapist must convince the family to follow the directive or task. This may be difficult unless each family member sees some payoff. Persuading a family to perform a task depends on the type of task, the family, and the kind of relationship the therapist has with the family (Haley, 1976). For example, there may not be a payoff for adolescents to talk in a session if they aren't certain that their parents care about them or if they can get their way without talking. In this case, the therapist's directive must provide some benefits (e.g., more privileges or parental concern) for the adolescent as well as for other members of the family.

Haley (1976) offers several suggestions to therapists for getting families to follow their tasks or directives:

1. *Discuss everything the family has done to try to solve the problem* By this device, the therapist can avoid making suggestions that have already been tried. The therapist should lead the family to the conclusion that everything has been tried but nothing has worked. At this point, the therapist is in a position to offer the family something different.

2. *Ask family members to discuss the negative consequences if their problem is not handled now (i.e., "What is going to happen if this problem is not resolved?")* Aversive consequences are probably different for different members of the family. Nevertheless, examining the negative consequences of

the problem for each family member emphasizes the intensity of the problem. A mother and her adolescent daughter, for instance, get into conflicts; both cry and are unhappy, and neither gets her way. The mother doesn't get the kind of respect she deserves and the daughter doesn't get any privileges. It is important for the therapist to emphasize these consequences and to project what might happen if the problem is not resolved.

3. *Assign a task that is reasonable and easily accomplished*   To ensure that the family can complete the task at home, it is often necessary to get them to complete the task in the session. For example, the therapist may want an adolescent daughter to have a conversation with her mother without interruptions by her father. Therefore, the therapist may ask the daughter to talk with her mother in session while the father reads a magazine. The therapist might suggest an activity that both of them might enjoy doing together. If the father interrupts before the mother and daughter complete the task, the therapist may wish to devise something else for the father to do, such as running an errand, so as to improve the chances that he does not interrupt when mother and daughter attempt to complete a conversation at home. The therapist can also ensure that the task is accomplished by providing adequate instructions. In this instance, the therapist focuses attention on the relevant and essential aspects of each family member's performance. Before the family begins the task, the therapist might instruct the father that it will be difficult for him to stay out of it and that he needs to occupy himself in some other way.

4. *Assign a task to fit the ability and performance level of the family members*   In the film *Family With a Little Fire* (Minuchin, 1974), the task is focused on the scapegoated child's fire setting. The therapist, Braulio Montalvo, asks the mother to spend 5 minutes each day teaching her daughter how to light matches correctly. He also instructs the parental child who stands between mother and child to watch the other children while the mother is teaching the child. This task is suited to each family member's level of ability.

5. *Use authority to get the family to follow the directive or task*   Sometimes the therapist must use his or her knowledge and expertise to get the family to comply. It is important for the therapist to accept the role of expert rather than asking the family what they think they should do. The therapist might say, for example, "From my experience, I'd say that this is a critical time for your son, and he needs time with his father." The therapist is really saying, "On the basis of my expertise, I believe that it is important for you to do this." Sometimes the therapist may ask whether the family or family member trusts him or her. If the family or family member says yes, the therapist might say, "Good. Then I want you to do this because it is important. Trust me." Here the therapist uses trust to gain control of the interview.

6. *Give clear instructions to each member of the family*   Everyone should know what his or her responsibilities are. If a therapist asks a father and daughter to do something together, then specific dates and times should be specified. By deciding in advance on a time, the father and daughter make a commitment to perform the task. Establishing a time also decreases the likelihood of interference by something else, such as work or TV. The therapist and the family should also decide who will take care of the other children and what the mother will be doing during that time. The therapist might ask family members to describe what they will be doing so that they are all clear about their roles. Family members should be encouraged to discuss anything that might interfere with the completion of the task.

Developing Rituals

Rituals can address a number of therapeutic goals related to rigid family rules and omitted developmental tasks in the life cycle. The Milan team (Selvini Palazzoli et al., 1978) designed specific strategic instructions in the form of family rituals. Their ritualized prescriptions were designed for "breaking up those behaviors through which each parent disqualifies and sabotages the initiatives and directions of the other parent in his relation with the children" (Selvini Palazzoli et al., 1978, p. 3). Such prescriptions can be repeated with the same format for any type of family. Rituals are used instead of interpretation, which is often ineffective in altering the rules of the system. At the end of an assessment period, the therapist helps the family develop a ritual. The following is a common Milan-style prescription:

> *On even days of the week—Tuesdays, Thursdays, and Saturdays—beginning from tomorrow onwards until the date of the next session and fixing the time between X o'clock and Y o'clock (making sure that the whole family will be at home during this time), whatever Z does (name of patient, followed by a list of his symptomatic behaviors), father will decide alone, at his absolute discretion, what to do with Z. Mother will have to behave as if she were not there. On odd days of the week—Mondays, Wednesdays, and Fridays—at the same time, whatever Z may do, mother will have full power to decide what course of action to follow regarding Z. Father will have to behave as if he were not there. On Sundays, everyone must behave spontaneously. Each parent, on the days assigned to him or her, must record in a diary any infringement by the partner of the prescription according to which*

he is expected to behave as if he were not there. (In some cases the job of re-
cording the possible mistakes of one of the parents has been entrusted to a
child acting as a recorder or to the patient himself if he is fit for the task.)
(Selvini Palazzoli et al., 1978, p. 5)

Selvini Palazzoli et al. (1978) note that the ritualized prescription oper-
ates at several levels. First, the rules of the game are changed to prevent inter-
ferences from occurring. Second, parents are blocked from competing for the
therapist's approval, since their efforts only serve to deflect attention from the
problem (relationship). Finally, the therapist gains information regardless of
whether the family follows the prescription. This information can be used to
design subsequent interventions.

The following guidelines are helpful in designing rituals:

1. *Prescribe one or more aspects of the problem. Those problematic*
   thoughts and behaviors then form the content of the ritual. For example,
   a boy who threw frequent "out-of-control" temper tantrums was
   asked to continue having his tantrums but to have them in a special
   place at home and only after school, when he really had time to
   throw one.
2. *Provide a rationale for the ritual to increase the likelihood of compliance.*
   For example, the therapist might suggest to the family that structuring the temper tantrums in this way helps family members gain control of the problem or helps the therapist better understand the
   problem.

Another type of ritual, suggested by Imber-Black, Roberts, and Whiting
(1988), helps families address unresolved developmental issues by grieving
traumatic losses, completing developmental milestones, or celebrating and
stabilizing progress. Such rituals form a part of many religious and societal traditions, but may have been overlooked as a family's problem was developing.
For example, if families have suffered a traumatic death or loss, the therapist
may develop special grieving rituals for the family to facilitate the further healing necessary to break a dysfunctional pattern. These rituals are most effective
when the influence of the loss on the presenting problem has been recognized
and the family becomes the author of the ceremony, determining the participants and the desired meaning of the ritual.

Sometimes, families skip important developmental milestones that later
become metaphors for the presenting problem. For example, when couples
elope or forgo a honeymoon, family therapists may use this as a metaphor for

skipping some important developmental task, such as creating a strong marital attachment. As the couple identifies elements of the marriage that were skipped and need to be developed, the planning of a honeymoon or special anniversary celebration can symbolize the completion of relationship tasks facilitated during the course of therapy.

Other rituals celebrate the completion of therapy as a rite of passage (Epston & White, 1992); for example, a triangulated child may be helped to disengage from the position of "marital therapist" and given a new position as "liberated sixth-grader," free to explore how children grow up when they don't have to worry about their parents' marriage. A concluding ritual then allows the family to celebrate such achievements in the company of significant others. Thus, the culmination of therapy is not seen as a private termination or as implying loss of the therapeutic relationship. Rather, such rituals help families to stay focused on the changes they have made. They also normalize therapy by incorporating societal traditions into the process.

❄ ADDRESSING CLIENT RESISTANCE

The term *resistance* has become a cliché in the field of psychotherapy. Most often, it connotes the client's lack of cooperation with the practitioner. However, in family therapy, there is a strong bias toward the notion that resistance is an interactional event characterized by the professional's lack of understanding about what is important to the family. For example, battered women are often considered resistant when they fail to follow professional advice that places physical safety above psychological safety. While there is widespread agreement about the importance of physical safety as a human right, professionals are frequently guilty of blaming the innocent when they label clients as resistant or stubborn without understanding the history that has influenced their beliefs about self, others, and the world around them. It is our observation that in many difficult cases involving elder abuse, domestic violence, and child sexual abuse, distinct perceptual patterns have a significant influence over the behavioral patterns that develop in family life. Thus, it is incumbent on family therapists to understand the unique thought processes of clients rather than to label them resistant or stubborn. As therapist skill develops in this area, client resistance diminishes.

When family therapists reach a therapeutic impasse, one way to address client thought processes is to search for a positive connotation to some element of the problem. For example, Selvini Palazzoli et al. (1978) describe a 10-year-old boy who exhibited psychotic symptoms following the death of his grandfather. At the end of the first session, the therapist told the boy that he was "doing a good thing" (p. 81). The therapist further noted that the grandfather was a "central pillar of the family" and kept the family together. The boy was told that he had assumed his grandfather's role to maintain balance in the family and that he should continue this role until the next session. Here the therapist used "positive connotation" to maintain homeostasis in the family rather than to challenge it. The boy had taken the grandfather's place to maintain a gender balance in a family that, following the grandfather's death, had been dominated by women. The use of positive connotation allows the therapist to join with the family at a time of crisis and to understand the problem in the light of complicated systemic dynamics.

If families fail to follow a prescription, the Milan team might write paradoxical letters that admit defeat or helplessness (e.g., "Your family has special power" or "I feel a sense of helplessness"). When therapists acknowledge their powerlessness, some families continue in therapy and discuss their influence on the therapist when they are united (Weeks & Abate, 1982). Furthermore, paradoxical letters allow the therapist to stop arguing for something that the family does not want. The family, in turn, often rebounds and begins changing on their own terms. Thus, the Milan team uses the family's resistance to produce change in the system. The paradoxical letters "allow the therapist or team to stay in a position from which maximum change can be achieved" (Hoffman, 1981, p. 303).

When symptoms have become chronic, even though numerous people are trying to help the family or individual to change, it is often wise to take a cautious position about the timing and amount of change: Restrain the family when it begins to show improvement. Restraining interventions are used to help the therapist move at a pace that is optimal for the family. In essence, the therapist is saying, "I'm not sure this change would be beneficial. I realize the problem has certain disadvantages, but there may be benefits to this situation that need to be identified first so that improvement in one part of your life won't lead to unforeseen consequences somewhere else. Can you think of any conditions that might get worse if this problem were to be resolved?" As families are encouraged and allowed to identify certain dilemmas that may have been covert, the therapist offers genuineness and warmth to the family in addressing these unforeseen consequences before change begins in earnest.

These examples are commonly referred to as "paradoxical interventions." However, we offer them not as strategic manipulations that may satisfy a practitioner's need for compliance, but as suggestions for understanding human nature at the deeper level of personal and relational dilemmas that often makes change a complicated process for families. If beginning practitioners address resistance as an issue of therapist inexperience rather than as a personal attribute of the client, therapeutic impasses become signals that this deeper level of understanding is needed to break the impasse. Then it is possible to return to the models of assessment reviewed in Chapter Six and choose another area of emphasis until the understanding is achieved.

In summary, the family is most able to resolve its problems when the therapist takes a directive approach to managing in-session process, mobilizes perceptual and behavioral change, and remains nonjudgmental toward unique client characteristics that may be at the heart of a treatment impasse. As beginning practitioners learn to integrate these areas of expertise, they become able to recognize how each model of family therapy addresses these elements in some way. Then they are able to develop their own innovations by combining various models to address the issues in a way that is most comfortable or useful for the family.

Chapter Nine

DEVELOPING A SHARED DIRECTION

DEVELOPING GOALS
Prioritizing Areas of Change
Making Goals Concrete and Specific
Developing Goals From Family Strengths
Building on Existing Strengths

INVOLVING FAMILY MEMBERS
Overcoming Initial Resistances
Connecting With Family Members

INVOLVING THE NETWORK
Interview Strategies
Developing a Collaboration Team
Guidelines for the Collaboration Team Interview
Obstacles to Collaboration

CHOOSING INTERVENTIONS

Treatment plans should be based on assessment data for the family. Each treatment plan should be individualized and should fit the unique characteristics of the family and interactive culture. For example, in one family with parent–child conflict, the treatment plan might call for conflict management skills. In another family with a similar problem but more hostility, the plan might call for separate sessions with the parent and child to establish trust. Sometimes a treatment plan can be presented in the initial contract for service. In these cases, clients already have their problem defined in concrete, behavioral terms, and the process of problem resolution is straightforward. For example, if the family is seeking a consultation to decide on a strategy for the long-term care of an elderly parent, the goal may be to decide who is responsible for which tasks after some psychoeducational sessions regarding the impact of long-term care on families. This direction could be decided on in the initial session and described to the family as part of the therapeutic contract.

In another case, parents may be seeking help for the behavioral problems of their daughter. Their goal may be for her to stop fighting with other children on the school playground. A common treatment plan for such a presenting problem is to explore the relationships between the family and the school, between the daughter and the playground group, and between the individual family members. The family therapist, the family, and the school might form a collaborative team. Then the family therapist can facilitate cooperation among all parties in developing corrective strategies. This direction might also be formulated in the initial session and suggested to the family for their consideration during the contracting stage of that session.

Regardless of the complexity of the case, most treatment plans involve some combination of the elements illustrated in these examples. First, goals are developed from assessment data to fit each unique situation. Second, the family and larger network are considered as potential participants. Third, interventions that fit the family's developmental level and the clinician's skill level are chosen either spontaneously or deliberately. This chapter reviews each of these elements of treatment planning.

❄ DEVELOPING GOALS

In most cases, client goals begin as abstract desires (e.g., "I want help dealing with my low self-esteem" or "We want to communicate better"). The family therapist helps the family clarify such desires until behavioral and perceptual elements of the problem are identified as specific goals ("I want to be able to go to a party and have something interesting to say" or "When we discuss finances, we'll be able to resolve the conflict to our satisfaction"). The treatment plan may be described as including the assessment process, which clarifies the nature of the problem and a subsequent plan of action, or as consisting only of the sequence of interventions set in motion as a result of the assessment process. In either case, the treatment plan should address the family's goals and hypotheses generated during the assessment process. A good treatment plan requires the therapist to analyze hypotheses to (a) prioritize areas of change, (b) make goals concrete and specific, (c) develop goals from family strengths, and (d) build on existing strengths.

Prioritizing Areas of Change

One of the greatest dilemmas a therapist faces is knowing where to start treatment. Where the intervention begins is often determined by the therapist's own theoretical framework. The structural family therapist might intervene by developing an interactional relationship with the family. The therapist probes both to elicit information about the problem and to realign the organization of the family. The strategic family therapist, on the other hand, might intervene through messages or directives. Directives require the client to respond or behave in a specific way. Likewise, the intergenerational therapist attempts to maintain objectivity from the outset by (a) asking "thinking" questions rather than "feeling" questions and (b) avoiding triangulation by asking each family member to speak to the therapist rather than to each other. The experiential family therapist, on the other hand, focuses more on the personhood of the therapist and how to intervene with the use of self to accomplish the therapeutic goal. When developing a treatment plan, we suggest that beginning practitioners avoid interventions that are model-specific until after the family's goals have been prioritized and clarified.

If the family presents several problem areas, the beginning therapist must set priorities for treatment. Four criteria are critical in making this determination. The first criterion is: Which problem is of most immediate importance to the family? The family must be asked to select the problem of greatest concern. For example, a couple may want to improve their marital relationship, a mother may want to get along better with her daughter, or two parents may need support in taking care of their infant. The therapist then must ask, "Which problem is most pressing to you?" or "Which problem must you solve now?" Alternatively, the therapist might say, "So, the first issue we need to resolve is _____ ." Unless the therapist has reasons for choosing another area to change, the family is told that the one selected will be addressed initially.

In many cases, additional criteria must be considered in prioritizing areas of change. The second criterion is: Which problem has the greatest negative consequence if not handled immediately? While a family member may feel that a specific problem is of greatest concern to her (e.g., loss of friends), another problem may have greater negative consequence (e.g., loss of a job or breakup of a marriage). A young adult may feel he needs to get along better with others, but unless he stops drinking, his health and safety are at risk. The therapist might ask the young adult what would happen if the drinking problem was not resolved. In this case, the consequences seem more severe for drinking than for lack of friends, thus warranting more immediate intervention.

By examining what has happened in the past with the same people under similar conditions, the therapist can better predict the consequences of the problem and weigh it accordingly. The therapist may ask, "What might happen if this problem is not resolved?" or "What would likely happen to you if _____ occurred?" Once this is determined, the third criterion comes into play: Which problem can be corrected most easily considering the resources and constraints? What forces (people, situations) stand in the way of problem resolution? What resources exist that could help solve the problem? For example, a mother who feels trapped by her children may list going to school to complete an advanced degree as a goal. If lack of money for a babysitter and her husband's resistance are obstacles, however, the therapist might ask, "What are some things that might prevent this problem from being solved?" and "What are some things that will help you resolve the problem?"

Finally, the fourth criterion for prioritizing change is: Which problems require handling before other problems can be solved? For example, it makes little sense to work on improving the marriage if both spouses are abusing alcohol. Likewise, before parents can control their children, they must learn to work cooperatively. The therapist might ask, "What would happen if the problem were solved?" "Would the couple improve their marriage?" "Would they do a better job parenting their children?"

In some cases, the therapist may wish to be more precise in determining the relative importance of each goal. Utilizing family goal recording, Fleuridas, Rosenthal, Leigh, and Leigh (1990) weigh each goal according to its relative importance to the family. They state:

> *Often a family claims that the target complaint (for example, Mom's alcoholism or Dad's abuse) is the primary concern and far outweighs the other goal areas. When such a preference is acknowledged, the therapist proceeds by asking the family if the target area is twice or three times as important as the other goal areas (in that subsystem unit). Through this process of*

questioning, approximate weights of importance can be assigned to each subsystem unit (the sum of the subsystems' weights = 100%). (p. 394)

Family goal recording permits the therapist to evaluate change in the presenting concerns of couples and families (see Chapter Ten).

Making Goals Concrete and Specific

In the problem definition stage, the therapist helps family members decide what they want changed. For example, the therapist might begin by asking, "How would you like things to be different in this family?" or "What would you like your son to be doing instead?" The responses eventually become goal behaviors ("If your husband doesn't pay attention to you, how would you like him to show that he is paying attention?"). Later, when tracking the interactional sequence that is maintaining the problem, the therapist might say, "And then he yells at you. What would you like him to do instead of that?" or "It sounds like when he talks to you that way you get angry and threaten him. How could he talk to you differently at that moment so you don't get angry with him?" Often, when tracking the interactional sequence, the therapist is asking family members to describe how they would like another family member to respond differently within the sequence of behavior preceding or following the identified problem. In earlier phases of the interview, the clinician is requesting only that family members give a general statement of what they want to be different. In this portion of the interview, the therapist can help family members become more specific in formulating observable goals.

Goals should be stated clearly so that everyone can agree when the goal has been reached. For example, if parents report that they want their child "to pay attention," then the therapist must question the parent to determine what the child will be doing "to pay attention." Likewise, labels such as "unhappiness" and "anger" must be stated in such a way that they can be resolved.

The following suggestions represent several different ways to help family members describe changes (goals) in more observable terms:

1. *Ask each family member to describe how he or she would like things to be different.* The therapist might ask, "What changes would you like to see in this family?" or "How would you like things to be different?"
2. *Ask family members to describe changes in positive rather than negative terms.* The therapist might comment, "I know you don't like the way your son said that. How would you like him to say it?"

3. *Ask family members to be specific about what they want changed.* The therapist might ask questions such as: "What do you mean by _____ ?" "What would your son be doing to show you that he can be trusted?" "How would you know that your mother cares about you?" "What is one way he could help you?" "How would she show you that she has an improved self-concept?"

The therapist may often establish intermediate goals, each of which represents a step toward the final goal. This process helps make the family's problem more manageable. Consider a mother who cannot get her 15-year-old son to come home on time. The family lives in the grandmother's home. The grandmother complains that her daughter (the mother) doesn't know how to handle the son. The grandmother and mother argue over who should be in charge of the boy. The boy is out of control; however, the intermediate goal might be to have mother and grandmother agree on how the mother will manage her son's behavior. The grandmother may also need to become involved in some outside activities. Once these intermediate goals have been reached, the therapist could focus on the final goal—how the mother (and grandmother, if necessary) can get her son to come home at the designated time.

Once the therapist and family have agreed on the goal, the next step is to specify conditions under which the goal behavior will occur. The conditions of the desired behavior are often interactionally based; that is, it may be that a mother needs to set limits with her son in the father's presence. The conditions under which the behavior is to occur indicate with whom and where the behavior is to take place. If family members are to plan an activity, the conditions state who will be present and where the activity will occur.

Once the goal has been specified in concrete terms, an acceptable level of performance must be established. This criterion specifies how well and how often the behavior is to be performed. For example, "complying with parental requests" is not very useful as an indicator of successful performance. However, if the goal is restated as "complying with household parental requests 80% of the time and never breaking curfew," then the therapist, family, and others will know when the goal has been reached. This helps ensure that observers (probation officers, teachers, or others) will agree whether the goal has been met.

In determining how much change is needed, it is essential to specify how family members are currently behaving. This provides some standard by which to measure the family members' progress toward their individual goals and to determine the amount of learning needed by the family members to achieve the change they want. The amount of change agreed on should be set low enough to ensure success; that is, the initial goals must be achievable. As a general rule, it is better to set the level of initial change too low rather than too high. If the criterion level is too high, the desired behavior often does not occur. Once an intermediate goal has been accomplished, it is possible to specify new changes that are now more achievable.

In defining the problem, family members are asked to describe changes that they would like to see in the family. These changes eventually are refined until they can be stated in the form of manageable and measurable goals. When therapists help family members specify measurable goals, they are making a therapeutic contract with the family to ensure a clear understanding of what everyone expects and how long it might take to reach the goals.

Developing Goals From Family Strengths

Goal setting should evolve out of family strengths rather than weaknesses. Focusing on the family's deficits without considering their strengths makes it difficult to establish a relationship where both the therapist and the family can be optimistic about change. Emphasizing strengths helps alter the family's self-image and gives family members hope that their goals can be attained.

In establishing goals based on strengths, the therapist and family work in partnership. Instead of selecting goals for the family, the therapist listens to what the family would like changed and encourages them to express what they would like to be different. Family members often feel hopeless; thus, it is important to put them in charge of deciding on changes (goals). In some cases, the family's goals may be different from those of the therapist. A parent may wish to take care of a legal problem or illness, whereas the therapist may be concerned about the parent's relationship with the children. Parents often feel overwhelmed because they have multiple problems. The therapist should respond to the family's concern around these basic needs before dealing with higher order needs such as parent–child relationships.

The therapist must interpret the family's definition of the problem in a different way to give it new meaning. This new interpretation helps the family get in touch with their own strengths. Sometimes this is referred to as reframing the problem. Such an intervention may have a paradoxical effect. When a mother says, "I can't get him to do anything. He won't pay any attention to me," the therapist helps the mother understand that her "caring" sometimes makes it difficult for her to set firm limits. When she perceives herself not as "weak" but as caring, she has a new way of thinking about the problem so that it can be resolved. Paradoxically, the therapist can then help her expand her sense of caring to include additional behaviors.

Another approach to the same problem might be to help the mother break down "pay any attention" into small goals that are attainable. The therapist might start by asking, "What is something your son does when he is paying attention?" Then the goal is to increase something that is already happening to a small extent (O'Hanlon & Weiner-Davis, 1989). When the therapist creates an environment based on strengths, family members are more likely to set goals that can be met successfully.

If therapists start treatment according to these assumptions, they will focus on those areas that are working. The therapist wants to start by looking for small positive changes before examining bigger changes. This can be done by focusing on those aspects of the family that seem most changeable. The therapist might ask, "What would be a small sign that things are changing?" or "What might be one thing you could do to change _____ ?" or "What are some things you could do now to handle _____ ?" When family members are able to make small positive changes, they are more hopeful about handling bigger changes (O'Hanlon & Weiner-Davis, 1989).

Building on Existing Strengths

Family members who are overwhelmed by difficulties often lose touch with their strengths. In that case, a good therapist helps them identify problem-solving strengths. This approach allows the family members to be more hopeful, to alter their view of themselves, and to feel more optimistic about change.

The following interview strategies are helpful in identifying strengths:

1. *Emphasize positive statements reported by family members* (e.g., "My mother listens to me when I have a problem"). It is also important to observe behaviors that reflect sensitivity, appreciation, or cooperation between family members.
2. *Encourage family members to share their story about themselves.* The therapist should pay particular attention to those aspects of their story that reveal how the family has coped successfully with problems.
3. *Note family interactions that reflect strengths and competence* (e.g., "I like the way you help your daughter find her own answers to the problem"). Underscoring positive family interactions helps the therapist identify other strengths and competencies.

4. *Emphasize times that family members enjoy together.* What are they do-ing? What makes it enjoyable? These questions offer opportunities to discuss strengths and capabilities.

5. *Reframe problems or negative statements in a more positive way* (e.g., "Your anger shows how much you care about him"). A therapist re-frames the problem by changing the conceptual or emotional view-point so as to change the meaning of the problem without changing the facts. The situation doesn't change, but the interpretation does.

6. *Emphasize the things that families do well.* All families have areas of strengths (e.g., patience, skills, and coping behavior). By asking questions, the therapist can learn how families utilize these strengths to solve problems (e.g., "What works best with your child?" "Tell me about the times you were able to get him to _____ . What did you do?" "How were you able to get him to _____ ? What does that say about your ability to get him to do that in the fu-ture?").

Eliciting family strengths helps the clinician understand how families cope with problems as well as how they promote growth and development.

These principles of treatment planning lay a foundation to maximize the effectiveness of any family therapy model that the clinician might prefer. This foundation is built on the following assumptions: (a) There are several poten-tially effective ways to begin treatment; (b) families have resources and strengths to resolve problems; (c) families often are aware of alternative ways to alter a problem; and (d) families are more likely to implement a solution to the problem if they suggest it. If further treatment planning indicates family or network involvement, the family therapist must be prepared to direct the pro-cess in a manner that maintains the foundation that is being built.

❄ INVOLVING FAMILY MEMBERS

When a family member first calls a therapist, the call can be regarded as an in-dividual request for help and an indicator of stress in the family. The clinician must attempt to gather information that reflects the effects of the problem on other family members and the family's view of the problem. If made aware of relational information about the problem during intake, the individual is more likely to understand why all family members should be present during therapy. Therapists should request the family's help in solving the problem.

In presenting a rationale for involving all family members, Garfield (1981) suggests:

> *When a family member begins to describe his problem, the therapist should listen sympathetically. He should also pay attention to the interactional aspects of the problem. For example, if a husband says, "I'm not getting along with my wife," or "My wife and I are having a terrible problem with our teenage daughter," or even "I've been awfully depressed and haven't discussed this with anyone in my family," he is already introducing interpersonal elements of the problem. The therapist may take note of this issue and return to it later when he explains the importance of including the other family members in the evaluation. If the person describes the problem in personal terms, e.g. "I've been suffering from severe headaches and my family doctor tells me it's my nerves," the therapist may inquire if anyone in the house is aware of this problem and how they have responded to it. This reframes the problem in interactional terms, and allows the therapist to find out who else lives in the house and how they may be involved in the problem. (p. 6)*

Therapists and intake workers should listen closely to how the caller describes the problem. For example, a wife may say, "We just don't communicate" or "We don't get along." In some cases, a parent may describe the problem in triangular terms: "She won't listen to us" or "He minds everyone but me." In such cases, the therapist should clarify to whom the caller is referring and their relationship to the problem (see Chapter Five). Whatever the request for help, all family members who are related to the problem should be asked to attend the initial session.

Overcoming Initial Resistances

Family members may often be resistant to attending therapy sessions, especially if they feel blame or responsibility for the problem. In particular, fathers and husbands characteristically have been reluctant to discuss matters that they regard as private with someone outside the family. These problems become more deep-seated when the wife protects her husband ("My husband would never talk to a therapist" or "He doesn't believe in counseling").

The beginning therapist must understand the protective nature of these responses and deal with them in a supportive manner. The real issue here seems to be who is responsible for bringing reluctant family members to therapy and how this might be accomplished. Some therapists (Minuchin, 1984) refuse to see the family unless all members are present. This obviously puts pressure on the family member to get the entire family to therapy. However, this tactic may backfire: The family member may drop out of therapy. Moreover, providing therapy only if the entire family attends may be inconsistent with the policies at many mental health centers or family service agencies.

Family members' reluctance to attend therapy often reflects the systemic nature of the problem. In this case, the therapist might first challenge the caller's belief system by saying, "I think you may be underestimating your husband" or "What makes you think he doesn't want to share his feelings?" Sometimes, the therapist can point out the benefits of therapy by saying, "It might be a relief for him to talk about this with someone else" or "It might be helpful if he heard what is really bothering you" or "I think your kids would learn to share their feelings if they were here."

Beginning family therapists and students should consult with their supervisors to assess the motivational level of family members who make initial contacts (W. Nichols & Everett, 1988). What is the role of these individuals in the family system? Do they in fact want other family members to be present? Important information can often be gained by discussing what would happen if the therapist took the responsibility of persuading reluctant members to attend therapy. The practitioner must pay attention to the individual's feelings and address each area of discomfort with a plan such that the proposed conjoint session could avoid the client's worst fears (e.g., "I'm afraid you will side with my husband against me"). However, if therapists do decide to make contact with other family members, they are taking responsibility away from the family. We believe that this should be attempted only when all efforts by family members have failed.

At that point, a therapeutic strategy for communicating with the reluctant family member should be discussed. When the absent spouse is uncooperative, the therapist might attempt to focus therapeutic efforts on the cooperating spouse. This procedure is often adopted in cases of substance abuse. David Treadway (1989) elaborates on a case where the husband is the reluctant partner:

> The other way I elicit the husband's cooperation is by asking him if he cares about his wife's anxiety and distress and if he would like to be helpful to her. This defines my work as help to her rather than an attempt to change him. I want him to take the position of aiding her in getting help with her part of the problem. Many drinkers will go along with this idea, because at least for the moment it takes the heat off them. For once their wives are being challenged about their own behavior. Anticipating and blocking the drinker's reactivity are essential to effective intervention with the spouse. (p. 40)

The strategy helps the therapist involve the resistant family member in therapy gradually. In the final analysis, the therapist must decide what to do in the event that not all the members of the family make their scheduled appointments. Many family therapists meet with whomever attends the sessions. These therapists believe that the family system can change by working with one member of the system (O'Hanlon & Weiner-Davis, 1989). However, when the entire family attends the initial session, the therapist can better anticipate the effect of individual changes on the whole system. Additionally, the therapist wants to consult with the family about treatment for individuals to help other family members cope and anticipate any changes in a positive way.

Connecting With Family Members

If family therapists are to be effective in this context, they must connect with the family. Connecting is both an attitude and a skill. To connect with the family, the therapist must convey acceptance of family members and respect for their way of seeing and doing things. It is critical to validate each family member and acknowledge his or her experience and actions. The therapist must let family members know that they are understood and their views are important. Family members must be encouraged to express themselves and to believe that their feelings and views are normal.

The therapist can join with family members in the following ways:

1. *Greet each member of the family by name.*
2. *Make friendly contact with each member.* The therapist asks the individual members what they do and where they live, shares information about the children, and so on.
3. *Respect the family hierarchy.* The therapist must begin with the parents when asking each member about his or her view of the problem.
4. *Acknowledge each member's experience, position, and actions* (e.g., "Ms. Jones, I know you have tried your best to help your son. It shows how much you care about him"). Reinforcing or validating a family member often helps other members view the problem differently.

When Boszormenyi-Nagy (1966) developed the strategy of multidirected partiality, one of his goals was to address the challenge of connecting with each member of the family. In his work, he systematically interacted with each family member to understand each position and to communicate that understanding for each member to ratify or clarify. As he did so, he was able to gain a clear picture of what each member thought about the presenting problem and what issues might become obstacles to change. In working with entire family groups or networks from the larger community, the skill of connecting with each member of the system becomes a trademark of the evolving family therapist.

❄ INVOLVING THE NETWORK

The purpose of this section is to assist the therapist in identifying sources of support and resources for the family. Sources of support vary along a continuum beginning with the family unit and moving outward to social organizations. Sources of support might include: (a) nuclear or immediate family (children, parents, household members); (b) relatives (blood and marriage); (c) informal network members (friends, neighbors, co-workers, and others); (d) social organizations (church, clubs, etc.); (e) educational organizations and agencies (family agencies, health organizations, schools, and day-care centers); (f) professional services (e.g., counseling and early intervention services); and (g) policymaking groups and individuals (agency directors, school boards, county and state governments, etc.) (Dunst, Trivette, & Deal, 1988).

   People who can be supportive to the family have many characteristics: (a) They are good at understanding others' needs; (b) they provide unconditional support (i.e., they don't demand something in return for their help); (c) they provide a variety of helping activities (emotional support, instrumental support such as getting groceries, repairs, etc.); and (d) their support is a reciprocal process that benefits both the helper and the family members.

Interview Strategies

Strategies that the therapist can employ to identify sources of support and resources in the family are as follows:

   1. *Ask the family what they have done to resolve the problem*   The following questions are useful in assessing the family's existing network: "Who else is concerned about this problem?" "How do you know they are concerned?" "With whom do you discuss this problem?" "What kind of help do you want from him or her?" "Is that helpful? How so?" "What do they expect from you?" "Is this a person who could be helpful to you here?"

2. Brainstorm a list of persons from human service who are in regular contact with the family The therapist might ask, "Are you involved with _____ ?" or "Who are you in contact with at this agency?" It is important to identify all human service personnel who come in contact with the family.

3. Identify neighbors or friends who can meet needs that cannot be met by the family The therapist might ask, "Is there someone else in your neighborhood who can help you with _____ ?" or "Is there anyone who can make sure your child gets to school on _____ ?"

4. Ask the family if there's anything that would stop them from asking a resource person for help A family may be able to identify people who could help them but may be reluctant to ask for their support. Perhaps a family member does not want to be indebted or dependent on others. In other cases, the family may desire to approach others but lack the prerequisite skills to do so. Identifying barriers utilizing resources assists the therapist in dealing with these obstacles.

It is usually advisable to draw on informal or natural supports before utilizing professional support and resources. Natural supports are people who are resourceful and empathetic to the family. Professional support personnel should not replace natural supports; rather, they should strengthen these relationships. Natural supports offer opportunities for reciprocal aid, a critical element in empowering families. When family members can repay the support person, it strengthens their sense that they have to give as well as take.

In spite of the benefits of informal supports, the practitioner should also be aware that there are several legitimate barriers to their use:

Family members may not have the skills to develop relationships with others.

Family members may be reluctant to ask for help when there are racial or ethnic differences.

Family members may be unwilling to approach others whom they don't know.

Family members may prefer to rely on themselves and not depend on others.

Family members may be closed and reluctant to let others know their business.

In such cases, the family must use the therapist for support. Then they will be more likely to acquire the competencies to obtain other support and re-sources. As the clinician works toward this end, collaboration with other pro-fessionals may also be helpful.

Developing a Collaboration Team

There are several ways to start a collaboration team:

1. *The therapist must develop good relationships with larger systems such as schools, hospitals, and social service agencies.* A beginning therapist might call to make an appointment to learn more about the organi-zation. In some cases, it might be helpful for the therapist to offer a free workshop or consultation on special cases.
2. *Therapists should provide feedback to referral sources (school counselors, social workers, etc.) about current cases when clients have given their per-mission.*
3. *Therapists should ask other professionals (collaborators) for their sugges-tions and ideas about cases.* Would they be willing to provide assis-tance if asked?
4. *Therapists should seek out professionals to form an interagency team that can deal with problems that come to the attention of various organizations.*

In many settings (schools, hospitals, social service and mental health agencies), the family is assigned to a case manager or team. While the thera-pist may treat the family, the case manager or team determines the nature of treatment. In these settings, the therapist may not have access to all family members nor have control over the welfare of the child. For example, in a school setting, the therapist does not have control over the educational plan for the child. The important issue here is how the therapist works with the team or network to empower the family.

A critical consideration is how the therapist can establish a collabora-tive relationship with team members to protect the boundaries of individual roles. Collaborative relationships are predicated largely on the problem-solving process. Team members (teachers, social workers, ministers, friends, and others) are encouraged to identify specific problems and generate solu-tions. The therapist facilitates full participation from all team members.

Working with team members as mutual partners within their prescribed roles, the therapist establishes mutual trust with the collaboration team. Finally, positive changes in the family are more likely to be maintained when team members are involved fully.

Guidelines for the Collaboration Team Interview

The collaboration team interview has evolved from the ecostructural model of Harry Aponte (1976a) and has been described more recently by O'Callaghan (1988) and Boyd-Franklin (1989). Brown and Vaccaro (1991) have developed a set of guidelines for the collaboration team based on these models (Box 9.1). The collaboration team interview is implemented currently with at-risk children and their families at public schools, social service agencies, and mental health centers.

The most essential consideration for the therapist in conducting the collaboration team interview is to remain neutral. Whether the therapist is inside or outside the system (school, social service agency, hospital, etc.), it is important not to be identified too closely with any particular part of the team. For example, a therapist too close to the staff in a school may have difficulty remaining neutral and side with the school against the family. The position of neutrality allows the therapist the greatest latitude for effecting change.

The family therapist can do several other things to maintain a collaborative relationship with team members:

BOX 9.1
Guidelines for Conducting a Family–School Collaboration Meeting

1. Establish a positive climate for change.
2. Report the purpose of the meeting.
3. Have each participant tell how he or she sees the problem.
4. Discuss the strengths of the child.
5. Let participants tell what results they hope to see.
6. Decide how this can be accomplished. Who will do what? When?
7. Decide if other people need to be involved in the intervention.
8. Discuss obstacles to the intervention (e.g., lack of transportation, schedule conflicts).
9. Decide how the participants will know if the intervention has been successful.
10. Decide if a follow-up meeting needs to be scheduled. If so, when?

1. *Try to understand the family problem and how the team member perceives it*   Inherent in this understanding is some discussion of the extent to which the problem is affecting the team member as well as the team member's expectations for the family. In this context, the therapist can clarify the team member's biases and unrealistic expectations.

2. *Make frequent use of the word "we" in developing a collaborative relationship with team members*   The word "we" helps build a sense of cooperation and support among team members. The therapist should avoid criticizing fellow team members.

3. *Examine attempted solutions on the part of team members*   Team members may want to refer the family to the family therapist without doing anything about the problem. For example, a school counselor may refer a child to a family therapist without attempting to address the problem itself. Unless the counselor has tried to solve the problem, the therapist may be unaware of its severity and uncertain of the school's commitment to do something about it. Moreover, if the counselor has intervened, the therapist needs to know the results of the attempted solution.

4. *Work with individuals within their prescribed roles*   For example, classroom problems should be handled by the classroom teacher, conduct problems at home by the parents, and so on. Friends should be asked to provide support without usurping the executive role of parents. Respecting roles helps establish a collaborative relationship with team members and avoids triangles and coalitions that interrupt the treatment plan.

Occasionally, the therapist may choose to shift to the role of advocate for a family if the family is having difficulty obtaining services or needs the weight of an expert to effect a change in the system. The second author has acted as an advocate for families, primarily around issues of educational placement, when appropriate procedures were not being followed or testing data were not being interpreted accurately to parents. But it is preferable to move back to a more neutral stance as quickly as possible. To step in and act as an advocate for parents reduces their own sense of power and competence and creates a coalition with the parents that restricts the range of therapy and limits the therapist's role with school personnel.

In summary, the increased emphasis on family preservation and home-based services has led to therapeutic practices characterized by collaboration between families and community organizations (schools, churches, and other agencies). Thus, the therapist must assist families to become aware of resources and support. Moreover, the therapist must move beyond simply making families aware of services and programs to helping them become effective and successful in accessing them. It is critical that the family be empowered to take action on their own behalf; the therapist cannot simply act for the family.

Obstacles to Collaboration

In preparing for collaboration, the beginning practitioner is well advised to anticipate as many potential problems as possible (Amatea & Sherrard, 1989). Amatea and Sherrard (1991, p. 6) list the following obstacles to collaboration in school settings. Their original words appear in italics:

1. *Educators and therapists are engaged in different systems and traditions, which often makes communication and team work problematic.* For example, educators often handle the needs of the school and community, which requires them to develop rules and expectations for that group. By contrast, therapists deal with the specific beliefs and patterns depicted by the family members before them.
2. *Therapists can often become triangulated in the pattern of blaming and counterblaming between adults at home and school.* The school can often blame the therapist because they perceive he or she is allied with the family. This may serve as an obstacle to working cooperatively with school personnel.
3. *Many therapists are unfamiliar with school contexts and learning/schooling issues.* Unless they are willing to become active learners about the realities of school life and educational practice from educators, they will not be able to collaborate effectively.
4. *The engagement of school personnel in addition to family members in the resolution of a child's problem requires a redefinition of traditional notions of family confidentiality and parameters as to what information is to be shared and with whom.*
5. *Insurance reimbursement is not organized to fund collaborative team efforts between family therapists and school personnel.* Collaborative team efforts often require additional time that does not get reimbursed by an insurance carrier.

When these obstacles are overcome, the collaboration process may become an intervention that effects change on its own. At other times, the collaboration sets the stage for other interventions that relate to specific hypotheses formulated by the family therapist through ongoing assessment. The next section reviews guidelines for choosing interventions.

❄ CHOOSING INTERVENTIONS

After the therapeutic goal has been established, a therapeutic intervention must be chosen; that is, after one or more problem behaviors have been selected, therapists must decide what they are going to do with the family to bring about the stated goals. More important, they must determine a logical rationale for using a particular intervention. The critical question about choosing an intervention is, "What intervention, by whom, is most effective for the family, with what specific problem, and under which set of circumstances?" (Paul, 1967, p. 111).

Given any specific family intervention, a therapist can build a rationale for working with almost any problem within a specific theoretical model. For instance, the structural therapist can readily give and support a rationale for dealing with most problems consistently using a structural approach. The behavioral family therapist, the strategic therapist, and the intergenerational therapist can do likewise. However, the therapeutic experience must meet the family's goal and not simply reflect the therapist's own theoretical biases. For instance, some approaches are differentially effective depending on the presenting problem. Psychosomatic problems have been treated most effectively with the structural approach (Aponte & Van Deusen, 1981), and there is little or no evidence of symptom substitution. On the other hand, couples who are in conflict often respond better to a communication and problem-solving approach (Jacobson, 1984).

In providing guidelines for determining an appropriate intervention, we do not intend to imply that only one particular approach can work with a particular type of problem. This is not the case, although certain interventions have proven more effective than others in ameliorating certain types of problems. In fact, there is some overlap between interventions that are effective in changing behavior problems. Although each strategy is discussed separately in Chapter Eight, more than one intervention will likely be used with any particular family in actual practice. For example, a couple lacking the skills to interact appropriately with each other may need a problem-solving and communication skills program. After learning how to communicate with each other, they may be given the in-session task of working out a curfew with their adolescent daughter without interruptions from the younger siblings.

While the major family therapy models offer a wide range of interventions, little has been written to guide the practitioner in deciding which model might be most effective with a given family. Wright and Leahey (1984) characterize common interventions in the field of family therapy along a continuum of *direct* and *indirect*. Direct interventions are compliance-based—straightforward attempts at change with cooperative clients. They include psychoeducation, task assignments, and directives. Indirect interventions are not based on compliance; they are less threatening attempts at change with clients who are less comfortable with the direction that the therapist has chosen. They include questions, strategic tasks, positive connotations, and paradoxes. Thus, the family therapist should explore the consequences of change with a given family to determine whether direct or indirect interventions are appropriate (e.g., "Can you think of anything negative that might occur when you solve this problem?").

Research studies on the family therapy of adolescent drug abusers have noted a developing trend regarding the choice of interventions (Selekman & Todd, 1991). Two studies reported that, when the family was more disorganized, a direct approach was more effective; when the family was more rigid, an indirect approach was more effective. Anderson, Reiss, and Hogarty (1986) have had success with a psychoeducational family approach to managing schizophrenic behavior in which education is combined with the development of a cooperative relationship with the family to provide ongoing care to a family member. Such approaches are pragmatic rather than model-specific; they develop hypotheses about how change will occur rather than about what the problem is and what is needed to correct it.

A minimum requirement in deciding on the intervention is that the therapist must make a thorough analysis of the context in which the problem occurs; that is, the therapist must have asked, and gotten answers to, the following questions before determining an appropriate intervention:

1. What is the problem and how often does it occur or how intense is it?
2. What are the consequences of the problem behavior to the family and to others in the environment (e.g., teachers, friends, and neighbors)?
3. What resources to promote change does the family have in their environment?
4. What effects would a change in the problem behavior have on the family and others?

In summary, the therapist must formulate hypotheses regarding the problem to determine an appropriate intervention plan. The therapist must examine nonverbal clues such as tone of voice, facial expressions, and eye contact with other family members. Why does the family believe this problem occurs? What do they feel would help resolve the problem? Who speaks for whom in deciding these issues? How do other family members view the problem? Using these data, the therapist formulates hypotheses and appropriate interventions. The therapist should be ready to alter the treatment plan if the family presents new information or rejects the initial proposal.

Chapter Ten

Maintaining Direction: Evaluations, Terminations, and Follow-Ups

Evaluating Family Process

Evaluating Therapeutic Process
Family Perceptions
Therapist Perceptions
Periodic Evaluations of the Process

Evaluating Outcomes of Family Therapy
Measuring Behavioral Changes
Goal Attainment Scales
Self-Reports

Evaluations for Termination and Follow-Up
Conducting Follow-Up Evaluations

Evaluations in Training

Evaluations As Clinical Research

Summary

In the course of family therapy, evaluations take place in many different ways. Chapter Four discussed evaluations as a final stage in the therapeutic process and as an ongoing review that happens as family therapists assess their effectiveness. In addition, evaluations of family process may occur during initial assessments if therapists employ formal evaluation measures such as objective questionnaires or research instruments. These forms of evaluation are used in treatment planning and in developing an understanding of family members' experience. Later in the process, evaluations may take the form of noting treatment outcomes that provide the impetus for a new treatment plan, termination, supervision, or research. If these forms are placed in an order corresponding to therapeutic process, the beginning practitioner could conceptualize the various forms of evaluation as follows:

1. Objective evaluations can be administered during the assessment stage of therapy to aid in understanding family process and in formulating treatment plans.
2. Ongoing microevaluations can take place session by session as a conversational feedback loop that informs the clinician how family members are reacting to the therapeutic process.
3. Outcome evaluations can gather qualitative (verbal) or quantitative (behavioral or numerical) information that helps the family therapist document the completion of goals or the need to revise treatment goals or plans.
4. Evaluations in training and research can document therapist skill levels and general therapeutic patterns.

This chapter focuses on these forms of evaluation and how they can be used at different points in the therapeutic process.

❄ Evaluating Family Process

Evaluations that relate specifically to client variables occur in a variety of situations. Clients may evaluate themselves with an expectation of improvement in some aspect of their well-being. Traditionally, therapists have adopted the role of expert and evaluated their clients. This may happen during the initial assessment phase in treatment and is sometimes formally accomplished by administering objective instruments. In addition, third parties, such as schools and social services, may desire some type of evaluation related to client behavior if they initiate referral. Because of this, even if family therapists hope to maintain a focus on the family's strengths, it is virtually impossible to escape situations where the goals of the client or others dictate that therapists provide an evaluation in their role as expert.

Family process measures are often designed as paper-and-pencil questionnaires that provide family therapists with a family member's self-report of his or her own behaviors or perceptions. Of the various instruments commonly in use, we discuss the Family Adaptability and Cohesion Evaluation Scale (FACES), the Locke-Wallace Marital Status Inventory (L-W), the Dyadic Adjustment Scale (DAS), the Marital Precounseling Inventory (MPI), and the Divorce Adjustment Inventories (DAI).

The Family Adaptability and Cohesion Evaluation Scale, third edition (FACES III), is based on the Olson Circumplex Model (Olson, Porter, & Ravee, 1985). This inventory measures family members' perceptions of family process and provides a score on the two dimensions of adaptability and cohesion. Adaptability refers to flexibility of roles, rules, and relationships during times of stress. Cohesion refers to the sense of emotional bonding experienced by family members. FACES III is the most recent version of the inventory and is widely used to discriminate between control groups and families with varying degrees of dysfunction. Family therapists often use FACES III in research and in obtaining a baseline of family functioning prior to treatment.

The Locke-Wallace Marital Status Inventory (Locke & Wallace, 1959) contains a set of true/false items that are used to assess steps toward dissolution of the marriage. According to Weiss and Perry (1979), the test was designed to provide "an intensity scale (for example, Guttman scale) such that any given step would necessarily include all preceding steps. Thus, before one sought legal aid for a divorce, it would be reasonable to assume that one had thoughts about divorce and engaged in behaviors preparatory to that of seeking legal advice" (p. 17). Because this inventory describes intensity, it is possible for the clinician to use the information in deciding whether crisis intervention is needed or whether a less dramatic treatment plan is warranted.

Spanier (1976) included many items from the Locke-Wallace inventory in his assessment scale. Weiss and Perry (1979) altered the items omitted by Spanier so that both measures are incorporated into one questionnaire called the Dyadic Adjustment Scale. The DAS is somewhat more modern in its wording than the Locke-Wallace inventory and provides four factor scales: Dyadic Consensus (e.g., problem solving), Dyadic Satisfaction (e.g., "good feelings" and "sentiment" in the relationship), Dyadic Cohesion (e.g., outside interests, exchange of ideas, cooperation), and Affectional Expression (e.g., sexual and emotional expression). The DAS is an easy instrument to score and may be very useful to the behavioral family therapist because it conceptualizes the marital relationship as a set of specific behaviors that may be targeted for increase or decrease.

The Marital Precounseling Inventory (Stuart & Stuart, 1972) is administered prior to treatment to aid treatment planning. The inventory is 11 pages long and provides assessment information in the following areas: daily activities of both spouses, general goals and resources for change, spouse satisfaction and targets for change in 12 areas of marital and family functioning, rationales for decision making, and level of commitment to the marriage (Stuart, 1976). The MPI serves several purposes. It provides the therapist with data for planning a treatment program, and it also helps orient the couple to treatment. Each spouse can often anticipate issues that will be discussed. At the end of treatment, the inventory can be completed to evaluate therapy.

The Divorce Adjustment Inventories (Brown, Eichenberger, Portes, & Christensen, 1991) provide both child and parent ratings of divorce adjustment. The DAI for parents consists of 31 Likert scale items that offer a numerical range of responses related to family functioning, children's coping skills, and social support systems before and after divorce. The DAI for children consists of 25 Likert scale items that assess the child's adjustment to divorce. Clinicians are able to help parents facilitate the adjustment of their children through the use and discussion of results.

These instruments serve a variety of assessment functions. First, they provide objective measures of overt and covert behavior important to the satisfaction of the relationship. Second, instruments often reveal information that family members might be reluctant to provide in an interview; for example, a spouse may find it embarrassing to discuss sexual issues in the interview. The therapist can often use this information to help family members focus on critical issues that might otherwise be avoided. Finally, instruments often provide an ongoing measure of subjective satisfaction that cannot be obtained through direct observation.

When using self-report scales and inventories, there are several considerations:

1. *Select instruments that measure specific areas of family functioning.* This is of critical importance. For example, the DAI (Brown et al., 1991) contains subscales that measure parental interaction and parent–child interaction, both critical variables in divorce adjustment.
2. *Select instruments that have been validated on similar populations.* If the instrument of choice is normed on a population similar (in terms of

socioeconomic status, race, ethnic group, etc.) to the client family, the scores can be compared with the norm group. If norms are not available for the client family's group, interpretations are likely to be unfair and negatively biased.

3. *Use the scales or checklists in conjunction with other evaluation data.* By using scales and inventories to corroborate other evaluation data—observations, goal attainment scales, and self-reports—the therapist can be more confident that change has actually occurred.

The biggest limitation in using scales or inventories is that they are global and often fail to pinpoint specific concerns of the family; that is, marital adjustment or satisfaction scales may provide an index of marital quality but may not be an adequate measure of the problem the family brings to therapy. Furthermore, scales and inventories may not be appropriate for minority families (if the appropriate cultural norms are not available), some family members who have little education, or families who are hesitant to disclose certain information before developing a comfortable relationship with the therapist. If a family has already suffered some degree of prejudice from a comparison to cultural norms, such instruments should be used with caution and with a neutral explanation of how results will be interpreted. For example, inventories that primarily describe internal family process can provide families with descriptive information about their relationships rather than a diagnostic score that indicates health or dysfunction.

❄ EVALUATING THERAPEUTIC PROCESS

The therapeutic relationship is central to the facilitation of change and should be monitored on many levels as family therapy progresses. This evaluation should include the perceptions of the practitioner and of the family. Without feedback from each side of the interaction, it is difficult for clinicians, supervisors, or researchers to account for strengths and weaknesses in the interpersonal process between therapist and family. What is the relationship like? Is it accomplishing the desired goals? Is it authoritarian, cooperative, or collegial? This assessment may focus on each person's role and expectations in the relationship as well as how these are manifest in therapeutic interactions. What type of communication patterns can be described in therapy sessions? Are therapist and family able to "communicate about their communication" with each other? This type of evaluation is subjective in nature and should be used regularly to avoid misunderstandings, to troubleshoot when the clinician feels a lack of therapeutic progress, and in situations where the clinician anticipates a potential problem from a subsequent part of the treatment plan.

Family Perceptions

Family members may be privately evaluating the therapist with respect to trustworthiness, empathy, safety, helpfulness, and so on. This level of evaluation is based on subjective criteria chosen by each person and is often related to first impressions of interpersonal comfort. At this level of evaluation, discussion must be initiated by therapists because the topic can be intimate and threatening for family and therapist. To ask families about how they are experiencing the process elicits information that may imply how therapists are doing their job. Nevertheless, beginning family therapists can minimize their sense of threat in such an interaction by regarding the clients' perceptions as information about what is most comfortable for them. Therapist competence is then related to a willingness to ask the questions and not to the content of the answers. Family therapists can conduct this type of evaluation in a spirit of reflection, communicating self-confidence and concern about the well-being of the client. Is the family feeling comfortable with the process? Does the process seem beneficial and hopeful? Is it too structured? Too unstructured? Too authoritarian? Relevant? Not relevant?

An interesting research project that addressed client perceptions of family therapists was conducted by Newfield, Kuehl, Joanning, and Quinn (1991) with families who had participated in family therapy as part of a study of adolescent substance abuse. In this qualitative study, independent interviewers asked participants to describe their experience of the family therapy process, their perceptions of the therapist, and their views of the outcome. The purpose of the project was to obtain qualitative information about therapy from a lay point of view. The investigators characterized professional clinicians as members of a culture (with a distinctive language and expectations) that is different from the culture of those who seek their services. This attention to the interplay of different cultures is borrowed from the field of anthropology. The main questions focused on what occurred in the process and the implications of these occurrences. The results of this research suggested that clients were most satisfied with treatment when therapy matched their conceptualizations of the problem. Consequently, an anthropological view of the therapeutic experience uses the natural language and expectations of clients to understand the process rather than technical theories that are rooted in the culture of the profession.

Often, beginning practitioners are most threatened by openly expressed anger, criticism, or despair from family members. However, we find it useful to help trainees anticipate their most feared stumbling blocks and develop a repertoire of questions and responses that encourages open discussion of client experience. For example, some clinicians give clients permission to express disagreement or discontent ("It's normal for family members to become upset over some aspects of the therapy process. Can you think of anything so far that has been upsetting or confusing for you?"). Family members may be uncomfortable with some part of the process (e.g., questions or responses from the therapist that inadvertently offend someone). When this is discovered, the therapist can legitimize their experience ("I'm sorry for the misunderstanding; you did the right thing to let me know about it") or put their feelings into a larger perspective ("I can understand how you would come to feel this way. You're not the only one who has had this type of experience, and sometimes we professionals need help in knowing how you're feeling about our work together"). Very often, anger can be reframed as pain, thereby alerting the practitioner to some aspect of the process that has become threatening for a family member. Dominance can be reframed as fear, which alerts the therapist to a covert sense of vulnerability. When clients express despair ("This isn't doing any good"), the therapist can inquire about expectations and priorities of the client that may need to be addressed more directly. Despair may also prompt the therapist to explain the process more fully and to shift the target of change—for example, from behavioral to cognitive or from cognitive to behavioral. Family members who are more literal or concrete (result-oriented) often want behavioral change to be manifest first. Family members who are more intuitive (process-oriented) often want cognitive change that impacts their internal experience.

It is recommended that practitioners ask for client perceptions of therapeutic process before and after various stages of assessment and treatment. For example, if a family has agreed to cooperate with the construction of a genogram in an initial interview, the practitioner may still want to ask the family at the beginning of the second session if they feel comfortable proceeding in that direction (e.g., "On a scale from 1 to 10, how comfortable are you with our plan for today?"). By acknowledging that some families are uncomfortable with the process or do not think it is a relevant exercise for their particular problem, the therapist provides the family with an opportunity to discuss their thoughts, second thoughts, or questions about the process. It also gives the therapist an opportunity to search for a rationale that makes sense to the family or to search for a different approach.

Careful observation of nonverbal messages is another important vehicle for gauging client perceptions. Many family members are too threatened to make direct disclosures about their experience. In that case, the observation of behavioral patterns and sequences over time provides useful information on how the process fits the clients. For example, family therapists may discover that clients respond to some direction, advice, or task with a "yes, but" pattern. This pattern can be interpreted as a nonverbal message that the direction or task does not fit. In addition, such a pattern should be thought of as a courteous power struggle between therapist and family member, which should be avoided through therapist flexibility. When the therapist can take a one-down position and state a desire to change the process so that the family feels more comfortable, the family is encouraged to trust the therapist more and to be more direct.

One way of learning from nonverbal messages involves noting how families respond to homework and out-of-session tasks. De Shazer (1985) lists five possible responses that clients may make to a given task assignment and five suggested responses from the therapist. Even when a family does something opposite to the task or fails to fulfill the assignment at all, therapists are encouraged to view the family's response as a message that the family is instinctively doing what is best for them. By such nonverbal observation, the therapist learns to understand messages that are sent through behavior instead of words.

As family therapists become skilled at eliciting microevaluations from family perceptions, they discover that such evaluations become interventions. These turning points of change in the therapeutic relationship become models for change in family relationships. In addition, the effectiveness of the therapeutic relationship is influenced by perceptions, beliefs, and attitudes that develop within the therapist. These will now be examined.

Therapist Perceptions

The therapist may be evaluating clients with respect to level of cooperation, severity of the problem, and so on. In addition to focusing on the family's perception of the process, clinicians must also pay attention to their own perceptions and misperceptions of the process. If a therapist is feeling stuck but finds that the client is satisfied with the process, what does that say about the theory that the practitioner is using as a lens? By the same token, if both therapist and client are feeling dissatisfied with the process, blame can be centered on the process and not on either party. Then, both parties can work together to cooperatively resolve their dissatisfaction. Besides modeling problem-solving skills, the family therapist also demonstrates a willingness to admit mistakes and to explore misunderstandings. When the client is feeling dissatisfied, but the practitioner believes that all is well, it is important for clinicians to distinguish assumption from fact or, in constructivist terms, to distinguish their personal reality from the reality of the client.

When reviewing their own perceptions, family therapists should remember that their behavior is often an extension of their beliefs and intentions. Using the Awareness Wheel from the Couple Communication Program (Miller, Nunnally, Wackman, & Miller, 1988), it is possible for the clinician to identify what thoughts and intentions may have been operating during problematic interactions. A therapist who has chosen a specific model of family therapy may also compare his or her own perceptions with the assumptions adopted by the model. For example, suppose a therapist's goal is to conduct a session from an intergenerational point of view. The fundamental assumptions of that model include an acknowledgment that past relationships and interactions affect present relationships and interactions and the assertion that thoughts and intentions are often taught by one generation to another. Thus, if the therapist inquires about family and cultural values, significant intergenerational relationships, and the evolution of the client's experience in the family of origin, these behaviors reflect an intergenerational point of view. However, if the therapist becomes concerned with a client's weight problem without directing therapeutic conversation toward how the weight is related to intergenerational dynamics, the therapist's conduct might indicate a lack of self-confidence in executing the model, a conflicting belief (e.g., "If I try to relate the problem to a larger issue, the client may disagree"), or a belief that eliminates the model altogether (e.g., "Weight is not related to intergenerational dynamics; it is related to present behavior and lifestyle").

Therapists should also take the opportunity to evaluate their own perceptions when they leave a session feeling angry, defeated, or confused. At these times, reflecting on expectations for self, client, and the process itself is in order. Is the therapist expecting too much from the family? Is the therapist becoming dependent on client behavior for a feeling of success? Has the therapist remembered to utilize strengths and idiosyncrasies of the family in the proposed solution to the problem? Has the therapist found a way to value the unique and sometimes contrary style of a family? By means of these questions, which constitute a form of self-supervision, clinicians are able to develop learning and process goals that can further their own cognitive and behavioral development. In addition, the traditional supervisory process can shed light on therapists' perceptions of the process. Objective evaluations can also provide an external review of therapeutic process.

Periodic Evaluations of the Process

In many instances, periodic evaluations of the process prevent impasses from occurring. Coleman (1985) suggests that treatment failures are often related to a variety of factors, including theoretical issues, process issues, motivation and consumerism, goal setting, the therapeutic alliance, personal issues of the therapist, and relationships with larger systems. If an impasse has occurred, an evaluation of these factors might provide a constructive resolution. For many beginning family therapists struggling to put their nascent skills to work, it is a challenge to initiate an evaluation. Since negative evaluations make learning difficult, it is human nature to avoid the possibility of criticism until more confidence is gained. However, such evaluations can be as simple as reviewing the history of therapy to date. Beginning practitioners can also use the outline from Chapter Six to analyze the beginning stages of therapy. Was any important topic skipped? Was the information about previous treatment history detailed? Was the discussion about goals and expectations candid? What might the client still be hesitant to disclose? What does the family need for the therapeutic relationship to become more comfortable? As clinicians begin to experiment with periodic evaluations of their own process through the eyes of the family, they discover the importance of such information in facilitating therapeutic progress.

While discussions about the therapeutic relationship may often be informal and impromptu, it is also possible to evaluate therapeutic interaction in a formal way for supervision or research. Supervisors may observe therapeutic exchanges firsthand to understand the nature of the therapeutic relationship. In some training programs, sessions are recorded on audiotape to enable beginning practitioners to review their communication patterns and to monitor their grasp of various skills. For example, a formal evaluation might consist of the practitioner reviewing a tape of a family therapy session and counting how many circular questions were asked of the family. If there was a part of the session when the therapist felt stuck, the evaluation could also include a review of circular questions to see which ones could have been asked during the period of difficulty.

In addition, therapeutic process can be formally evaluated through models of interactional analysis that are used for research. The Couple Communication Program can be used for this purpose, since communication may readily be broken down into each category of the Awareness Wheel and then quantified by noting the frequencies in each category. The Relational Coding Scheme is another model that analyzes communication into categories such as questions, support, assertions, talkovers, and so on (Ericson & Rogers,

1973). An analysis of therapeutic interaction with this method categorizes each message from each person and quantifies how many of each type of statements were made. In additional analyses, this coding scheme produces data that describe the sequence and patterns of each exchange over time. For example, if the client made frequent assertions that were often followed by the therapist asking frequent questions, this recurring pattern could be noted by the formal analysis.

Thus, it is possible to conduct formal and informal evaluations of each person's experience in the therapeutic process, the nature of specific micro-interactions within the relationship, and the ongoing relationship and its effectiveness. In focusing on therapeutic process in these ways, the beginning practitioner begins to see that the process of family therapy is, indeed, a complex set of interactions that accommodates multiple points of view and is experienced on multiple levels. These interactions become the means used by the clinician to bring about change. Such change is measured at another level of clinical evaluation, which usually focuses on treatment outcomes.

❄ Evaluating Outcomes of Family Therapy

There are several formal methods for determining whether goals have been met in therapy: measuring behavioral changes, goal attainment scales, self-reports, and behavioral checklists. These methods may be used separately or in combination to determine whether goal behaviors have been successfully reached.

Measuring Behavioral Changes

Of the various evaluation designs the therapist may utilize, the most useful for tracking specific behavioral changes are time-series designs, where data are collected over different points in time. Some of these have been developed for experimental purposes and, therefore, may not be practical for the therapist, who, in many cases, must change the family's behavior in the shortest possible time. Only those designs that are of practical use in family therapy are discussed here.

The AB Design   The simplest time-series approach is the AB design. Here the therapist or family first records baseline rates of target behaviors (positive interactions, arguments, etc.). Having plotted the baseline level of behavior, the therapist and family set an objective. It is helpful to specify the number of consecutive days on which the criterion must be achieved to provide an objective determination of when the goal has been reached. The therapist or family gathers a second set of data during the implementation phase of the program. Data may be collected continuously throughout the program or at specific times. For example, during baseline, a couple averaged only 3 minutes of positive interaction per day for 1 week. On the basis of this information, the therapist and family decided the couple should set a goal of at least 15 minutes each day for positive (problem-free) interaction. Figure 10.1 illustrates that the goal was reached. The AB design in this instance provides an easy means of evaluating one behavior of one family in one setting. The therapist may only need to collect baseline data for several days (until there is some consistency in the rate), then set a reasonable objective, and continue collecting data to measure changes. By graphing data, the therapist and family can set realistic goals and monitor those goals on a daily basis.

The therapist should be mindful that other events might also be influencing the behavior of the family. For example, although the couple set aside time for positive interaction, both spouses may have been getting encouragement from friends and family to do more things with each other. However, even though this design does not control for error resulting from competing events, it is an acceptable means for determining whether an objective has been met.

The Multiple Baseline   In some instances, therapists may be interested in more than one target behavior for a particular family, or they may want to

Figure 10.1

measure changes on a specific behavior for more than one family or situation. In that case, a multiple baseline is used. For example, a second target behavior for the couple just discussed was the amount of time spent arguing with their son. When they reached the first goal (15 minutes per day of positive interaction), the family, under the therapist's guidance, set a second goal: to reduce the amount of negative interaction with their son from 25 to 5 minutes daily.

Figure 10.2 illustrates an increase in the couple's positive interaction time when exposed to the first intervention (i.e., structured time for positive interaction), while the amount of negative interaction time with the son (which is not being treated) shows little change. The latter quantity only decreases when the second intervention is introduced. By exposing each target behavior—positive couple interaction and negative interaction time with the son—to the intervention, the therapist can determine if the intervention is actually responsible for meeting the goal; that is, each family behavior should change only as it is exposed to the intervention and not before. It should be noted that the behaviors studied in the multiple baseline are not necessarily isolated. For example, positive interactions probably impact on negative interactions, and vice versa.

There are many instances when the target behavior occurs in more than one situation (home, school, work, neighborhood, etc.). In this case, the therapist can use the multiple baseline to evaluate the target behaviors of the

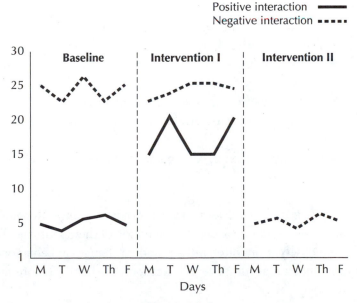

Figure 10.2

family in different situations. For example, negative requests (complaints or demands) by a child can be monitored both at home and at school. If parents are able to successfully reduce the child's negative requests at home, while the level of negative requests remains the same at school, then a similar intervention can be implemented at school with the assistance of the therapist and the family. The multiple baseline is useful here in determining the success of an intervention when the problem occurs in more than one setting.

Comparative Data From Taped Interviews   Although the graphing procedures just described were applied primarily to discrete behaviors that can be easily observed and recorded, the same principle can be applied to data that are more difficult to observe and quantify. For instance, the therapeutic goal may be to improve marital satisfaction as measured by the number of positive statements each spouse makes about the other. Marital satisfaction can obviously be measured in other ways; the important thing is that all goals be operationalized so that there is some way of measuring progress. For instance, if the goal is stated only as improvement in the relationship, this may mean different things to different people, and it is difficult to measure success. Assuming that the number of positive statements that each spouse makes about the other is a reasonable measure of marital satisfaction, the therapist can tape interviews and record the number of positive versus negative statements. Using the first session or two as a baseline, the therapist can then chart this behavior as intervention is implemented.

Even when objectives are operationalized, there are varying ranges of objectivity. For example, the therapist must often depend on clients' self-reports of behaviors such as anxiety, marital discord, and drug use, and there may be no way to verify the accuracy of such reports. Still, if the evaluation data are to be obtained by the self-recording of client behavior, there is some evidence that the very act of self-recording is itself effective in promoting the desired behavior.

The therapist must follow several guidelines when using behavioral observation:

1. *Use repeated observations to evaluate behavior change.* Repeated measures provide a more accurate evaluation of therapeutic goals. Infrequent observations often reflect random changes in behavior and fail to provide an accurate representation of behavior before and after treatment.

2. *Ask family members to practice self-observation.* For example, a family member might be taught to observe and record the number of angry thoughts he or she has about another family member.

3. *Record behavioral observations on a prepared form.* The form should include the date, session number, family member's name, observer, operational definition of the problem, times of observation, length of interval, and setting or activity.

4. *Provide a graphic summary of the behavior.* The therapist should enter the time of recording (minutes, days, etc.) on the horizontal axis, from far left to far right, and the number of target behaviors on the vertical axis.

5. *Determine whether further observations are necessary.* If baseline or pretreatment data are characterized by extreme variation or a gradual increase or decrease, further observations should be collected until some stability is noted. Of course, these considerations must be weighed against the need for prompt treatment; if the problem behavior is severely disturbing (as in the case of violence), treatment should supersede behavioral observation. Too much time spent in collecting baseline data may reduce the time available for treatment, which is of greater importance.

There are several limitations to self-observation as a means of recording behavior change. First, family members may change their behavior during the period of observation to please the therapist. This is particularly true for family members who have a need to please others. Second, some family members may not follow through with monitoring behavior change because of the time or effort required to keep accurate records. This is often the case when the therapist has not chosen a focus that is meaningful to family members. Finally, since self-observation can often produce a behavior change, the data may not accurately reflect the situation in the absence of observation (Barlow, Hayes, & Nelson, 1984).

Goal Attainment Scales

A second method for evaluating goals specifies the level or amount of change—how much families must do to reach the desired goal. In this case, the level of attainment determines whether the goals have been successfully reached. Cormier and Cormier (1991) offer an example:

Suppose a client wants to increase the number of assertive opinions she expresses orally with her husband. If she now withholds all her opinions, her level of change might be stated at a lower level than that defined for another client who already expresses some opinions. And if the client's husband is accustomed to her refraining from giving opinions, this might affect the degree of change made, at least initially. The counselor's and client's primary concern is to establish a level that is manageable, and that the client can attain with some success. (p. 233)

Achievable goals should be determined by the current level of problem behavior, the desired level of goal behavior, available support and resources, and the desire to change. One way to establish achievable and measurable goals is through the use of goal attainment scaling. This procedure (Kiresuk & Sherman, 1979) involves three basic steps and ends with a written product mutually agreeable to the therapist and the family.

Box 10.1 is an adaptation of goal attainment scaling, which is titled "Goal Attainment Review." This shows a completed goal attainment review for a family. Note that the goals are stated in performance terms and specify the criteria for success. Consequently, measurement is relatively simple, and evaluation of goal attainment is straightforward.

There are several procedures to follow in using the goal attainment scale:

1. *State the goal in measurable terms.* Goals should be stated clearly and should be decided on mutually by the therapist and family. It is important to select goals that can be changed.
2. *Assign a weight to each goal.* Some goals are more important than others and should be weighted to show their comparative value. These weights are relative and may be ranked on a scale of 1 to 3, where 1 is the least important and 3 is the most important. It should be noted that it is the relative rather than the absolute weight that is imperative (some goals may be assigned the same weight).
3. *Determine the expected level of attainment.* The central questions that must be asked are: What is the current amount or duration of behavior? What is a reasonable or expected level of goal attainment? To answer these questions, the family must have some knowledge of their current level of behavior (baseline). This information should be entered in the column "expected level of attainment."
4. *Determine other levels of attainment.* Once the expected level of attainment has been determined, the next step is to determine levels that are "more than expected" and "most favorable outcome." Likewise

BOX 10.1

CASE NAME   Mary Goddard   DATE   3/28/93

CASE NUMBER   MA-03285   PHONE NUMBER   477-8240

GOAL ATTAINMENT REVIEW*
(Client Constructed Outcome Goals)

		Contract Goal 1	Contract Goal 2	Contract Goal 3	Contract Goal 4
Weight of Goal (1–3) Expected Level of Attainment (1–2)		Weight = 3 Attainment = 1	Weight = 3 Attainment = 2	Weight = 2 Attainment = 2	Weight = Attainment =
G U I D E T O G O A L S	MUCH LESS THAN EXPECTED RESULTS = 0	Robbie will not complete his homework every night.	Robbie will complete his assigned work at school 2 or fewer days per week.	Robbie will argue with his mother more than 1 time per day.	
	EXPECTED OR MOST LIKELY RESULTS = 1	Robbie will complete his homework every night.	Robbie will complete his assigned work in school 3 out of every 5 days.	Robbie will argue with his mother no more than 1 time per day.	
	MUCH MORE THAN EXPECTED RESULTS = 2		Robbie will complete his assigned work in school 4–5 per week.	Robbie will argue with his mother fewer than 1 time per day.	
P R O G R E S S	3-MONTH REVIEW Treatment __ Terminated _x_ Discontinued __	Case terminated 6/16/93 Progress __ Follow-up _1_ Date 6/22/93	Progress __ Follow-up _1_ Date 6/22/93	Progress __ Follow-up _2_ Date 6/22/93	Progress ___ Follow-up ___ Date _____
F O L L O W - U P	6-MONTH REVIEW Treatment __ Terminated __ Discontinued __	Progress ___ Follow-up ___ Date _____	Progress ___ Follow-up ___ Date _____	Progress ___ Follow-up ___ Date _____	Progress ___ Follow-up ___ Date _____
	9-MONTH REVIEW Treatment __ Terminated __ Discontinued __	Progress ___ Follow-up ___ Date _____	Progress ___ Follow-up ___ Date _____	Progress ___ Follow-up ___ Date _____	Progress ___ Follow-up ___ Date _____

Box 10.1 *(continued)*

		Contract Goal 1	Contract Goal 2	Contract Goal 3	Contract Goal 4
Weight of Goal (1–3) Expected Level of Attainment (1–2)		Weight = 3 Attainment = 1	Weight = 3 Attainment = 2	Weight = 2 Attainment = 2	Weight = Attainment =
c o n t i n u e d	12-MONTH REVIEW Treatment __ Terminated __ Discontinued __	Progress __ Follow-up __ Date _____	Progress __ Follow-up __ Date _____	Progress __ Follow-up __ Date _____	Progress __ Follow-up __ Date _____
	15-MONTH REVIEW Treatment __ Terminated __ Discontinued __	Progress __ Follow-up __ Date _____	Progress __ Follow-up __ Date _____	Progress __ Follow-up __ Date _____	Progress __ Follow-up __ Date _____

*The Goal Attainment Review is a derivative of the GAS.

wise, the therapist and family must specify a "less than expected" and "most unfavorable outcome." In some cases, the appropriate levels may only be 1 or 2, as in the case of alcohol consumption, violence, or curfew. These levels should be entered in the lefthand column.

Goal attainment reviews have several limitations: (a) Families often have difficulty in knowing what to expect from therapy; stating goals in objective terms or measurable terms may be very difficult; (b) family members often have difficulty presenting problems and specifying what is an "expected" or an acceptable level of attainment; moreover, they may have even more difficulties specifying "less than expected" levels of attainment; (c) the therapist and family may have difficulty completing a goal attainment review during the initial intake session. Adequate time must be allotted to complete a goal attainment review. In some cases, a second session may be necessary.

Self-Reports

Self-reports are simply what family members say about their condition in the interview; that is, improvement is determined by what family members report to the therapist. This approach assumes that if the family is improving, family members will report the improvement ("Everyone seems to be getting along better"). Likewise, little improvement is characterized by statements such as, "Things are about the same" or "I can't see any change." Self-reports are the easiest way for the therapist to evaluate changes in the family.

Here are some considerations:

1. *Develop some specific questions to evaluate the family's progress.* Questions such as, "How are things different than they were before?" or "Tell me how things used to be and how they are now" help determine the effectiveness of therapy.
2. *Ask family members to scale their improvement.* The therapist can ask the family to describe their ability to handle the problem on a scale from 1 "not able to handle the problem" to 10 "able to handle the problem." These questions can be asked prior to, during, and following treatment.
3. *Ask family members how satisfied they are with therapy.* The therapist might ask, "Was therapy helpful? How so? What was most helpful to you?"
4. *Ask family members to describe what still needs to change.* When asking the family to identify anything that still needs to be done, the therapist may need to remind them of some issues that were raised but not worked on during sessions.

Although self-reports are the most common type of outcome evaluation, family therapists should be aware of their limitations. First, self-reports are open to bias because family members may report what they believe will please the therapist. Thus, self-reports are quite subjective and may not accurately represent the family's progress in treatment. Second, family members may be able to report how they feel today, but may not be able to reliably describe their behavior between sessions. Day-to-day behavioral changes are often difficult to recall without some written record. Finally, self-reports are nonstandardized and are often determined by therapeutic leads (nonverbal cues) that seek to elicit a certain description of behavior change. Different leads at different points in therapy may result in different descriptions of progress.

❊ EVALUATIONS FOR TERMINATION AND FOLLOW-UP

Two criteria should be used in determining whether to continue therapy. First, family goals should be met. In some cases, the family or others (teachers, social workers, friends, or relatives) may feel the problem no longer exists. However, if family data fail to support this, therapy should continue until family goals have been met. Second, the goal may have been met, but the family or others in the environment may not be satisfied with the change produced, in which case a new goal should be established. In other cases, the family may wish to pursue another related goal. When goals have been reached and no new goals have been set, the therapist and family can focus on the maintenance of behavior change.

In some cases, families terminate by not returning. This may occur for several reasons. The family may feel that therapy is not working, or they may become upset with the therapist. Occasionally, the family may be unwilling to change some of their behavior. Unless the therapist works through these concerns early in therapy, termination may be premature.

There are several guidelines the therapist should follow when terminating with the family:

1. *Plan for termination in advance*   The therapist should be careful not to withdraw therapy abruptly because in such cases the problem behavior generally returns to the pretreatment level. Families should be given an approximate estimate for the length of therapy. The use of a contract specifying a fixed number of sessions ensures a periodic review of therapy (Barker, 1981). Setting a specific time for termination helps the family and therapist plan for change. The therapist should be flexible about the frequency of sessions, which depends on the nature of the problem. The frequency of sessions should decrease when initial goals have been met (Wright & Leahey, 1984).

2. *Plan to gradually withdraw therapy*   If families have been heavily dependent on therapy (as sometimes happens in cases of severe crisis), they are less likely to resist termination if therapy is withdrawn gradually. One method of gradual withdrawal is to increase the amount of time between sessions (perhaps to between 3 and 5 weeks). This step should be taken if families are unsure they can maintain the desired changes. Todd (1986) discusses this withdrawal process as follows:

> As therapy begins to be successful in achieving the agreed-upon goals, the sessions are usually spaced at wider time intervals, such as moving to alternate weeks and progressing to once a month. This allows the spouses to do more of the work themselves and helps ensure that they can maintain the changes without the therapist. (p. 81)

Wright and Leahey (1984) suggest that families are more likely to believe they have the resources to deal with this problem when the therapist gives them credit for change. If families believe they were responsible for alleviating the presenting problem, they are likely to be more confident they can handle future problems. Statements such as, "You handled this; you'll be able to handle a similar problem if it comes up" help the family believe in their abilities outside of therapy.

3. *Summarize the major themes*   In terminating, the therapist should summarize the major themes of therapy (e.g., growing up) and observe closely to see whether the family agrees or disagrees with the summary statement. If the family disagrees, the therapist should note this and give them the opportunity to discuss their views. On some occasions, the therapist may ask the family to summarize the therapy.

4. *Ask the family to decide what needs to happen for them to return to therapy*   It is important for the therapist to help the family decide when they no longer can manage the problem and need to return to therapy. The therapist might say, "What would be the first sign that you no longer can handle this problem?" Tomm and Wright (1979) ask, "What would each of you have to do to bring the problem back?" Such questions should help family members understand the specific changes they have made in therapy. The therapist should help the family understand that returning to therapy does not mean the family has failed. Instead, a follow-up session can be framed as a booster shot to help the family maintain desired changes. Then, if further services are sought, the therapist can reiterate that this is not an indicator of failure; instead, additional therapy sessions are likely to be brief because the family has demonstrated an ability to solve their problems (Todd, 1986).

5. *Reassure the family that they have the strengths and resources to deal with future problems*   In some cases, a family presents a new problem at the time of termination. If the problem is not serious, the therapist must reassure the family that they have the skills to deal with this problem on their own without therapeutic intervention. If therapists have difficulty letting go of the family (e.g., the therapist may get special nurturance and support from the family or may need the family to work out some unresolved issue), they should discuss such matters in supervision to minimize client dependence as well as their own.

Conducting Follow-Up Evaluations

Once termination has been discussed, follow-up allows the therapist to find out how the family is progressing and to discuss new problems if any have developed. Follow-up can be short-term (2 to 4 weeks) or long-term (3 to 6 months) after termination of treatment. When setting a date for follow-up, the therapist should assess the amount of time the family will need to maintain goal behaviors without therapeutic intervention.

There are several reasons for follow-up contact with the family. First, many families, particularly those who require intensive services, need a booster shot following termination. For example, family preservation programs that offer intensive in-home family crisis intervention often provide weekly or biweekly follow-up visits in the home. The purpose of these visits is to support desired behavior changes or to troubleshoot any problems that the family may have in implementing the program (Kinney, Haopala, & Booth, 1991). Second, follow-up helps assess the effectiveness of the intervention program, particularly the long-term effects of therapy. Third, planned follow-up encourages the family to monitor their own change program and thus benefit from contact with the therapist.

There are several ways the therapist can conduct follow-up:

1. *Conduct a follow-up interview in the home or office.* Follow-up interviews provide an opportunity for the family to discuss what is working and what still needs to change. Interviews are useful for reinforcing desired changes and problem solving if necessary.
2. *Make a telephone call.* Telephone calls can be useful in assessing the effectiveness of the intervention and they also provide a cost-effective way of determining whether a follow-up interview is warranted.
3. *Mail a questionnaire to the family.* This is another way to assess the effectiveness of the program. Unfortunately, families may only report what they think will please the therapist; this method may lack objectivity.

❄ EVALUATIONS IN TRAINING

Formal evaluations of therapists are often model-specific; that is, they evaluate the trainee's mastery of the therapeutic process specified by a certain school of family therapy. For example, those learning structural family therapy might be evaluated according to their ability to mark boundaries or to set up enactments in a session. Those learning intergenerational family therapy might be evaluated according to how well they construct genograms and how effectively they facilitate intergenerational dialogue. Other models might emphasize the therapist's use of self or the therapist's ability to design specific directives and tasks.

Piercy, Laird, and Mohammed (1983) have developed a therapist rating scale that integrates several models of family therapy into a supervisory rating of the student or trainee. In this rating scale, each major school is represented as a cluster of behaviors that each family therapist can be challenged to master as part of his or her education and training. The rating scale provides a guide for the supervisor and therapist in setting training goals.

In addition to these formal methods of evaluating trainees, it is important for family therapists to monitor their own progress and development in personal ways. Clinicians can do this by being responsible for their own well-being as professionals and by becoming aware of times when their physical or mental health may have a negative impact on their ability to provide effective service. While this type of evaluation is often underemphasized as part of formal training, it can help practitioners focus on personal factors that make them vulnerable to job stress and burnout. In addition, when family therapists evaluate their own patterns of fatigue and stagnation, their own creativity and growth can be maximized.

❄ EVALUATIONS AS CLINICAL RESEARCH

As a group, clinicians are rarely apt to call themselves researchers or scientists. Very often, they are so immersed in the implicit subtleties of therapeutic experience that they dismiss scientific inquiry as irrelevant to clinical work. Particularly with beginning therapists, their energy is often directed exclusively toward skill mastery in specific sessions as they discover what works with their clients. In addition, those learning family therapy often hold the belief that scientific rigor fails to acknowledge the human aspects of therapeutic experience.

In the traditional use of the term, research connotes an interest in the explicit, observable, and quantifiable parts of human experience. However, if research is defined as systematic inquiry, family therapists are more likely to see that clinical research can have great relevance to their work; one example is the growing trend toward qualitative research. Ethnographic studies on client perceptions can provide therapists with a mirror of their professional role (Newfield et al., 1991). In addition, Selekman and Todd (1991) argue in favor of "empirically-based clinical practice." From studies on family therapy effectiveness, they conclude that family-based research shows which type of intervention is most effective with which type of family. In their review, chronic, discouraged families did not respond well to "zealous optimism and pushy methods" (p. 321).

Thus, clinicians can participate in systematic inquiry for formal and informal research. Any time family therapists ask the same question in each case, they are engaging in systematic inquiry. When therapists notice similarities between families, presenting problems, and eventual solutions, this is a form of research. As clinicians begin to observe and understand these patterns, their work can be influenced by the new information. For example, they can begin to routinely ask families at the end of successful treatment what they remember as the least important topic discussed during sessions. Even though the answers may be diverse, family therapists can use the information as a mirror from which to view themselves in therapy. They may decide to emphasize or minimize aspects of the process on the basis of such client feedback.

An example of formal inquiry in clinical practice might be the categorization of completed cases according to presenting problems, type of family, number of sessions, type of intervention, and outcomes. Over time, the practitioner can begin to determine whether certain characteristics emerge as similarities or patterns that can be anticipated at the beginning of treatment to improve treatment effectiveness. For example, studies in adolescent drug abuse found that a structural-strategic model worked well with a variety of intact and single-parent families as long as they did not have parental or multiple drug abuse, unresolved losses, or financial or community problems. However, when these problems were present, an indirect approach such as that used by the Milan team was more successful (Selekman & Todd, 1991). Family therapists are currently learning more about the relevance of quantitative and qualitative research. As this continues, they will be able to identify parts of their clinical experience that are naturally occurring methods of research.

❄ SUMMARY

Evaluation is an important part of the treatment process, but it is often omitted by beginning family therapists. However, the process of therapy is sometimes stalemated without a mechanism to provide ongoing feedback and reflection about families and their therapy. While objective assessment instruments often provide quantitative information about family variables and therapy outcomes, informal feedback loops can provide qualitative information about the effectiveness of the therapeutic relationship and the fit between family, intervention, and clinician.

When evaluation is integrated into the practice of family therapy, beginning practitioners become flexible and responsive to the individual needs of families and family members. In addition, treatment planning becomes more systematic and effective. Family therapists develop a shared reality with their families rather than a reality created in isolation from those who are expected to receive its benefits. Although considered here as a skill to be learned by the beginner, evaluation is also a threshold into intermediate and advanced practice. Learning from experience and refinement on the basis of feedback are fundamental to advanced practice.

Chapter Eleven

INTEGRATING TREATMENT THROUGH CASE REVIEWS

THE BURNS FAMILY

JEAN AND DAN

COMPONENTS OF FAMILY THERAPY

As the beginning practitioner starts to implement assessment and treatment skills, confusion and anxiety inevitably attend the learning process. However, as in-session experience accumulates, practitioners become able to review their own therapeutic behavior, assessing what parts of the process may need attention. Because therapeutic process is so complex and fast-paced, it is sometimes only in retrospect that the practitioner can make sense of it. Although the elements discussed thus far have often been thought of as separate skills, they are rarely that distinct in practice. Thus, professional growth and development often depend on therapists' willingness to reflect on the therapeutic process, which cannot be expected to conform to a step-by-step recipe; instead, beginning practitioners must endeavor to identify missing elements or possible options for improving the experience.

In this chapter, two cases are reviewed to help clinicians understand how the practice of family therapy can evolve in many different ways. The clients were seen long before this book was written; therefore, the cases vary according to the style of the practitioner. However, they are used to contrast ways in which basic skills can be implemented. The first case is an example of a short strategic intervention; the second illustrates a more lengthy assessment process before treatment of the presenting problem begins. In addition, different models are used to conceptualize the problem, and different family types influence the choice of interventions.

❄ THE BURNS FAMILY

Mrs. Burns, a single parent, and her 10-year-old son, Keith, were referred by the school counselor because of Keith's fighting and poor grades. In the initial intake interview, Mrs. Burns reported that since her divorce she had worked nights and hadn't been able to spend enough time with Keith. Mrs. Burns attended the first session alone because Keith was ill.

Therapist: *I'm glad you could get off from work, and I'm sorry Keith is ill today.*

Mrs. Burns: *Well, I've been looking forward to talking with you. Keith has been very difficult for me to handle for a while, but he seems to be*

In this sequence, the therapist joins with the client by asking questions to attain greater specificity and by clarifying her thoughts and regarding the problem she has identified.

getting even worse recently. He's just about too much for me to handle.

Therapist: *Tell me what you mean.*

Mrs. Burns: *You know, he just won't mind or do his schoolwork. I just don't know what to do with him.*

Therapist: *Sounds like you're really frustrated with him.*

Mrs. Burns: *That's for sure. I'm glad for days he has activities after school because he keeps me stressed out. Then I feel guilty about not wanting him there.*

Therapist: *Your feelings are mixed then. Although you know the house is more pleasant when he's not there, you think you should want him to be there.*

Mrs. Burns: *Yes. It doesn't make much sense, does it?*

Therapist: *What contact have you had with the school?*

During the sequence, the client gives some clues as to her expectation about the role of the therapist as advocate, go-between, and so on. The therapist helps clarify the process by which he can fulfill such a role.

Mrs. Burns: *Not much. I've talked with Mrs. Brown about his schoolwork. I've never talked with her alone, though. Do you think you could do that? I think you might get something out of her. She won't tell me why he does the things he does.*

Therapist: *Well, Mrs. Burns, I might call her just to get more information about Keith, but I'd prefer that you meet with her and his teacher to figure out how to get him to behave better.*

As the therapeutic relationship evolves, the therapist creates the expectation for change and asks for client cooperation in the process. "Trying some different things" becomes an informal description of the direction of therapy. Then, the therapist pursues a more specific definition of the problem.

Mrs. Burns: *I've really tried every-thing I know. I can't imagine doing anything else with him.*

Therapist: *Are you willing to try some different things?*

Mrs. Burns: *Yes, but I can't think what.*

Therapist: *Well, I'm sure we'll think of some things. But first, I'd like to better understand what Keith does that you don't like.*

Mrs. Burns: *Okay. I told you he won't mind and he does poorly at school.*

Therapist: *What do you mean when you say he doesn't mind?*

The therapist asks more questions to help define the problem in terms of interactional sequences on the assumption that behavioral patterns consist of circular repeating cycles.

Mrs. Burns: *Just that. If I tell him to pick up his clothes or be home on time, he just doesn't do it. When I tell him to do his homework, he just ignores me.*

Therapist: *Does he tell you he's not going to do what you tell him or does he just act as though he will and then not follow through?*

The problem is operationalized by means of questions that put the cycles in behavioral terms with specific reports of what was actually done or said.

Mrs. Burns: *Keith says things like, "Okay, later," and then just doesn't do it.*

Therapist: *When does this usually happen?*

Mrs. Burns: *Mostly right after school when he wants to watch TV.*

Therapist: What happens when he doesn't do it?

Mrs. Burns: Sometimes I get mad and yell at him, but there's not much I can do.

Therapist: So you want Keith to do what you tell him. And you mentioned his poor schoolwork. Tell me more about that.

The therapist helps the client identify all problem areas before beginning to prioritize.

Mrs. Burns: Last grading period, he got three Ds and he's always done well in school before. His teacher says he doesn't turn in his assignments and that he disrupts the class by talking out loud and talking to other students when they're supposed to be working. I've spoken to him about this and told him not to do it, but he denies that he talks to other students.

Therapist: You'd like to see him talk less, then, turn in more assignments, and get better grades.

Mrs. Burns: Right! That would certainly make life easier for all of us.

Therapist: We now have him minding you, completing assignments, and improving grades. Are there other things you're concerned about?

Mrs. Burns: Yes. Really, I'm bothered that Keith has so few friends. Well, really, he doesn't have any close friends. I think Keith just doesn't know how to act around other kids.

Therapist: How does he act?

Mrs. Burns: He's silly.

Therapist: What does he do that's silly?

There is continued clarification to obtain behavioral descriptions of what family members report.

Mrs. Burns: He hits people to get attention, or he will interrupt and talk very loudly. I don't know how he is at school.

Therapist: We could probably have a talk with his teacher sometime to find out.

Mrs. Burns: That would help. As I said, I just don't know what to do now.

Therapist: Okay. You've mentioned three problem areas: Keith's failure to mind, his poor grades, and his peer relationships. Are there others?

Mrs. Burns: No. Those about cover everything.

Therapist: Which of these problems is of most immediate concern to you? Which would you want to change first?

After exploring the areas of greatest concern to the client, the therapist and client prioritize the problems and clarify the issues regarding the most pressing of them.

Mrs. Burns: Getting him to mind. If he did that, it would help me.

Therapist: All right. Let's work on that one first. You've said he minds least right after school when he's watching TV. Is there a particular place where you have the biggest problem?

Mrs. Burns: Yes. Usually in the TV room. For one thing, half the time he doesn't seem to hear me. When I tell him to do something, he may not respond at all.

Therapist: You mentioned before that he sometimes says, "Okay, later."

The problem behavior is operationalized, and who owns the problem is determined.

Mrs. Burns: Yes. When I raise my voice, he makes a promise to do it later. If I talk in a tone of voice like I'm using with you now, he probably wouldn't even answer.

Therapist: How do you usually react when he doesn't answer?

Mrs. Burns: It depends on what I want him to do or what kind of mood I'm in. Sometimes I just go on and do it myself. Other times I yell at him. Then he promises to do it later, and it usually turns into a yelling match because he doesn't do it at all.

Therapist: Does anyone else have difficulty getting him to mind?

Mrs. Burns: Primarily me. My boyfriend occasionally gets mad at him, but he actually asks Keith to do very few things. I think Keith does what he's told to do at school except for assigned work. Mrs. Brown says he isn't really a discipline problem, but that he just doesn't finish his work.

Therapist: You're the one who is mainly concerned about getting him *to mind more then. What have you tried so far to get him to mind?*

Mrs. Burns: *Yelling. Threatening him.*

Therapist: *How has it worked?*

Mrs. Burns: *It hasn't. That's why I'm here.*

Therapist: *Let's work on it together. Now, are you satisfied with first working on getting Keith to mind and then attacking the other concerns?*

With a specific problem identified, the therapist develops a contract for change in which the structure (who will attend and the order of the process) is agreed on.

Mrs. Burns: *Fine.*

Therapist: *It would be important for Keith to be at our next session.*

Mrs. Burns: *Yes. He should be okay by then. So next week at this time?*

Therapist: *Yes, if that will work for you.*

In the second session, Keith was present. In the early part of the session, the therapist joined with Keith. Later, the therapist worked with Mrs. Burns and Keith to find a solution to the problem.

Therapist: *Tell me some things about yourself, Keith.*

Keith: *I like to play ball.*

Therapist: *What kind of ball?*

Keith: *Oh, basketball and baseball.*

Therapist: *Do you play with your neighbors?*

Since Keith was absent from the first session, it is important to spend time joining with him before addressing the identified problem from the first session.

Keith: *Yeah.*

Therapist: *Play at school too?*

Keith: *Yes. I play intramurals.*

Therapist: *Good! What else do you like to do?*

Keith: *Not much. I like to listen to music.*

Therapist: *What kind?*

Keith: *Peaches.*

Therapist: *I'm showing my age! What do they play?*

Keith: *Soft rock.*

Therapist: *Okay. Do you listen to music with your friends?*

Keith: *Yeah.*

Therapist: *Good. Well, your mother and I had a chance to talk. Maybe she can share her concerns first, and then I would like to hear from you.*

Mrs. Burns: *Well, I would like you to mind. When I ask you to do something, I would like you to do it. I want you to quit promising to do things and start doing them.*

Keith: *Like what?*

Mrs. Burns: *Doing chores, coming in on time, doing your homework.*

Keith: *I do those things.*

Mrs. Burns: *Yes, sometimes. But only after I get after you.*

It is important to return to the process of defining the problem to develop a collaborative relationship with the person who was previously absent. In this case, the information that comes forth from Keith helps highlight the relational nature of the problem. Since there are different points of view, the therapist can now change the original definition of the problem from "Keith won't mind" to "We have a disagreement."

Keith: *I do my work.*

Therapist: *So there seems to be some disagreement. Keith, you seem to believe that you get your work done and, Mom, you say he gets it done once in a while but only after you hound him.*

Mrs. Burns: *Yes.*

Keith: *(Nods)*

Therapist: *I'm wondering if you could both keep a record of what is happening. Mrs. Burns, maybe you could write down each time you ask Keith to do something. Let's put this in the left-hand column. Next to it, write down how many times you ask him, and in the right-hand column write whether he does it. Would you be willing to keep a chart of these things?*

Mrs. Burns: *Yeah. It might keep me really busy writing it all down.*

Therapist: *I know you care about him and want him to be responsible.*

Mrs. Burns: *I'll do it. Do I write down every time I ask him to do something?*

Therapist: *Yes. And, Keith, I would like you to record each time you do something when your mother requests it. (shows Keith the chart) If you do this until next Tuesday, it will give us 6 days of information.*

Mrs. Burns: *Okay. You want us back at the same time?*

Rather than trying to establish truth in the midst of the disagreement, the therapist takes advantage of the disagreement to develop a therapeutic task that will implicitly bring about behavioral change if the clients are able to carry it out, because they are being asked to change from trying to solve the problem to simply gathering information. At the same time, the nature of the task sets the stage for the cognitive changes that may come about from information gained in the task.

Although the therapist is remaining neutral in prescribing the task, he continues to provide reassurance and support by noting the mother's good intentions (resources).

Therapist: Yes.

Mrs. Burns: Fine.

Therapist: Just remember, you are just getting the information; you are not trying to change anything.

Mrs. Burns: Right.

Keith: (Nods)

In the third session, the therapist discussed the information with Mrs. Burns and Keith.

Therapist: Well, how did it go?

Mrs. Burns: I got everything written down here. What I found out was that he really does what I tell him to do sometimes and I guess I don't remember those times.

Therapist: Let's take a look at your chart.

During the remainder of the third session, the therapist noted that Mrs. Burns was making an average of ten requests per day of Keith. In addition, Keith reported that Mrs. Burns's boyfriend, Max, made an average of three requests per day. Sometimes, Mrs. Burns and Max were making requests simultaneously. Both Mrs. Burns and Keith reported that Keith's average level of compliance with his mother was 40%. In addition, Keith complied with all three of Max's requests. The therapist praised Mrs. Burns's and Keith's efforts and asked that Mrs. Burns bring Max to the next session.

In the fourth session, the therapist suggested that Mrs. Burns and Max come to an agreement about what Keith's daily responsibilities should be. With Keith, they could then decide how those duties should be carried out. Mrs. Burns should be the one to communicate with Keith about his tasks. The therapist also suggested that no more than five requests be made of Keith per day. Max agreed to help monitor the program and to support Mrs. Burns and

Keith. If Keith completed all his responsibilities on 4 of 5 days, he would be permitted to go to the Rollerdome on Saturday. The therapist encouraged both of them to continue recording Mrs. Burns's requests and Keith's compliance rate.

Three weeks later, a follow-up session found Mrs. Burns pleased that Keith was complying with each request on 4 of 5 days. Keith and Max also reported satisfaction with the program. The therapist encouraged the family to maintain the same procedures so that they could be more aware of their requests and Keith's reaction to their requests. The family was encouraged to call if they had further difficulties.

A successful treatment program was established when Mrs. Burns and Max were able to agree on Keith's responsibilities and the consequences from compliant behavior. The self-recording procedure that Mrs. Burns and Keith carried out helped them become aware of specific interactional sequences as they occurred. By minimizing instructions, the therapist was able to empower the family to manage the problem. Moreover, Max was able to play a neutral but supportive role to each, an important structural consideration for a third party who becomes involved with a single-parent family.

This case illustrates how self-observation can help family members be more aware of their behavior and how they interact with each other. In the follow-up session, the therapist assesses with the family whether the program is progressing satisfactorily. If there are problems in implementing the program or if the program is not working, the therapist helps troubleshoot with the family. In this case, there were no particular problems after Mrs. Burns reduced the number of demands on her son. If problems were to arise in the future, the therapist would again go through the problem-solving process with the family and determine alternative procedures to be administered.

❇ JEAN AND DAN

Jean and her husband, Dan, came to counseling at Jean's request because of her frustration and admitted lack of bonding with her 2-year-old son, Jason. She stated that she was often angry and disappointed with his responses to her attempted nurturing and was feeling increasingly violent toward him. She had been referred to the family therapist by a friend and by a local social service agency. When she called for an appointment, the therapist asked if she would be willing to invite her husband and if she thought her husband was willing to attend the first session. Jean responded positively to both suggestions and brought Dan to the first session. The initial discussion elicited observations from Dan and Jean about the problem.

As a baby, Jason was "not cuddly," "wanted to be up" most of the time, and was very active. Jean also described him as a "textbook boy." Jason skipped the crawling stage and was walking by his 8th month. Such accelerated development occurred in spite of seizures at 7 months and repeated ear infections during infancy. Jean said she felt rejected by Jason and was lonely. Dan indicated that his wife's problems had left him feeling lonely as well. Jean stated that she wanted help with parenting and also with her depression, for which she was currently on medication. Dan indicated that Jean "had a history" of these problems.

The family therapist began to explore recent events and the specific process that brought them to the point of seeking counseling. That process included the following factors:

1. Shortly after Jason was born, Jean went back to work "too soon" as a labor and delivery nurse. She became emotionally and physically exhausted after 6 weeks and stopped working. At that time, she reported feeling guilty about leaving the baby and feeling rejected by Jason's behavior. As she became increasingly

The therapist used the problem-definition stage to join with the couple. Jean was given the opportunity to describe her experience and perceptions without being challenged. Dan was asked for his point of view as well. The therapist gained an understanding of their experience by summarizing what was heard and by asking questions. An important aspect was the therapist's curiosity about how the problems affected each of them. Such inquiry helped identify areas of pain for both partners. Since Jean was the client of record, the therapist was looking for issues that could motivate Dan to participate for his own well-being. Both partners implied that the problem was Jean's "condition." Thus, at this stage, the therapist was alerted to the need to define the goals of counseling in a conjoint way.

The referral process was explored for two reasons: (a) to understand Jean's level of motivation for counseling and to determine if she had felt pressured into calling by well-meaning social service personnel and (b) to understand the progression of recent events leading up to the referral, which might signal the level of desperation or danger *depressed, a psychiatrist prescribed an antidepressant and met with her periodically to monitor the medication; however, he provided no ongoing counseling.*

2. During a difficult period with Jason, Jean heard an announcement on TV about a program that offered help to parents who were feeling abusive toward their children. She called the program and went for an initial screening. During this screening, Jean was given the opportunity to join a support group for parents at risk and to participate in an educational program. In addition, the worker suggested that Jean seek counseling, something that agency did not provide.

At this point, the therapist asked if the couple was considering any other sources of help and added counseling to the list, which now included:

1. Psychiatrist
2. Support group
3. Educational program (possibly)
4. Counseling (possibly)

The couple mentioned that a member of the clergy had been consulted but was not giving any ongoing help at that time.

After listing these sources of help for the couple to reflect on, the family therapist expressed concern

experienced by family members. These inquiries revealed Jean's personal activation for counseling (internal rather than external) and a number of other sources of help that she had identified. While she was distraught, her lack of isolation helped neutralize the danger that she might become violent. However, the number of potential "authorities" involved was a signal for the therapist to clarify her role and determine how each of these helpers impacted each other. The ultimate question was: Who in this network can support therapeutic progress and who might unwittingly interfere in the process?

During this stage of the process, the therapist assumed the role of director as the couple and therapist determined the best working relationship. The therapist provided leadership in developing priorities; however, the client provided the ranking of importance so that the direction remained client-centered. The therapist was prepared to advise them to delay therapy if they had listed it last in their order of priorities. However, since Jean validated the therapist's hypothesis that information overload had become an additional problem, the organizational focus by the therapist became an intervention as well as a preliminary contract for service.

*that they might be feeling over-
whelmed because of the number of
helpers involved with the problem
and an overload of information for
each of them. Agreeing with this assessment, Jean described how she
had been "going in all directions" in
her desperation to get help and be
responsible. The therapist asked the
couple to discuss which of the helpers were the most important to them
and offered to help them organize a
course of action with the other helpers before focusing attention on the
presenting problem. The rationale
provided was that Jean would probably not be able to benefit from the
counseling if there were too many
people offering diverse points of view.
Thus, the initial goal became that of
prioritizing her sources of help and
coordinating the most important ones
to develop a compatible treatment
plan. Since Jean stated that counseling was more important to her than
the educational program, she was
helped to take a more directive role in
delaying her enrollment in this optional program. In addition, since her
medication and the support group
were very helpful to her, the family
therapist discussed possible ways of
coordinating counseling services with
these other sources of help. Jean was
asked whether she thought she might
be in danger of hurting Jason between
the first and second sessions. She re-
plied, "No." The first session ended
with an initial contract to develop a*

Sometimes, beginning practitioners fail to see the benefit in taking extra time to clarify the politics
of the larger system (client and
helpers) and the smaller therapeutic
system (therapist and client). However, a therapist in a practice with
voluntary clients has no control, but
only potential influence, over the
larger system, which may play an
important role in certain aspects of
the therapeutic process. Thus, by focusing on how clients can organize
the other influences, the therapist
can proceed with appropriate support but with minimal interference
from other agencies. In addition,
this is an effective intervention for
clients who already feel out of control in some part of their life. Their
sense of empowerment further dissi-
pates potential danger and creates a
hopeful, collegial relationship with
the therapist before the presenting
problem is addressed. Since the clients understand that the preliminary goal helps the therapeutic
system become more effective, they
are satisfied that their concerns are
being addressed. If the potential for
violence had been greater in this
situation, the therapist would have
helped the couple develop a plan for
safety first (see Chapter Five), then
addressed the larger system, and left
the traditional therapeutic goals for
last. The assignment helped Jean
understand the expectations she
had for the therapist and it also

plan of coordination between all parties involved. When this was accomplished to everyone's satisfaction, the presenting problem would then be addressed in greater detail.

In the second session, Jean and her husband brought back information from the psychiatrist that clarified his role as simply monitoring and prescribing medication. He was open to discussing Jean's situation with the family therapist, but was not providing counseling services at that time. In addition, Jean was able to clarify what she hoped to accomplish in counseling that would be different from her experiences with her support group.

With these issues clarified, the therapeutic system could move ahead in developing goals and a contract for service that would specifically address Jean's original concern—her problems with her son. By this time, the family therapist had joined with the couple through empowering them to be more assertive with outside influences in their lives. In addition, Dan had expressed his own frustrations, thereby providing the therapist with an opportunity to engage him more personally in the therapeutic contract.

Therapist: *Dan, it sounds like things haven't been too good for you lately. You mentioned last week how lonely your marriage had been since Jason was born.*

Dan: *That's true. Things haven't been all that rosy.*

helped the therapist understand what role could complement, and not conflict with, the influence of Jean's support group.

Although Dan had agreed to come to the first session and was willing to help Jean, there was no explicit understanding that he would address his own concerns except as they related to solving the problem of Jean's frustration and depression.

Therapist: *Well, I'm wondering if you would be interested in an agreement for counseling in which we state that we'll not only work to make things better for Jean, but we'll also take a look at how things could be better for you, too.*

Dan: *That would be okay.*

Jean: *I know I'm not being a very good wife right now.*

Therapist: *That may be how it seems right now, but that's not what I was referring to. Usually, when a couple first marries and has complications such as you have with a first child, it's very common for spouses to go through a period of stress and conflict. [To Dan:] Although Jean's problems were your motivation for coming, I feel a responsibility to help you with those problems in a way that will strengthen rather than threaten your marriage. The best way to do that is to involve you and include you in the problem-solving process.*

Dan: *I'd like that.*

Therapist: *Jean, would it be okay with you if we include Dan, rather than you coming by yourself?*

Jean: *Yes. I think it would help. We don't communicate very well.*

Therapist: *Dan, what do you think about Jean's observation?*

Dan: *She's right. We need some help. I'll come if it will help.*

Therefore, the therapist initiated a conversation with Dan to understand whether he was comfortable with the idea of identifying and admitting that he wants positive outcomes for himself.

If he had responded negatively, the therapist would have accepted Dan's response and acknowledged Dan's wisdom in recognizing his limits and in being firm about what is best for him. Then, the therapist could ask Dan to describe more fully what aspect of the therapy process seemed problematic for him. At that point, the therapist might be able to address those concerns. If not, Dan might be willing to act as an intermittent consultant, agreeing to attend occasional sessions, or he might be willing to make occasional check-ins with the therapist by telephone. These would be used to continue the joining process and to learn more about how the therapy process could be sensitive to his needs.

Since the therapist was able to engage Dan, the goal of therapy can be expanded to include a strengthening of the relationship. In this way, the marriage becomes a focus for change as well as a resource in solving the presenting problem. Such an orientation carries with it the assumption that presenting problems are influenced by the significant relationships of those who define the problem. By involving significant others

Therapist: *So, if our agreement included the strengthening of your relationship, does that sound like it might make things better for you at home?*

Dan: *Yes. That sounds good.*

in solving the presenting problem, the family therapist makes a choice to facilitate a solution that impacts the client's relational system in the best possible way.

At this point, noting that their observations and definition of the problem had already been discussed at length, the therapist suggested that they participate together in a thorough assessment process as a means of reviewing the many changes and adjustments that had taken place in their young married lives. Such an assessment could also provide them with a perspective that would be useful in developing strategies to solve the present problem and to meet other challenges that occur as a natural part of family life. The assessment process was described as a series of three to five sessions that would help the family therapist understand their unique experiences together and help them select the best strategy for finding a solution. The couple agreed to this contract; the husband characterized his involvement as a way to strengthen their relationship. The therapist asked Jean if her feelings of violence toward Jason were so strong that a 5-week delay before the beginning of treatment might be dangerous. She indicated that knowing she was now getting help made her feel better and said she could call members of her support group if she began to feel too desperate.

The third and fourth sessions were spent reviewing information that the couple identified as important for the therapist. Jean reported having suicidal thoughts and wanting to find a way to escape the stresses she was now feeling. She stated that she had no plan and did not want to die; however, she continued to feel overwhelmed and guilty about her relationship with Jason. In reviewing the history of these feelings, she revealed a suicide attempt during her high school years and described her pattern of coping during emotional difficulties. She found it hard to prioritize and often felt disorganized, not knowing where to begin. At the same time, she would become angry at Dan for his inability to be more helpful. Dan felt depressed and wished he had more confidence in himself. He said he had been feeling increasingly discouraged and was considering dropping out of electronics school. Both partners said they wanted to make changes in these areas and wanted to save face as well because they were embarrassed about their problems and wanted to look more competent in the eyes of their families.

The fifth session was devoted to a developmental review of the couple's courtship, marriage, and early married life. Keeping in mind Jean's initial goal of feeling better about her son and eliminating all feelings of violence toward him, the family therapist used these sessions to discover and highlight information that might put Jean's feelings in a larger context to allow the couple to redefine the problem in some way that would lead to its resolution. As the couple described the ups and downs of their lives, the therapist portrayed these events not as problems to be solved, but rather as life experiences from which they were learning new skills. The review process became a vehicle for increased intimacy between Jean and Dan, who took the opportunity to reflect on their life together and to develop a shared understanding about their strengths and weaknesses. In addition, the family therapist identified how existing strengths in the couple could be used to develop additional problem-solving skills.

As Jean and Dan reviewed their early courtship, they recalled their attraction to each other: Dan perceived Jean as "sincere, cute, and together"; Jean perceived Dan as "handsome and shy." Their early married life was characterized by financial struggles, followed by a pregnancy after the first year. Because of complications, Jean was ordered to bed by her doctor during the month in which she was scheduled to take her state nursing exam. During this period, the couple began to feel alienated from each other, and Jean's depression began to surface.

The therapist used the telling of the couple's story to point out their accomplishments in spite of the hardships. Jean had graduated from college. Dan was being used at school as a tutor because of his competence. They had felt close and hopeful in spite of financial problems. As they began to experience increased

The therapist noticed that the initial attraction between Jean and Dan included clues about what they might be expecting from each other. If Dan thought Jean was "together," he might be unprepared for a wife who would need his help and support. In addition, when Jean thought of Dan as "shy," she may have assumed that this would be a relationship where her sense of initiative and willingness to nurture could be valued. The therapist identified the complemenarity of the couple (one as giver and one as receiver) as a possible locus of developmental crisis: Now that Jean had been stretched to her limit by life experiences and unforeseen complications, she felt guilty that she could not fulfill her unspoken role in the marriage. Dan also felt disappointed that the previous relational patterns were not being maintained. In addition, Jean's anger at Dan could be *distance and frustration, they remained committed to the marriage and continued trying to improve the situation. Their endurance was identified as a strength, and their patience under the onslaught of complications was emphasized.*

During the sixth session, Jean reported that her suicidal thoughts had resumed, as she remembered her sexual permissiveness during her courtship with Dan. She felt guilty for violating the standards of her family of origin and remembered her role in her family as a "shining star." The therapist suggested that they spend more time understanding the patterns related to each spouse's family of origin; however, Jean asked for a session alone to discuss a problem with her employer that had reached a crisis. The therapist cooperated with Jean's request, and the seventh and eighth sessions were spent developing strategies to help Jean be more assertive with her supervisor.

When Dan returned to the ninth session, Jean reported that she had begun to understand her feelings toward Jason as part of her personal need to be a perfect shining star. As she began to notice these feelings dominating her, she started to address her internal process as a way of detaching from her negative feelings toward Jason. She began to realize that this need for perfection was an unrealistic goal, which had come

seen as an indication that she was aware of the imbalance and was asking for a change.

Since the complementarity of the couple followed traditional gender stereotypes, the therapist was careful not to characterize Jean's anger at Dan as weak, since Jean perceived a lack of reciprocity in the marriage. At the same time, the therapist empathized with Dan's disappointment, treating it as an understandable by-product brought on by life events that rendered Jean unable to maintain her role unconditionally. In such discussions, the couple was invited to consider how their roles could be more flexible, how they could take turns in the supportive role, rather than polarizing to a rigid extreme. However, when Jean began to discuss her feelings of hopelessness, the therapist decided to delay more extensive marital intervention until Jean's depression improved.

Although the therapist wanted to help with the developmental task of negotiating boundaries with in-laws, it was more important to cooperate with what Jean felt was an impending crisis. By remaining flexible and democratic, the therapist maintained a collegial relationship with Jean and cooperated with her priorities. With the depression still pronounced, it was also necessary for the therapist to empower Jean by validating what was most relevant to her.

*Ffrom her role in her amily of origin.
The couple had agreed that Jean's
family was sometimes a help and
sometimes a hindrance for their well-
being. As family-of-origin issues were
explored, the couple successfully executed a new plan in which Dan could
support Jean when she was more assertive with her parents. She had
feared their disapproval all her life.
Rather than let them know when she
was fearful or feeling inadequate, she
had constantly tried to live up to her
shining star image. She was able to understand her earlier suicide attempt as
a time in her life when she was keeping negative feelings to herself and was
driven by high expectations from self
and family. As Jean and Dan both became more assertive with their families,
they also began to feel a sense of equal
status with their parents and a sense of
increased competence. By the 15th session, both were enjoying Jason more
and were feeling a sense of accomplish-
ment in their progress.*

*Two months passed before the
next group of sessions. Jean and Dan
reported heavy work schedules, which
they had no choice but to endure. On
returning, both were feeling distant
and out of control. They expressed a
need to have time for each other.
Marital and health issues were addressed during the remaining 15 ses-
sions.The therapist used reports of
conflict to reframe arguments as opportunities for increased communication. Couple interaction patterns were*

At this time, the client vol-
unteered clues about how she was
integrating information from the
larger context (e.g., life cycle,
marital dynamics, family of origin)
with the presenting problem. However, if the client had not indicated that the therapeutic process
was still relevant to the presenting
problem, it would have been the
therapist's responsibility to raise
the question and review the sessions to date, with the intent of re-
negotiating a clearer understanding of what needed to be addressed
(child management strategies,
marital communication, or other
issues). At the middle stage of
therapy, if the initial issues are no
longer the focus, it is important to
clarify who initiated the change of
focus.

When clinicians initiate the
change (e.g., from feelings toward
son to feelings toward family of
origin), they should also initiate a
discussion about how this change
affects the client. Does the change
seem relevant to the client? Does
the therapist's rationale satisfy a
client's questions? Is there a direction that seems more relevant to
the client?

In this case, the process had
influenced the couple to view
the problem developmentally, as
they reviewed their marital development—and now Jean's personal development— through

Reported: Jean would become upset and "blow up" but then recant her complaint and back down. Dan would try to pacify Jean and "jump around" as he tried to guess what she really wanted.

In addition, they began to identify a pattern of overresponsibility in Jean and underresponsibility in Dan. She was consistently the initiator in the marriage; most decisions were her idea. Dan would comply rather than negotiate with Jean around his preferences or differing point of view.

When the couple began to use their arguments as opportunities to negotiate differences, Dan became more involved in decisions and Jean felt more support with household responsibilities. They began to experience improved marital communication, largely because they became more assertive with each other, rather than avoiding conflict through distance. Ultimately, they concluded therapy so they could begin saving their money instead to buy a home. The therapist complimented them on their ability to prioritize and take control of their lives in such an assertive manner. They were left with the option of returning for support if needed. Two years later, they successfully purchased their first home and, in approximately two more years, they had a second child with no complications and reported that they are doing fine.

many life transitions. Jean was taking the initiative to move in the direction of her family issues, and Dan was willing to explore his own family-of-origin relationships as a result.

At this point in the process, the couple felt no further need to address Jean's original concerns regarding Jason. Instead, they brought a definition of the problem that had clear relational components and was explicitly marital in nature. This gave the therapist the opportunity to address earlier hypotheses regarding the complementarity in the marriage.

In earlier stages of therapy, the therapist had remained indirect, addressing only the most immediate aspects that related to the original presenting problem. However, the small pragmatic changes that had been made months before were not enough to challenge the couple's original "private marital contract" and its complementarity, which spread to other aspects of their relationship. Dan had become more involved with child care and home management; however, these were seen as necessary to help Jean, not as a rewriting of significant marital expectations.

Now that Jean's depression had lifted and the couple was asking for marital counseling, the therapist could resurrect previous hypotheses about the relationship and address them directly. Drawing on literature about gender relationships and birth-order roles, the therapist took a psychoeducational approach by raising the issue of over- and under-responsibility.

After tracking interactional sequences, the therapist asked them to describe the outcomes they would have preferred and what each person's options were for bringing about more satisfying interactions. In response to the therapist's coaching and reassurance, the couple learned to tolerate each other's anger and to understand the thoughts and intentions that were influencing their behaviors. As communication brought a deeper level of intimacy and more concrete requests for behavioral changes, their marital roles became broader and more flexible. Emotional support became more reciprocal: Dan realized that he had strength to offer Jean, and Jean realized that she had the right to ask Dan to make some sacrifices for the relationship.

This case illustrates the convergence of culture, gender, life-cycle, family structure, family-of-origin, and personal constructs in the formation of the presenting problem. When a couple has a child, the three automatically form a triangle (family structure influenced by life-cycle changes). Jean became close to Jason and developed depression when he did not respond according to her expectations (personal constructs). Her expectations of self and Jason came from her role as a shining star (culture and family of origin influencing personal constructs). The couple's pattern of over- and underresponsibility was addressed at the parenting level and, later, at the level of marital roles and communication (gender issues influencing family structure). The therapist first intervened with the family and larger system by helping them challenge cultural assumptions about seeking help. Next, Dan was engaged as an important player in the therapeutic process. This intervention created a context for change in gender balances and family structure. Problem solving around Jean's work issues validated her ability to take charge of her life and became a positive prelude to addressing her issues with her family of origin in a more assertive way. As the couple worked together on these earlier issues, they developed the trust and intimacy needed to become more assertive and negotiable with each other. And what about Jason? The presenting problem was redefined in light of all these factors, and positive changes occurred as each systemic issue became an area of growth for both parents.

To sum up, we have attempted to integrate treatment concepts through two case reviews. In the Burns family, the therapist got the family to agree on the problem and a self-observation procedure to assess the interactional patterns around the problem. By reducing Mrs. Burns's frequency of requests and getting her boyfriend to support her and Keith in their new behavior, the therapist empowered the family to manage the problem. In the case of Jean and Dan, the therapist provided an integration of treatment models to create a context for change in gender roles and family structure.

The treatment offered to both of these families is not presented as a model to be replicated and therefore is deliberately not recorded in specific detail. Instead, both case reviews serve only as a guide for integrating treatment concepts and methods. Therapists are obligated to use their own sensitive, creative, and flexible ideas in integrating treatment with their client families. As such integrations develop, evaluative feedback from clients can help the family therapist maintain a relevant and individualized direction.

❄ COMPONENTS OF FAMILY THERAPY

Returning to the four integrative components of family therapy, we can see that each case contains structural, experiential, relational, and directional processes that are implemented by the therapist. With the Burns family, treatment is brief. Thus, the first session contains all four components as the therapist (1) provides clarity around roles and describes the therapeutic process,

(2) explores interactions and intentions in order to define the problem, (3) emphasizes relational aspects of the problem, and (4) prioritizes and develops a contract for change. Subsequent sessions focus more on experiential and relational processes since Keith had to be engaged in the second session and the therapist had to foster his cooperation with the contract. We think of this process alone as a significant intervention.

With Jean and Dan, the four components of family therapy occur as segments of the first four sessions. Sessions One and Two are devoted largely to structural and directional issues because of the influence of the larger system. Sessions Three and Four explore relevant client experience as a means of highlighting relational resources and strengths. Subsequent sessions become combinations of experiential and relational components as various problems are addressed pragmatically.

To help with treatment planning, Box 11.1 summarizes various tasks that are associated with each of the four components. While not exhaustive, this list serves as a reminder of what we consider to be key processes in marital and family therapy. It provides a foundation of abilities that will develop more fully with exploration and dedication. Like driving a car, after the basics are mastered, it is the driver who determines how each adventure is approached, how each challenge is addressed, and the meaning that is ultimately given to the relationships that are encountered along the way. As family therapists, we encourage a journey that will contain enough courage to enter the unknown, enough hope to believe in positive possibilities, and enough compassion to find value in the uniqueness of all people.

Box 11.1
Basic Components of Marital and Family Therapy

I. Provide structure
   A. Initiate the therapeutic relationship
   B. Organize treatment
   C. Explain the process
   D. Promote give and take
   E. Develop rationales for specific directions
   F. Negotiate changes in the process
   G. Verify assumptions and intentions

II. Explore client experience related to the problem
   A. Understand client expectations for the session
   B. Understand client expectations for treatment
   C. Understand the client's definition of the problem
   D. Assess beliefs and behaviors related to the problem
   E. Assess levels of experience
      1. Individual
      2. Structural
      3. Intergenerational
      4. Life transitions
      5. Race and culture
      6. Gender

III. Address relationships
   A. Identify important interpersonal influences
   B. Involve family members and/or the network
   C. Within the system, establish the range of opinions about the problem
   D. Emphasize relational resources and strengths
   E. Encourage new beliefs and behaviors related to relationships
   F. Choose interventions that target relationships

IV. Develop a unified direction
   A. Clarify assumptions and expectations
   B. Address each person's needs
   C. Use client resources
   D. Instill hope (The glass is always half full.)
   E. Propose options
   F. Elicit feedback
   G. Decide on a plan
   H. Set goals
   I. Facilitate contracts

REFERENCES

Amatea, E., & Sherrard, P. (1989). Reversing the school's response: A new approach to resolving persistent problems. *American Journal of Family Therapy, 17,* 15–26.

Amatea, E., & Sherrard, P. (1991, October). Systematic practice in schools provides a new frontier. *Family Therapy News,* pp. 5–6.

American Association for Marriage and Family Therapy. (1998). AAMFT *code of ethics.* Washington, DC: Author.

Anderson, C., Reiss, D., & Hogarty, G. (1986). *Schizophrenia and the family: A practitioner's guide to psycho-education and management.* New York: Guilford Press.

Anderson, H. (1991). Opening the door for change through continuing conversations. In T. C. Todd & M. D. Selekman (Eds.), *Family therapy approaches with adolescent substance abusers* (pp. 176–189). Needham Heights, MA: Allyn & Bacon.

Anderson, S., & Bagarozzi, D. (Eds.). (1989). *Family myths: Psychotherapy implications.* New York: Haworth Press.

Aponte, H. (1976a). The family–school interview. *Family Process, 15,* 464–477.

Aponte, H. (1976b). Underorganization in the poor family. In P. J. Guem, Jr. (Ed.), *Family therapy: Theory and practice* (pp. 432–448). New York: Guilford Press.

Aponte, H., & Van Deusen, J. (1981). Structural family therapy. In A. S. P. Gurman & D. Kniskern(Eds.), *Handbook of family therapy* (pp. 310–360). New York: Brunner/Mazel.

Barker, P. (1981). *Basic family therapy.* Baltimore, MD: University Park Press.

Barlow, P. H., Hayes, S. C., & Nelson, R. O. (1984). *The scientist practitioner: Research and accountability in clerical and educational settings.* New York: Pergamon Press.

Barton, C., & Alexander, J. F. (1981). Functional family therapy. In A. S. Gurman & D. P. Kniskern (Eds.), *Handbook of family therapy* (Vol. 1, pp. 403–443). New York: Brunner/Mazel.

Bateson, G. (1972). *Steps to an ecology of mind.* New York: Dutton.

Bateson, G. (1979). *Mind in nature: A necessary unity.* New York: Dutton.

Bateson, G., Jackson, D., Haley, J., & Weakland, J. (1956). Toward a theory of schizophrenia. *Behavioral Science, 1*(4), 251–264.

Baucom, D. H., Epstein, N. R., & Rankin, L. A. (1995). Cognitive aspects of cognitive-behavioral marital therapy. In N. S. Jacobson & A. Gurman (Eds.), *Clinical handbook of couple therapy* (pp. 65–90). New York: Guilford Press.

Baucom, D. H., Epstein, N., Sayers, S., & Sher, T. G. (1989). The role of cognitions in marital relationships: Definitional, methodological, and conceptual issues. *Journal of Consulting and Clinical Psychology, 57,* 31–38.

Baucom, D. H., Sayers, S., & Sher, T. G. (1990). Supplementing behavioral marital therapy with cognitive restructuring and emotional expressiveness training: An outcome investigation. *Journal of Consulting and Clinical Psychology, 58,* 636–645.

Bernal, G., & Flores-Oitiz, Y. (1991). Contextual family therapy with adolescent drug abusers. In T. Todd & M. Selekman (Eds.), *Family therapy approaches with adolescent substance abusers* (pp. 70–92). Needham Heights, MA: Allyn & Bacon.

Bodin, A. (1981). The interactional view: Family therapy approaches of the mental health institute. In A. S. Gurman & D. P. Kniskern (Eds.), *Handbook of family therapy* (pp. 267–309). New York: Brunner/Mazel.

Boscolo, L., Cecchin, G., Hoffman, L., & Penn, P. (1987). *Milan systemic family therapy: Conversations in theory and practice.* New York: Basic Books.

Boszormenyi-Nagy, I. (1966). From family therapy to a psychology of relationships: Fictions of the individual and fictions of the family. *Comprehensive Psychiatry, 7,* 408–423.

Boszormenyi-Nagy, I. (Ed.). (1987). *Foundations of contextual therapy: Collected papers.* New York: Brunner/Mazel.

Boszormenyi-Nagy, I., & Framo, J. (Eds.). (1965). *Intensive family therapy.* New York: Harper & Row.

Boszormenyi-Nagy, I., & Krasner, B. (1986). *Between give and take: A clinical guide to contextual therapy.* New York: Brunner/Mazel.

Boszormenyi-Nagy, I., & Spark, G. M. (1973). *Invisible loyalties: Reciprocity in intergenerational family therapy.* New York: Harper & Row.

Bowen, M. (1978). *Family therapy in clinical practice.* New York: Aronson.

Boyd-Franklin, N. (1989). *Black families in therapy: A multi-system approach.* New York: Guilford Press.

Breunlin, D. (1985). Expanding the concept of stages in family therapy. In D. Breunlin (Ed.), *Stages: Patterns of change over time* (pp. 95–120). Rockville, MD: Aspen.

Breunlin, D. C., Schwartz, R. C., & Mac Kune-Karrer, B. M. (1992). *Metaframeworks: Transcending the models of family therapy.* San Francisco: Jossey-Bass.

Brock, G., & Barnard, C. (1988). *Procedures in family therapy.* Needham Heights, MA: Allyn & Bacon.

Broderick, C. B., & Schrader, S. S. (1991). The history of professional marriage and family therapy. In A. S. Gurman & D. P. Kniskern (Eds.), *Handbook of family therapy* (pp. 3–40). New York: Brunner/Mazel.

Brown, J., Brown, C., & Portes, P. (1991). *The families in transition program.* Louisville, KY: University of Louisville Press.

Brown, J., & Christensen, D. (1986). *Family therapy: Theory and practice.* Pacific Grove, CA: Brooks/Cole.

Brown, J. H., Eichenberger, S. A., Portes, P., & Christensen, D. N. (1991). Family functioning factors associated with the adjustment level of children of divorce. *Journal of Divorce and Remarriage, 17,* 81–95.

Brown, J. H., & Vaccaro, A. (1991). *A manual for resource and youth services coordinators.* Louisville, KY: University of Louisville and Cities in Schools.

Campbell, D., Draper, R., & Crutchley, E. (1991). The Milan systemic approach to family therapy. In A. S. Gurman & D. P. Kniskern (Eds.), *Handbook of family therapy* (Vol. 2, pp. 324–362). New York: Brunner/Mazel.

Carter, B., & McGoldrick, M. (Eds.). (1989a). *The changing family life cycle: Framework for family therapy* (2nd ed.). Needham Heights, MA: Allyn & Bacon.

Carter, B., & McGoldrick, M. (1989b). Forming a remarried family. In B. Carter & M. McGoldrick (Eds.), *The changing family life cycle: Framework for family therapy* (2nd ed., pp. 399–432). Needham Heights, MA: Allyn & Bacon.

Colapinto, J. (1982). Structural family therapy. In A. M. Horne & M. M. Ohlsen (Eds.), *Family counseling and therapy* (pp. 112–140). Itasca, IL: F. E. Peacock.

Colapinto, J. (1991). Structural family therapy. In A. S. Gurman & D. P. Kniskern (Eds.), *Handbook of family therapy* (Vol. 2, pp. 417–443). New York: Brunner/Mazel.

Coleman, S. (Ed.). (1985). *Failures in family therapy.* New York: Guilford Press.

Commission on Accreditation for Marriage and Family Therapy Education (COAMFTE). (1997). *Manual on accreditation.* Washington, DC: Author.

Cormier, W. H., & Cormier, L. S. (1991). *Interviewing strategies for helpers: Fundamental skills and cognitive behavioral interventions* (3rd ed.). Pacific Grove, CA: Brooks/Cole.

Crando, R., & Ginsberg, B. G. (1976). Communication in the father–son relationship: The parent–adolescent relationship development program. *The Family Coordinator, 4,* 465–473.

Cross, T. L. (1995). Understanding family resiliency from a relational world view. In H. I. McCubbin, E. A. Thompson, A. I. Thompson, & J. E. Fromer (Eds.), *Resiliency in ethnic minority families: Native and immigrant American families* (Vol. 1, pp. 143–157). Madison: University of Wisconsin–Madison Center for Family Studies.

De Shazer, S. (1985). *Keys to solution in brief therapy.* New York: Norton.

Duncan, B., & Parks, M. B. (1988). Integrating individual and systems approaches: Strategic-behavioral therapy. *Journal of Marital and Family Therapy, 14,* 151–161.

Dunst, C., Trivette, C., & Deal, A. (1988). *Enabling and empowering families: Principles and guidelines for practice.* Cambridge, MA: Brookline Books.

Durrant, M. (1988). Gwynne: A new recipe for life [Special edition]. *Case Studies.*

Duvall, E. (1977). *Marriage and family development* (5th ed.). Philadelphia: Lippincott.

Efran, J., Lukens, M., & Lukens, R. (1990). *Language, structure and change.* New York: Norton.

Epston, D., & White, M. (1992). *Experience, contradiction, narrative and imagination: Selected papers of David Epston and Michael White, 1989–1991.* Adelaide, Australia: Dulwich Center Publications.

Erickson, M., & Rossi, E. (1979). *Hypnotherapy: An exploratory casework.* New York Irvington.

Ericson, P., & Rogers, L. E. (1973). New procedures for analyzing relational communication. *Family Process, 12*(3), 245–268.

Falicov, C. (1988). *Family transitions: Continuity and change over the lifecycle.* New York: Guilford Press.

Falloon, I. R. (1991). Behavioral family therapy. In A. S. Gurman & D. P. Kniskern (Eds.), *Handbook of family therapy* (Vol. 2, pp. 65–95). New York: Brunner/Mazel.

Ferreira, A. (1963). Family myth and homeostasis. *Archives of General Psychiatry, 9,* 457–463.

Figley, C., & Nelson, T. (1989). Basic family therapy skills. I: Conceptualization and findings. *Journal of Marital and Family Therapy, 4*(14), 349–366.

Fleuridas, C., Nelson, T., & Rosenthal, D. M. (1986). The evolution of circular questions: Training family therapists. *Journal of Marital and Family Therapy, 12*(27), 113–128.

Fleuridas, C., Rosenthal, D. M., Leigh, G. K., & Leigh, T. E. (1990). Family goal recording: An adaptation of goal attainment scaling for enhancing family therapy assessment. *Journal of Marital and Family Therapy, 16,* 389–406.

Framo, J. (1976). Family of origin as a therapeutic resource for adults in marital and family therapy: You can and should go home again. *Family Process, 15,* 193–210.

Framo, J. (1981). The integration of marital therapy with sessions with family of origin. In A. S. Gurman & D. P. Kniskern (Eds.), *Handbook of family therapy* (pp. 133–158). New York: Brunner/Mazel.

Gambino, R. (1974). *Blood of my blood: The dilemma of Italian-Americans.* New York: Doubleday.

Garcia-Preto, N. (1982). Family therapy with Puerto Rican families. In M. McGoldrick, J. K. Pearce, & J. Giordano (Eds.), *Ethnicity and family therapy* (pp. 164–186). New York: Guilford Press.

Garfield, R. (1981). Mourning and its resolution for spouses in marital separation. In J. C. Hansen & L. Messinger (Eds.), *Therapy with remarriage and families* (pp. 1–15). Rockville, MD: Aspen.

Garfield, S., & Bergin, A. (1978). *Handbook of psychotherapy and behavior change* (2nd ed.). New York: Wiley.

Garfield, S. L. (1994). Research on client variables in psychotherapy. In A. E. Bergin & S. L. Garfield (Eds.), *Handbook of psychotherapy and behavior change* (4th ed.). New York: Wiley.

Gergen, K. (1985). The social constructionist in modern psychology. *American Psychologist, 40,* 266–275.

Goldner, V. (1988). Generation and gender: Normative and covert hierarchies. *Family Process, 27,* 17–31.

Goldstein, A. (1973). *Structured learning therapy.* New York: Academic Press.

Gonzales, N. A., Hiraga, Y., & Cauce, A. M. (1995). Observing mother–daughter interaction in African-American and Asian-American families. In H. I. McCubbins, E. A. Thompson, A. I. Thompson, & J. A. Futrell (Eds.), *Resiliency in ethnic minority families: African-American families* (Vol. 2, pp. 259–286). Madison: University of Wisconsin–Madison Center for Family Studies.

Goolishian, H. A., & Anderson, H. (1992). Strategy and intervention versus nonintervention: A matter of theory? *Journal of Marital and Family Therapy, 18*(1), 5–15.

Gurman, A. S., & Kniskern, D. P. (Eds.). (1981). *Handbook of family therapy.* New York: Brunner/Mazel.

Gurman, A. S., & Kniskern, D. P. (Eds.). (1991). *Handbook of family therapy* (Vol. 2). New York: Brunner/Mazel.

Haley, J. (1967). Toward a theory of pathological systems. In G. H. Zuk & I. Boszormenyi-Nagy (Eds.), *Family theory and disturbed families* (pp. 11–27). Palo Alto, CA: Science and Behavior Books.

Haley, J. (Ed.). (1976). *Problem-solving therapy.* San Francisco: Jossey-Bass.

Haley, J. (1980). *Leaving home: The therapy of disturbed young people.* New York: McGraw-Hill.

Hanna, S. M. (1995). On paradox: Empathy before strategy. *Journal of Family Psychotherapy, 6*(1), 85–88.

Hanna, S. M. (1997). A developmental-interactional model. In T. D. Hargrave & S. M. Hanna (Eds.), *The aging family: New visions in theory, practice, and reality* (pp. 101–130). New York: Brunner/Mazel.

Hanna, S. M., & Hargrave, T. D. (1997). Integrating the process of aging and family therapy. In T. D. Hargrave & S. M. Hanna (Eds.), *The aging family: New visions in theory, practice, and reality* (pp. 19–38, 122). New York: Brunner/Mazel.

Hansen, J., Pound, R., & Warner, R. (1976). Use of modeling procedures. *Personnel and Guidance Journal, 54,* 242–245.

Hardy, K. V., & Laszloffy, T. A. (1995). The cultural genogram: Key to training culturally competent family therapists. *Journal of Marital and Family Therapy, 21*(3), 227–237.

Hare-Mustin, R. (1978). A feminist approach to family therapy. *Family Process, 17,* 181–194.

Hargrave, T., & Anderson, W. (1992). *Finishing well: Aging and reparation in the intergenerational family.* New York: Brunner/Mazel.

Hargrave, T. D., & Hanna, S. M. (1997). *The aging family: New visions in theory, practice, and reality.* New York: Brunner/Mazel Inc.

Hiebert, W., Gillespie, J., & Stahmann, R. (1993). *Dynamic assessment in couples therapy.* New York: Lexington Books.

Hirschmann, M. J., & Sprenkle, D. H. (1989). The use of therapeutic paradox among members of the American Association for Marriage and Family Therapy. *The American Journal of Family Therapy, 17*(4), 348–358.

Hoffman, L. (1981). *Foundations of family therapy.* New York: Basic Books.

Hoffman, L. (1983). A co-evolutionary framework for systemic family therapy. In J. Hansen & B. Keeney (Eds.), *Diagnosis and assessment in family therapy* (pp. 35–62). Rockville, MD: Aspen.

Hoffman, L. (1998). Setting aside the model in family therapy. *Journal of Marital and Family Therapy 24*(2), 145–156.

Holtzworth-Munroe, A., & Jacobson, N. S. (1991). Behavioral marital therapy. In A. S. Gurman & D. P. Kniskern (Eds.), *Handbook of family therapy* (Vol. 2, pp. 96–133). New York: Brunner/Mazel.

Hosford, R., & de Visser, C. (1974). *Behavioral counseling: An introduction.* Washington, DC: American Personnel and Guidance Press.

Howard, J. (1978). *Families.* New York: Simon & Schuster.

Imber-Black, E. (Ed.). (1993). Secrets in families and family therapy. New York: Norton.

Imber-Black, E., Roberts, J., & Whiting, R. (1988). *Rituals in families and family therapy.* New York: Norton.

Jacobson, N. S. (1984). A component analysis of behavioral marital therapy: The relative effectiveness of behavior exchange and problem solving training. *Journal of Consulting and Clinical Psychology, 52,* 295–305.

Jacobson, N. S., Holtzworth-Munroe, A., & Schmaling, K. B. (1989). Marital therapy and spouse involvement in the treatment of depression, agoraphobia, and alcoholism. *Journal of Consulting and Clinical Psychology, 57,* 5–10.

Jacobson, N. S., & Margolin, B. (1979). *Marital therapy: Strategies based on social learning and behavior exchange principles.* New York: Brunner/Mazel.

Jenkins, A. (1991). *Invitations to responsibility.* Adelaide, Australia: Dulwich Centre Publications.

Karpel, M. (1986). Questions, obstacles, and contributions. In M. A. Karpel (Ed.), *Family resources: The hidden partner in family therapy* (pp. 3–64). New York: Guilford Press.

Keith, D., & Whitaker, C. (1985). Failure: Our bold companion. In S. Coleman (Ed.), *Failures in family therapy* (pp. 8–26). New York: Guilford Press.

Kerr, M. (1981). Family systems theory and therapy. In A. S. Gurman & D. P. Kniskern (Eds.), *Handbook of family therapy* (pp. 226–266). New York: Brunner/Mazel.

Kinney, J., Haopala, P., & Booth, C. (1991). *Keeping families together: The home builders model.* New York: Aldine De Gruyter.

Kiresuk, T. J., & Sherman, R. E. (1979). Goal attainment scaling: A general method for evaluating community mental health programs. *Community Mental Health, 4,* 443–453.

Kramer, J. (1985). *Family interfaces: Transgenerational patterns.* New York: Brunner/Mazel.

Krumboltz, J., Varenhorst, B., & Thoresen, C. (1967). Nonverbal factors in effectiveness of models in counseling. *Journal of Counseling Psychology, 14,* 412–418.

Kuehl, B. P. (1995). The solution-oriented genogram: A collaborative approach. *Journal of Marital and Family Therapy, 21*(3), 239–250.

Lambert, M. J., & Bergin, A. E. (1994). The effectiveness of psychotherapy. In A. E. Bergin & S. L. Garfield (Eds.), *Handbook of psychotherapy and behavior change* (4th ed.). New York: Wiley.

Landau-Stanton, J. (1986). Competence, impermanence, and transitional mapping: A model for systems consultation. In L. C. Wynne, S. H. McDaniel, & T. T. Weber (Eds.), *Systems consultation: A new perspective for family therapy* (pp. 253–269). New York: Guilford Press.

Landau-Stanton, J., & Stanton, M. D. (1985). Treating suicidal adolescents and their families. In M. Pravder Mirkin & S. Koman (Eds.), *Handbook of adolescents and family therapy* (pp. 309–328). New York: Gardner Press.

Lankton, S. (1988). *Ericksonian hypnosis application, preparation and research* (Ericksonian Monograph No. 5). New York: Brunner/Mazel.

Lankton, S., & Lankton, C. (1983). *The answer within: A clinical framework of Ericksonian hypnotherapy.* New York: Brunner/Mazel.

Lankton, S., Lankton, C., & Matthews, W. (1991). Ericksonian family therapy. In A. S. Gurman & D. P. Kniskern (Eds.), *Handbook of family therapy* (Vol. 2, pp. 239–283). New York: Brunner/Mazel.

Lebow, J. L. (1987). Training psychologists in family therapy in Family Institute setting. *Journal of Family Psychology, 1,* 219–231.

Lewis, R., Piercy, F., Sprenkle, D., & Trepper, T. (1991). Family based interventions for helping drug abusing adolescents. *Journal of Adolescent Research, 5,* 82–95.

Locke, H., & Wallace, K. (1959). Short marital-adjustment and prediction tests: The reliability and validity. *Marriage and Family Living, 21*, 251–255.

Madanes, C. (1981). *Strategic family therapy.* San Francisco: Jossey-Bass.

Mahoney, M. J. (1991). *Human change processes.* New York: Basic Books.

McCubbin, H. I., Thompson, E. A., Thompson, A. I., & Fromer, J. E. (Eds.). (1995). *Resiliency in ethnic minority families: Native and Immigrant American families.* Madison: University of Wisconsin–Madison Center for Family Studies.

McCubbin, H. I., Thompson, E. A., Thompson, A. I., & Futrell, J. A. (Eds.). (1995). *Resiliency in ethnic minority families: African-American families.* Madison: University of Wisconsin–Madison Center for Family Studies.

McGoldrick, M. (1982). Ethnicity and family therapy: An overview. In M. McGoldrick, J. K. Pearce, & J. Giordano (Eds.), *Ethnicity and family therapy* (pp. 3–30). New York: Guilford Press.

McGoldrick, M., & Gerson, R. (1985). *Genograms in family assessment.* New York: Norton.

McGoldrick, M., & Giordano, J. (1996). Overview: Ethnicity and family therapy. In M. McGoldrick, J. Giordano, & J. K. Pearce (Eds.), *Ethnicity and family therapy* (2nd ed., pp. 1–27). New York: Guilford Press.

McGoldrick, M., Pearce, J., & Giordano, J. (Eds.). (1982). *Ethnicity and family therapy.* New York: Guilford Press.

Menses, G., & Durrant, M. (1987). Contextual residential care: The application of the principles of cybernetic therapy to the residential treatment of irresponsible adolescents and their families. *Journal of Strategic and Systemic Therapies, 6*, 3–15.

Metcalf, L., Thomas, F., Duncan B. L., Miller, S. D., & Hubble, M. A. (1996). What works in solution-focused brief therapy: A qualitative analysis of client and therapist perceptions. In S. D. Miller, M. A. Hubble, & B. L. Duncan (Eds.), *Handbook of solution-focused brief therapy.* San Francisco: Jossey-Bass.

Miller, S., Nunnally, E., Wackman, D., & Miller, P. (1988). *Connecting with self and others.* Littleton, CO: Interpersonal Communication Programs.

Miller, S. D., Duncan, B. L., & Hubble, M. A. (1997). *Escape from Babel: Toward a unifying language for psychotherapy practice.* New York: Norton.

Minuchin, S. (1974). *Families and family therapy.* Cambridge, MA: Harvard University Press.

Minuchin, S. (1984). *Family kaleidoscope.* Cambridge, MA: Harvard University Press.

Minuchin, S. (1987). My many voices. In J. K. Zeig (Ed.), *The evolution of psychotherapy* (pp. 5–28). New York: Brunner/Mazel.

Minuchin, S., & Fishman, H. C. (1981). *Family therapy techniques.* Cambridge, MA: Harvard University Press.

Minuchin, S., Montalvo, B., Guerney, B., Rosman, B., & Schumer, F. (1967). *Families of the slums: An exploration of their structure and treatment.* New York: Basic Books.

Napier, A., & Whitaker, C. (1978). *The family crucible: The intense experience of family therapy.* New York: Harper & Row.

Newfield, N. A., Kuehl, B. P., Joanning, H., & Quinn, W. H. (1991). We can tell you about "psychos and shrinks": An ethnography of the family therapy of adolescent drug abusers. In T. Todd & M. Selekman (Eds.), *Family therapy approaches with adolescent substance abusers* (pp. 277–316). Needham Heights, MA: Allyn & Bacon.

Nichols, M., & Schwartz, R. (1991). *Family therapy: Concepts and methods* (2nd ed.). Needham Heights, MA: Allyn & Bacon.

Nichols, W., & Everett, C. (1988). *Systemic family therapy: An integrative approach.* New York: Guilford Press.

O'Callaghan, J. B. (1988). *Family school consultation, state of the art analysis and blueprint.* Workshop presented at the 46th annual conference of the American Association for Marriage and Family Therapy, New Orleans.

O'Hanlon, W. H. (1982). Two genetic patterns in Ericksonian therapy. *Journal of Strategic and Systemic Therapies, 1*(4), 21–25.

O'Hanlon, W. H. (1987). *Taproots.* New York: Norton.

O'Hanlon, W. H. (1991). *Acknowledgement and possibility.* Paper presented at the Family and Children's Agency, Louisville, KY.

O'Hanlon, W. H., & Weiner-Davis, M. (1989). *In search of solutions: A new direction in psychotherapy.* New York: Norton.

Olson, D. H., Porter, J., & Ravee, Y. (1985). *FACES I.* St. Paul: Family Social Science, University of Minnesota.

Papp, P. (1980). The use of fantasy in a couples group. In M. Andolfi & I. Zwerling (Eds.), *Dimensions of family therapy* (pp. 73–90). New York: Guilford Press.

Papp, P. (1983). *The process of change.* New York: Guilford Press.

Paul, G. L. (1967). Strategy of outcome research in psychotherapy. *Journal of Consulting Psychology, 31,* 109–118.

Paul, N., & Paul, B. B. (1975). *A marital puzzle.* New York: Norton.

Penn, P. (1982). Circular questioning. *Family Process, 19,* 267–280.

Petker, S. (1982). The domino effect in a system with two or more generations of unresolved mourning. *The Family, 9*(2), 75–79.

Piercy, F., Laird, R., & Mohammed, Z. (1983). A family therapist rating scale. *Journal of Marital and Family Therapy, 9,* 49–59.

Piercy, F., & Sprenkle, D. (1986). *Family therapy source book.* New York: Guilford Press.

Pinsof, W. M., & Catherall, D. (1986). The integrative psychotherapy alliance. *Journal of Marital and Family Therapy, 12,* 137–152.

Pittman, F. (1991). The secret passions of men. *Journal of Marital and Family Therapy, 177*(17), 17–23.

Pittman, F., DeYoung, C., Flomenhaft, K., Kaplan, D., & Langsley, D. (1966). Crisis family therapy. In J. H. Masserman (Ed.), *Current psychiatric therapies* (Vol. 6, pp. 187–196). New York: Grune & Stratton.

Prochaska, J. O., DiClemente, C. C., & Norcross, J. C. (1992). In search of how people change. *American Psychologist, 47,* 1102–1114.

Quinn, W., & Davidson, B. (1984). Prevalence of family therapy models: A research note. *Journal of Marital and Family Therapy, 10*(4), 393–398.

Rappaport, A. F. (1976). Conjugal relationship enhancement program. In D. H. L. Olson (Ed.), *Treating relationships* (pp. 41–66). Lake Mills, IA: Graphic Publishing.

Rogers, C. (1961). *On becoming a person.* Boston: Houghton Mifflin.

Ruesch, J., & Bateson, G. (1951). *Communication: The social matrix of psychiatry.* New York: Norton.

Sager, C. (1981). Couples therapy and marriage contracts. In A. S. Gurman & D. P. Kniskern (Eds.), *Handbook of family therapy* (pp. 85–132). New York: Brunner/Mazel.

Satir, V. (1972). *People making.* Palo Alto, CA: Science and Behavior Books.

Scalise, J. (1992). Life or death: A family suicide watch. *GrassRoutes: Stories from Family and Systemic Therapists, 1*(1), 22.

Segal, L., & Bavelas, J. B. (1983). Human systems and communications theory. In B. B. Wolman & G. Strickler (Eds.), *Handbook of family and marital therapy* (pp. 11–27). New York: Plenum.

Selekman, M. D., & Todd, T. (1991). Major issues from family therapy research and theory: Implications for the future. In T. Todd & M. D. Selekman (Eds.), *Family therapy approaches with adolescent substance abusers* (pp. 311–325). Needham Heights, MA: Allyn & Bacon.

Selvini Palazzoli, M. (1978). *Self starvation.* New York: Aronson.

Selvini Palazzoli, M. (1985). The problem of the sibling as the referring person. *Journal of Marital and Family Therapy, 11*(1), 21–34.

Selvini Palazzoli, M. (1986). Towards a general model of psychotic family games. *Journal of Marital and Family Therapy, 12,* 339–349.

Selvini Palazzoli, M., Boscolo, L., Cecchin, G., & Prata, G. (1978). *Paradox and counter paradox.* New York: Aronson.

Selvini Palazzoli, M., Boscolo, L., Cecchin, G., & Prata, G. (1980a). Hypothesizing, circularity, neutrality: Three guidelines for the conduct of the session. *Family Process, 19*(1), 7–19.

Selvini Palazzoli, M., Boscolo, L., Cecchin, G., & Prata, G. (1980b). Why a long interval between sessions? The therapeutic control of the family-therapist supersystem. In M. Andolfi & I. Zwerling (Eds.), *Dimensions of family therapy* (pp. 161–169). New York: Guilford Press.

Selvini Palazzoli, M., Cirillo, S., Selvini, M., & Sorrentino, A. M. (1989). *Family games: General models of psychotic processes in the family.* New York: Norton.

Selvini Palazzoli, M., & Prata, G. (1982). Snares in family therapy. *Journal of Marital and Family Therapy, 8*(4), 443–450.

Sheinberg, M. (1992). Navigating treatment impasses at the disclosure of incest: Combining ideas from feminism and social constructionism. *Family Process, 31*(3), 201–216.

Sheinberg, M., & Penn, P. (1991). Gender dilemmas, gender questions and the gender mantra. *Journal of Marital and Family Therapy, 17*(1), 33–44.

Simon, R. (1992). *One on one: Conversations with the shapers of family therapy.* Washington, DC: The Family Therapy Networker.

Sluzki, C. (1992). Transformations: A blueprint for narrative changes in therapy. *Family Process, 31*(3), 217–230.

Snider, M. (1992). *Process family therapy.* Needham Heights, MA: Allyn & Bacon.

Spanier, G. B. (1976). Measuring dyadic adjustment: New scales for assessing the quality of marriage and similar dyads. *Journal of Marriage and the Family, 38,* 15–28.

Spiegel, J. (1982). An ecological model of ethnic families. In M. McGoldrick, J. K. Pearce, & J. Giordano (Eds.), *Ethnicity and family therapy* (pp. 31–51). New York: Guilford Press.

Stanton, M. D. (1981). Strategic approaches to family therapy. In A. S. Gurman & D. P. Kniskern (Eds.), *Handbook of family therapy* (pp. 361–402). New York: Brunner/Mazel.

Stanton, M. D. (1992). The time line and the "why now?" question: A technique and rationale for therapy, training, organizational consultation and research. *Journal of Marital and Family Therapy, 18*(4), 331–344.

Stanton, M. D., Todd, T. C., & Associates. (1982). *The family therapy of drug abuse and addiction.* New York: Guilford Press.

Steinglass, P., Bennett, L., Wolin, S., & Reiss, D. (1987). *The alcoholic family.* New York: Basic Books.

Stuart, R. B. (1976). An operant interpersonal program for couples. In D. H. L. Olsen (Ed.), *Treating relationships* (pp. 119–132). Lake Mills, IA: Graphic Publishing.

Stuart, R. B. (1980). *Helping couples change: A social learning approach to marital therapy.* Champaign, IL: Research Press.

Stuart, R. B., & Stuart, F. (1972). *Marital pre-counseling inventory.* Champaign, IL: Research Press.

Todd, T., & Selekman, M. D. (Eds.). (1991). *Family therapy approaches with adolescent substance abusers.* Needham Heights, MA: Allyn & Bacon.

Todd, T. C. (1986). Structural-strategic marital therapy. In N. S. Jacobson & A. S. Gurman (Eds.), *Clinical handbook of marital therapy* (pp. 71–106). New York: Guilford Press.

Tomm, K. M. (1984). One perspective on the Milan systemic approach: 1. Overview of development, theory and practice. *Journal of Marital and Family Therapy, 10,* 113–125.

Tomm, K. M., & Wright, L. M. (1979). Training in family therapy: Perceptual, conceptual and executive skills. *Family Process, 18,* 227–250.

Treadway, D. (1989). *Before it's too late: Working with substance abuse in the family.* New York: Norton.

Van Deusen, J., Stanton, M. D., Scott, S., Todd, T., & Mowatt, D. (1982). Getting the addict to agree to involve his family of origin: The initial contact. In M. Stanton & T. Todd (Eds.), *The family therapy of drug abuse and addiction* (pp. 39–59). New York: Guilford Press.

Waldegrave, C. (1990). Social justice and family therapy. *Dulwich Centre Newsletter, 1,* 6–45.

Wamboldt, F., & Wolin, S. (1989). Reality and myth in family life: Changes across generations. In S. Anderson & D. Bagarozzi (Eds.), *Family myths: Psychotherapy implications* (pp. 141–166). New York: Haworth Press.

Warner, R., & Hansen, J. (1970). Verbal-reinforcement and model-reinforcement group counseling with alienated students. *Journal of Counseling Psychology, 14,* 168–172.

Warner, R., Swisher, J., & Horan, J. (1973). Drug abuse prevention: A behavioral approach. *NAASP Bulletin, 372,* 49–54.

Watzlawick, P., Beavin, J., & Jackson, D. (1967). *Pragmatics of human communication.* New York: Norton.

Watzlawick, P., Weakland, J. H., & Fisch, R. (1974). *Change: Principles of problem formation and problem resolution.* New York: Norton.

Weakland, J., Fisch, R., Watzlawick, P., & Bodin, A. (1974). Brief therapy: Focused problem resolution. *Family Process, 13,* 141–168.

Weber, T., McKeever, J., & McDaniel, S. (1985). The beginning guide to the problem-oriented first family interview. *Family Process, 24*(3), 356–364.

Weeks, G. R. (1991). *Promoting change through paradoxical therapy.* New York: Brunner/Mazel.

Weeks, G. R., & Abate, L. (1982). *Paradoxical psychotherapy: Theory and technique.* New York: Brunner/Mazel.

Weiss, R. L., & Perry, B. A. (1979). *Assessment and treatment of marital dysfunction.* Eugene, OR: Marital Studies Program.

Whitaker, C. (1976). Comment: Live supervision in psychotherapy. *Voices, 12*, 24–25.

Whitaker, C. A. (1982). The ongoing training of the psychotherapist. In J. R. Neill & D. P. Kniskern (Eds.), *From psyche to system: The evolving therapy of Carl Whitaker* (pp. 121–138). New York: Guilford Press.

White, M. (1986). Negative explanation, restraint, and double description: A template for family therapy. *Family Process, 25*(2), 169–184.

White, M. (1990, October). *Couple therapy and deconstruction.* Paper presented at the meeting of the American Association for Marriage and Family Therapy, Washington, DC.

White, M., & Epston, D. (1991). *Narrative means to therapeutic ends.* New York: Norton.

Williamson, D. (1981). Personal authority via termination of the intergenerational hierarchical boundary: A "new" stage in the family lifecycle. *Journal of Marital and Family Therapy, 7*, 441–452.

Wright, L., & Leahey, M. (1984). *Nurses and families: A guide to family assessment and intervention.* Philadelphia: Davis.

Zeig, J., & Lankton, S. (1988). *Developing Ericksonian therapy: State of the art.* New York: Brunner/Mazel.

APPENDIX A
AAMFT CODE OF ETHICS

The Board of Directors of the American Association for Marriage and Family Therapy (AAMFT) hereby promulgates, pursuant to Article 2, Section 2.013 of the Association's Bylaws, the Revised AAMFT Code of Ethics, effective July 1, 1998.

The AAMFT Code of Ethics is binding on Members of AAMFT in all membership categories, AAMFT Approved Supervisors, and applicants for membership and the Approved Supervisor designation (hereafter, AAMFT Member).

If an AAMFT Member resigns in anticipation of, or during the course of an ethics investigation, the Ethics Committee will complete its investigation. Any publication of action taken by the Association will include the fact that the Member attempted to resign during the investigation.

Marriage and family therapists are strongly encouraged to report alleged unethical behavior of colleagues to appropriate professional associations and state regulatory bodies.

1. RESPONSIBILITY TO CLIENTS

Marriage and family therapists advance the welfare of families and individuals. They respect the rights of those persons seeking their assistance, and make reasonable efforts to ensure that their services are used appropriately.

> 1.1 Marriage and family therapists do not discriminate against or refuse professional service to anyone on the basis of race, gender, religion, national origin, or sexual orientation.

1.2 Marriage and family therapists are aware of their influential position with respect to clients, and they avoid exploiting the trust and dependency of such persons. Therapists, therefore, make every effort to avoid dual relationships with clients that could impair professional judgment or increase the risk of exploitation. When a dual relationship cannot be avoided, therapists take appropriate professional precautions to ensure judgment is not impaired and no exploitation occurs. Examples of such dual relationships include, but are not limited to, business or close personal relationships with clients. Sexual intimacy with clients is prohibited. Sexual intimacy with former clients for two years following the termination of therapy is prohibited.

1.3 Marriage and family therapists do not use their professional relationships with clients to further their own interests.

1.4 Marriage and family therapists respect the right of clients to make decisions and help them to understand the consequences of these decisions. Therapists clearly advise a client that a decision on marital status is the responsibility of the client.

1.5 Marriage and family therapists continue therapeutic relationships only so long as it is reasonably clear that clients are benefiting from the relationship.

1.6 Marriage and family therapists assist persons in obtaining other therapeutic services if the therapist is unable or unwilling, for appropriate reasons, to provide professional help.

1.7 Marriage and family therapists do not abandon or neglect clients in treatment without making reasonable arrangements for the continuation of such treatment.

1.8 Marriage and family therapists obtain written informed consent from clients before videotaping, audiorecording, or permitting third party observation.

2. CONFIDENTIALITY

Marriage and family therapists have unique confidentiality concerns because the client in a therapeutic relationship may be more than one person. Therapists respect and guard confidences of each individual client.

2.1 Marriage and family therapists may not disclose client confidences except: (a) as mandated by law; (b) to prevent a clear and immediate danger to a person or persons; (c) where the therapist is a defendant in a civil, criminal, or disciplinary action arising from the therapy (in which case client confidences may be disclosed only in the course of that action); or (d) if there is a waiver previously obtained in writing, and then such information may be revealed only in accordance with the terms of the waiver. In circumstances where more than one person in a family receives therapy, each such family member who is legally competent to execute a waiver must agree to the waiver required by subparagraph (d). Without such a waiver from each family member legally competent to execute a waiver, a therapist cannot disclose information received from any family member.

2.2 Marriage and family therapists use client and/or clinical materials in teaching, writing, and public presentations only if a written waiver has been obtained in accordance with Subprinciple 2.1 (d), or when appropriate steps have been taken to protect client identity and confidentiality.

2.3 Marriage and family therapists store or dispose of client records in ways that maintain confidentiality.

3. PROFESSIONAL COMPETENCE AND INTEGRITY

Marriage and family therapists maintain high standards of professional competence and integrity.

3.1 Marriage and family therapists are in violation of this Code and subject to termination of membership or other appropriate action if they: (a) are convicted of any felony; (b) are convicted of a misdemeanor related to their qualifications or functions; (c) engage in conduct which could lead to conviction of a felony, or a misdemeanor related to their qualifications or functions; (d) are expelled from or disciplined by other professional organizations; (e) have their licenses or certificates suspended or revoked or are otherwise disciplined by regulatory bodies; (f) are no longer competent to practice marriage and family therapy because they are impaired due to physical or mental causes or the use of alcohol or other substances; or (g) fail to cooperate with the Association at any point from the inception of an ethical complaint through the completion of all proceedings regarding that complaint.

3.2 Marriage and family therapists seek appropriate professional assistance for their personal problems or conflicts that may impair work performance or clinical judgment.

3.3 Marriage and family therapists, as teachers, supervisors, and researchers, are dedicated to high standards of scholarship and present accurate information.

3.4 Marriage and family therapists remain abreast of new developments in family therapy knowledge and practice through educational activities.

3.5 Marriage and family therapists do not engage in sexual or other harassment or exploitation of clients, students, trainees, supervisees, employees, colleagues, research subjects, or actual or potential witnesses or complainants in investigations and ethical proceedings.

3.6 Marriage and family therapists do not diagnose, treat, or advise on problems outside the recognized boundaries of their competence.

3.7 Marriage and family therapists make efforts to prevent the distortion or misuse of their clinical and research findings.

3.8 Marriage and family therapists, because of their ability to influence and alter the lives of others, exercise special care when making public their professional recommendations and opinions through testimony or other public statements.

4. RESPONSIBILITY TO STUDENTS, EMPLOYEES, AND SUPERVISEES

Marriage and family therapists do not exploit the trust and dependency of students, employees, and supervisees.

4.1 Marriage and family therapists are aware of their influential position with respect to students, employees, and supervisees, and they avoid exploiting the trust and dependency of such persons. Therapists, therefore, make every effort to avoid dual relationships that could impair professional judgment or increase the risk of exploitation. When a dual relationship cannot be avoided, therapists take appropriate professional precautions to ensure judgment is not impaired and no exploitation occurs. Examples of such dual relationships include, but are not limited to, business or close personal relationships with students, employees, or supervisees. Provision of therapy to students, employees, or supervisees is prohibited. Sexual intimacy with students or supervisees is prohibited.

4.2 Marriage and family therapists do not permit students, employees, or supervisees to perform or to hold themselves out as competent to perform professional services beyond their training, level of experience, and competence.

4.3 Marriage and family therapists do not disclose supervisee confidences except: (a) as mandated by law; (b) to prevent a clear and immediate danger to a person or persons; (c) where the therapist is a defendant in a civil, criminal, or disciplinary action arising from the supervision (in which case supervisee confidences may be disclosed on in the course of that action); (d) in educational or training settings where there are multiple supervisors, and then only to other professional colleagues who share responsibility for the training of the supervisee; or (e) if there is a waive previously obtained in writing, and then such information may be revealed only in accordance with the terms of the waiver.

5. Responsibility to Research Participants

Investigators respect the dignity and protect the welfare of participants in research and are aware of federal and state laws and regulations and professional standards governing the conduct of research.

5.1 Investigators are responsible for making careful examinations of ethical acceptability in planning studies. To the extent that services to research participants may be compromised by participation in research, investigators seek the ethical advice of qualified professionals not directly involved in the investigation and observe safeguards to protect the rights of research participants.

5.2 Investigators requesting participants' involvement in research inform them of all aspects of the research that might reasonably be expected to influence willingness to participate. Investigators are especially sensitive to the possibility of diminished consent when participants are also receiving clinical services, have impairments which limit understanding and/or communication, or when participants are children.

5.3 Investigators respect participants' freedom to decline participation in or to withdraw from a research study at any time. This obligation requires special thought and consideration when investigators or other members of the research team are in positions of authority or influence over participants. Marriage and family therapists, therefore, make every effort to avoid dual relationships with research participants that could impair professional judgment or increase the risk of exploitation.

5.4 Information obtained about a research participant during the course of an investigation is confidential unless there is a waiver previously obtained in writing. When the possibility exists that others, including family members, may obtain access to such information, this possibility, together with the plan for protecting confidentiality, is explained as part of the procedure for obtaining informed consent.

6. RESPONSIBILITY TO THE PROFESSION

Marriage and family therapists respect the rights and responsibilities of professional colleagues and participate in activities which advance the goals of the profession.

6.1 Marriage and family therapists remain accountable to the standards of the profession when acting as members or employees of organizations.

6.2 Marriage and family therapists assign publication credit to those who have contributed to a publication in proportion to their contributions and in accordance with customary professional publication practices.

6.3 Marriage and family therapists who are the authors of books or other materials that are published or distributed cite persons to whom credit for original ideas is due.

6.4 Marriage and family therapists who are the authors of books or other materials published or distributed by an organization take reasonable precautions to ensure that the organization promotes and advertises the materials accurately and factually.

6.5 Marriage and family therapists participate in activities that contribute to a better community and society, including devoting a portion of their professional activity to services for which there is little or no financial return.

6.6 Marriage and family therapists are concerned with developing laws and regulations pertaining to marriage and family therapy that serve the public interest, and with altering such laws and regulations that are not in the public interest.

6.7 Marriage and family therapists encourage public participation in the design and delivery of professional services and in the regulation of practitioners.

7. FINANCIAL ARRANGEMENTS

Marriage and family therapists make financial arrangements with clients, third party payors, and supervisees that are reasonably understandable and conform to accepted professional practices.

7.1 Marriage and family therapists do not offer or accept payment for referrals.

7.2 Marriage and family therapists do not charge excessive fees for services.

7.3 Marriage and family therapists disclose their fees to clients and supervisees at the beginning of services.

7.4 Marriage and family therapists represent facts truthfully to clients, third party payors, and supervisees regarding services rendered.

8. ADVERTISING

Marriage and family therapists engage in appropriate informational activities, including those that enable laypersons to choose professional services on an informed basis.

General Advertising

8.1 Marriage and family therapists accurately represent their competence, education, training, and experience relevant to their practice of marriage and family therapy.

8.2 Marriage and family therapists assure that advertisements and publications in any media (such as directories, announcements, business cards, newspapers, radio, television, and facsimiles) convey information that is necessary for the public to make an appropriate selection of professional services. Information could include: (a) office information, such as name, address, telephone number, credit card acceptability, fees, languages spoken, and office hours; (b) appropriate degrees, state licensure and/or certification, and AAMFT Clinical Member status; and (c) description of practice. (For requirements for advertising under the AAMFT name, logo, and/or the abbreviated initials AAMFT, see Subprinciple 8.15, below.)

8.3 Marriage and family therapists do not use a name which could mislead the public concerning the identity, responsibility, source, and status of those practicing under that name and do not hold themselves out as being partners or associates of a firm if they are not.

8.4 Marriage and family therapists do not use any professional identification (such as a business card, office sign, letterhead, or telephone or association directory listing) if it includes a statement or claim that is false, fraudulent, misleading, or deceptive. A statement is false, fraudulent, misleading, or deceptive if it (a) contains a material misrepresentation of fact; (b) fails to state any material fact necessary to make the statement, in light of all circumstances, not misleading; or (c) is intended to or is likely to create an unjustified expectation.

8.5 Marriage and family therapists correct, wherever possible, false, misleading, or inaccurate information and representations made by others concerning the therapist's qualifications, services, or products.

8.6 Marriage and family therapists make certain that the qualifications of persons in their employ are represented in a manner that is not false, misleading, or deceptive.

8.7 Marriage and family therapists may represent themselves as specializing within a limited area of marriage and family therapy, but only if they have the education and supervised experience in settings which meet recognized professional standards to practice in that specialty area.

Advertising Using AAMFT Designations

8.8 The AAMFT designations of Clinical Member, Approved Supervisor, and Fellow may be used in public information or advertising materials only by persons holding such designations. Persons holding such designations may, for example, advertise in the following manner:

❊   *Jane Doe, Ph.D., a Clinical Member of the American Association for Marriage and Family Therapy.*

Alternately, the advertisement could read: *Jane Doe, Ph.D., AAMFT Clinical Member.*

❊   *John Doe, Ph.D., an Approved Supervisor of the American Association for Marriage and Family Therapy.*

Alternately, the advertisement could read: *John Doe, Ph.D., AAMFT Approved Supervisor.*

❊   *Jane Doe, Ph.D., a Fellow of the American Association for Marriage and Family Therapy.*

Alternately the advertisement could read: *Jane Doe, Ph.D., AAMFT Fellow.* More than one designation may be used if held by the AAMFT Member.

8.9   Marriage and family therapists who hold the AAMFT Approved Supervisor or the Fellow designation may not represent the designation as an advanced clinical status.

8.10   Student, Associate, and Affiliate Members may not use their AAMFT membership status in public information or advertising materials. Such listings on professional resumes are not considered advertisements.

8.11   Persons applying for AAMFT membership may not list their application status on any resume or advertisement.

8.12   In conjunction with their AAMFT membership, marriage and family therapists claim as evidence of educational qualifications only those degrees (a) from regionally accredited institutions or (b) from institutions recognized by states which license or certify marriage and family therapists, but only if such state regulation is recognized by AAMFT.

8.13   Marriage and family therapists may not use the initials AAMFT following their name in the manner of an academic degree.

8.14   Marriage and family therapists may not use the AAMFT and/or the abbreviated initials AAMFT or make any other such representation which would imply that they speak for or represent the Association. The Association is the sole owner of its name, logo, and the abbreviated initials AAMFT. Its committees and divisions, operating as such, may use the name, logo, and/or the abbreviated initials, AAMFT, in accordance with policies.

8.15 Advertisements of Clinical Members under the AAMFT name, logo, and/or the abbreviated initials AAMFT may include the following: the Clinical Member's name, degree, license or certificate held when required by state law, name of business, address, and telephone number. If a business is listed, it must follow, not precede the Clinical Member's name. Such listings may not include AAMFT offices held by the Clinical Member, nor any specializations, since such a listing under the AAMFT name, logo, and/or the abbreviated initials, AAMFT, would imply that this specialization has been credentialed by AAMFT. The Clinical Member logo shall be used in accordance with stated guidelines.

8.16 Marriage and family therapists use their membership in AAMFT only in connection with their clinical and professional activities.

8.17 Only AAMFT divisions and programs accredited by the AAMFT Commission on Accreditation for Marriage and Family Therapy Education, not businesses nor organizations, may use any AAMFT-related designation or affiliation in public information or advertising materials, and then only in accordance with AAMFT policies.

8.18 Programs accredited by the AAMFT Commission on Accreditation for Marriage and Family Therapy Education may not use the AAMFT name, logo, and/or the abbreviated initials, AAMFT. Instead, they may have printed on their stationery and other appropriate materials a statement such as: The (name of program) *of the* (name of institution) *is accredited by the AAMFT Commission on Accreditation for Marriage and Family Therapy Education.*

8.19 Programs not accredited by the AAMFT Commission on Accreditation for Marriage and Family Therapy Education may not use the AAMFT name, corporate logo, and/or the abbreviated initials, AAMFT. They may not state in printed program materials, program advertisements, and student advisement that their courses and training opportunities are accepted by AAMFT to meet AAMFT membership requirements.

NAME INDEX

SUBJECT INDEX

AB design, 269–270
Actions, as elements of self awareness, 60–63
Adolescent stage, 49
Adoptive families, 54
African American families, 42
  genograms and, 173–174
  mother-daughter interactions in, 78
Alcoholics Anonymous (AA), 162
Alcohol issue, 160, 162
Alienation, 45, 106
Alternative solutions, generating, 222–223
American Association for Marriage and Family Therapy (AAMFT), code of ethics, 70, 323–332
Ascribing noble intentions, 88
Asian American families, mother-daughter interactions in, 78
Assessment process, 167–201
  case study, 185–200
  circular questioning, 174-177
  genograms, 168–174, 180, 183, 189–190
  tracking interactional sequences, 177–179
Assumptions, 60
Attitudes of therapist, 79–80

Balance, in families, 57–58
Behavioral change, 75–77, 107
  measuring, 269–273
Behavioral tasks, 113

Behaviors, integration of practice and, 69, 83–95
Beliefs, 60
Belief systems, reconstructing, 213–222
Black Families in Therapy (Boyd-Franklin), 42
Boundary, concept of, 35, 56, 57
Boundary marking, 209–210
Brainstorming, 222–223, 251
Brief therapy, 12, 75–76, 81

Change:
  behavioral, 75–77, 107
  naturalistic, 71–73
  perceptual, 75–77, 107
  prioritizing areas of, 240–242
  relational, 75–77, 107
  therapeutic, 73–75
Chronic problems, 135–136
Circular questioning, 23, 24, 59, 84–86, 174–177
Client-centered therapy, 149
Client competence, perception of, 81–83, 111
Client resistance, 235–237, 247–249
Clinical information, intake process and, 126, 127, 130–131
Clinical research, evaluations as, 281–282
Coalitions, concept of, 35, 56, 57
Cognitive-behavioral family therapy (CBFT), 6–7, 22, 28–31, 73, 75, 94–95

TO THE OWNER OF THIS BOOK:

We hope that you have found *The Practice of Family Therapy: Key Elements Across Models*, Second Edition, useful. So that this book can be improved in a future edition, would you take the time to complete this sheet and return it? Thank you.

School and address: _____

Department: _____

Instructor's name: _____

1. What I like most about this book is: _____

_____

_____

2. What I like least about this book is: _____

_____

_____

3. My general reaction to this book is: _____

_____

4. The name of the course in which I used this book is: _____

_____

5. Were all of the chapters of the book assigned for you to read? ____

   If not, which ones weren't? _____

6. In the space below, or on a separate sheet of paper, please write specific suggestions for improving this book and anything else you'd care to share about your experience in using the book.

_____

_____

_____

_____

Optional:

Your name: _____ Date: _____

May Wadsworth quote you, either in promotion for *The Practice of Family Therapy: Key Elements Across Models,* Second Edition, or in future publishing ventures?

Yes: _____ No: _____

Sincerely,

Suzanne Midori Hanna
Joseph H. Brown

FOLD HERE

FOLD HERE

DATE DUE
